THE COMPLETE BOOK OF
CLASSIC
GM MUSCLE

BUICK • CHEVROLET • OLDSMOBILE • PONTIAC

First published in 2008 by Motorbooks, an imprint of MBI Publishing Company, 400 First Avenue North, Suite 300, Minneapolis, MN 55401 USA

Motorbooks titles are also available at discounts in bulk quantity for industrial or sales-promotional use. For details write to Special Sales Manager at MBI Publishing Company, 400 First Avenue North, Suite 300, Minneapolis, MN 55401 USA.

To find out more about our books, join us online at www.motorbooks.com.

Library of Congress Cataloging-in-Publication Data

Mueller, Mike, 1959-
  Complete book of classic GM muscle / Mike Mueller.
    p. cm.
  Includes index.
  ISBN 978-0-7603-3228-3 (hb w/ jkt)
  1. General Motors automobiles—History—20th century. 2. Muscle cars--United States—History—20th century. 3. Antique and classic cars—United States—History—20th century. I. Title.
  TL215.G4M84 2008
  629.222—dc22

                          2008009199

On the frontispiece: 1964 Impala SS

On the title pages: 1968 Camaro SS/RS

On contents page: Prototype 1970 Oldsmobile Hemi

On the back cover, main: 1969 Chevelle SS 396

Inset, left to right: 1970 Chevelle SS 396, 1971 Gran Sport Stage I, 1969 Hurst/Olds, 1967 4-4-2 W-30, 1967 GTO, 1969 Camaro Pace Car

Editor: Chris Endres
Designer: Laura Rades

Printed in China

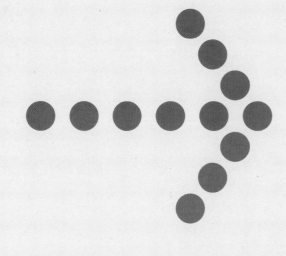

CLASSIC
GM MUSCLE

motorbooks

·⁚∻ Contents

01 ···> Full Size Flyers 22

02 ···> Founding Father 50

03 ···> Numbers Game 88

10 ···> Lengthy Legacy 296

11 ···> Power Shift 314

Acknowledgments

I've been writing about and photographing cars for nearly 25 years now because, plain and simply, I am a car guy. Have been since I was knee-high to a chrome reversed wheel. I come from car guys. Most of my friends have been car guys. Even a couple of my ex-wives were car guys. Hell, if it weren't for cars, I'd probably be working a real job right now. Yikes!

I owe so many thanks to so many other car guys out there, all the folks who made both my career and my latest book possible. There's my pa, Jim Mueller, back in Champaign, Illinois, who taught basic auto mechanics the hard way—"I don't care how much snow is on the driveway, get under there and yank out that tranny!" There's my brother, Dave Mueller, the greatest car guy I know. And there's fellow brother Jim Mueller Jr., who will requalify as a darned good car guy if he ever gets his license back. As for my youngest sibling Kenny… well, he's one heckuva little brother. Throw in my brother-in-law, Frank Young, recently retired from the Illinois State Police, and I've got the best free labor pool a freelance automotive photo/journalist could ask for. Keep up the good work, guys.

Like my so-called career, this book has been many years in the making. Guess you could say the following pages began forming about the time Donald Farr gave me my first magazine job with Dobbs Publishing in Florida in 1987. There, I was fortunate enough to cross paths with former *Muscle Car Review* editor Paul Zazarine and present *Musclecar Enthusiast* potentate Steve Statham, two super-duper car guys who I owe almost everything to—kinda like the IRS and my ex-wives. While at Dobbs, I also hooked up with John Scherer, who I followed from Florida to Georgia, to his utter dismay. John introduced me to countless car guys down Ft. Lauderdale way back in the eighties; today he never fails to come to the rescue whenever I'm in need of some free groceries, not to mention a complimentary Old Milwaukee or two.

Speaking of freebies, I probably would've never survived to miss so many deadlines during this project's progression if not for my new best friends, the Alabama Family McGee, now of Kennesaw, Georgia. Great chow and good times are guaranteed whenever the Big Hoss, Jason McGee, is in da house. Trophy wife Elizabeth only enhances the attraction, while their offspring, Hannah and Matthew, are a hoot to boot. Don't let me forget the McGees' wiener dog, Otis, who never fails to leave a parting gift in my guest bedroom whenever he visits. Maybe I'll return the favor someday. As for what I owe you, Ely, the check is almost in the mail.

On the deadline end of things, I've got to thank my longtime friend at MBI Publishing, Zack Miller, for once more trusting me with an assignment, this one of epic proportions. Zack passed the buck to editor Lindsay Hitch, who I still miss dearly after working with her on three MBI projects. Lindsay, on the other hand, is probably glad to see her hair growing back at her new job. In her place came Chris Endres, another true car guy. Chris picked up where Lindsay left off and never missed a beat, unlike me.

Like Lindsay and Chris, Peggy Vezina at GM Media Archives also deserves mucho kudos for putting up with me. She made incredibly quick work of my historical photo requests, and did so with a friendly flair that renewed my faith in corporate bureaucracies. Peggy, any chance your next job will be with the Internal Revenue Service?

Other photography came from the veteran drag-racing historian Geoff Stunkard and the aforementioned Steve Statham, now editor of *Musclecar Enthusiast* magazine. Judy Badgley, of the Hurst/Olds Club of America (www.hurstolds.com, 304 S. Clippert Street, Lansing, Michigan 48912), also came through at the last moment with a few bits of supportive artwork.

Additional archival support was delivered by various old friends: Pontiac historian Jim Mattison; Kim Miller at the AACA Library in Hershey, Pennsylvania; and Mark Patrick and Barbara Thompson at the Detroit Public Library's National Automotive History Collection. Countless other car clubs, far too numerous to list here, were of priceless help, too, during the years of work leading up to this project's culmination

Last, but certainly not least, I simply can't close without a tip of my hat to all the vehicle owners who graciously allowed me to photograph their pride and joys over the past couple decades while working my way toward this end. This list also is too cumbersome for these pages, but I definitely know who all you car guys (and gals) are.

Many thanks to each and every one.
—Mike Mueller

Introduction

The General Leads the Way

They don't call it *General* Motors for nothing. Like George Washington, Ulysses S. Grant, and ol' "Blood and Guts" Patton, Detroit's dominating automotive conglomerate has demonstrated leadership in its field like no other, at least from a domestic perspective. Accusations of monopolistic bullying during the 1960s aside, GM has long managed to sell more cars than Ford Motor Company and Chrysler Corporation simply by being better and stronger in nearly all facets compared to its American rivals. Superiority in engineering and design has been an unofficial GM trademark dating back almost to this megacorporation's earliest days.

Established in September 1908 by former carriage maker William Crapo Durant, the General Motors Company at first encompassed the fledgling firm named after

engineering pioneer David Dunbar Buick. The Buick Manufacturing Company, founded in 1902, had floundered before Durant came aboard to right the ship in 1904. He then used Buick to get GM rolling and quickly brought Oldsmobile into the fold late in 1908. Durant also acquired Cadillac and Oakland in 1909, with the latter firm eventually evolving into Pontiac.

But, just as General George Smith Patton discovered during World War II, a successful leader sometimes can be too strong and too aggressive for his or her own good. Concerned bankers, alarmed by Durant's rampant expansionist practices, booted him out on his wallet in 1910. Yet he bounced right back, opening Chevrolet in November 1911. This new company's success allowed him to buy a return

Top Left
William Durant (at the wheel of this 1906 Buick) founded General Motors in 1908, using the Buick Manufacturing Company as a base for his soon-to-be-giant empire. Oldsmobile joined the GM fold that year, followed by Cadillac and Oakland in 1909.

Top Right
Billy Durant also founded Chevrolet in 1911. Famous race driver Louis Chevrolet appears here at the wheel of a 1911 experimental Chevy. Full production started in 1912.

ticket into GM via stockholder channels. With 54.5 percent of corporate stock in hand, he marched in and regained control in September 1915. Three years later, in May 1918, he made Chevrolet a GM division. Further expansion followed as Durant captured more than 30 other companies during the teens. By 1929, GM was offering 72 models, including both cars and trucks.

The rest is history, as was Billy Durant after an economic recession caused GM stock to nosedive in 1920. He was shown the door a second time, never to return to such lofty heights. Another much smaller Durant empire did rise again but was defeated by the Great Depression in the early 1930s. General Motors, meanwhile, simply shrugged off such trials and tribulations and continued its offensive against

entrenched leader Ford, as well as a new combatant, this one founded by Walter P. Chrysler in 1924.

By the time World War II came along to temporarily shut down civilian automotive production, GM was showing the other Big Three players how to build Detroit's best cars. Make that best-*looking* cars once Harley Earl made the scene. Renowned for the rakish custom bodies he had designed during the 1920s for some of Hollywood's flashiest characters, Earl left California for Detroit in 1927 to work for GM's Fisher Body division, where he created the lovely LaSalle, Detroit's first truly styled car done in-house rather than by an outside contractor. Thoroughly impressed, GM President Alfred Sloan opened his Art and Colour Section in June 1927 and made Earl its head.

To this crowd, "muscle car" means carburetors, not electronically controlled fuel injectors; tire smoke, not traction control; distorted 8-track tunes, not crisply clear CD serenades.

Art and Colour instantly helped transform GM cars into Detroit's most fashionable offerings and at the same time effectively rang the death knell for this country's independent coachworks.

In 1937, the name was changed to Styling Section, and Earl and his people then became officially known as "stylists." Notable feathers stuck in Earl's rather large cap after the war included the fabled tailfin and trendy wraparound windshield, styling sensations copied by nearly all other automakers in short order. He also popularized the long, low lines that, along with heaping helpings of chrome, defined the American automobile during the fabulous 1950s. Back then, when Harley Earl spoke, everyone came to attention. Everyone.

The famed fin man was also responsible for Chevrolet's introduction of its fiberglass-bodied Corvette, this country's first and for decades "only" sports car. First, that is, from a modern perspective—let's not forget jaunty prewar (make that World War I) roadsters like Mercer's Raceabout and Stutz's Bearcat. And "first *sports car*" from a Yankee point of view—many critics still claim the Corvette always has been too big, too comfortable and convenient, basically too American to be allowed into the sporting fraternity.

Chevrolet officials themselves finally cooled on the tag "America's only sports car." Nowadays their fantastic plastic two-seater runs with the "muscle car" crowd, which is only right considering it offers 400 thoroughly buff horses in standard form—a brutal 505 in the special-edition Z06's case. Dodge's latest, greatest

Viper may lead the way now on paper, with 510 horsepower, but the 2007 Z06 features nearly as many rarin'-to-run ponies for far fewer dollars, making it easily the world's best high-performance buy. General Motors once again sets the pace for all others to follow, though Ford's 2007 Shelby GT500 Mustang, priced even less than the Z06 and fit with 500 horses, isn't far behind. But no worries: as Ford's stronger GT500KR is being announced for 2008, work is progressing on an even more muscular Corvette to counter push with shove.

Today's muscle cars are far and away the wildest rides ever built in Detroit, yet many horsepower hounds still prefer to play with the breed's earliest examples, which—wouldn't you know it—the General also deserves credit for fathering. To this crowd, "muscle car" means carburetors, not electronically controlled fuel

Above
Originally called the "Kettering engine," in honor of the veteran GM engineer who contributed so much to the development of modern high-compression, short-stroke, overhead-valve engines, Oldsmobile's Rocket V-8 debuted in 1949 with 135 horsepower and 7.25:1 compression. That latter figure was considered well up the scale back then. *Mike Mueller*

Above
Chevy's long-running small-block V-8 set the low-priced field on fire in 1955. By 1957, the top-shelf fuel-injected version of this high-winding engine was making 1 horsepower per cubic inch. The 283-cubic-inch V-8 was enlarged to 327 cubes in 1962, and the last "fuelie" (shown here) was offered in 1965. Maximum output for the 1965 injected small-block was 375 horsepower. *Mike Mueller*

Mopar fans like to claim that Chrysler introduced the muscle car in 1955 after rolling out the first of its legendary letter-series 300 models. The 300-C combined lavish luxury with maximum performance to a degree not seen since Duesenberg disappeared in the 1930s. Beneath the hood was a 300-horsepower hemi-head V-8. *Mike Mueller*

injectors; tire smoke, not traction control; distorted 8-track tunes, not crisply clear CD serenades. And, in most of their opinions, America's first muscle car was born in 1964, with Pete Estes, John De Lorean, and all the other excitable boys at Pontiac Motor Division standing tall as proud papas. Jim Wangers' ads touted it as the "Tiger." The name on the street was "Goat." But Pontiac Motor Division (PMD) promotional people preferred "GTO," at the time an already

While sports car purists cringed, speed-sensitive Americans were lining up to buy 1964 GTOs faster than Pontiac could build them.

Chevrolet's venerable Super Sport legacy began in 1961, appearing first in full-size Impala form. SS versions of the Nova, Chevelle, Camaro, El Camino, and Monte Carlo followed. The 454 SS pickup debuted in 1990, and another half-ton hauler, the Intimidator SS (shown here), appeared in 2006 in honor of NASCAR legend Dale Earnhardt. *Mike Mueller*

famous moniker they unabashedly copped from Ferrari with nary a blush or apology.

While sports car purists cringed, speed-sensitive Americans were lining up to buy 1964 GTOs faster than Pontiac could build them. Production doubled in 1965 and eventually peaked at more than 87,000 in 1968. Up until 1969, the Goat was America's best-selling high-performance automobile, which early on hit the streets carrying the "supercar" banner, at least according to quick-thinking automotive

journalists like David E. Davis Jr., Eric Dahlquist, and Brock Yates. Sometime around 1970, that nickname evolved into the more familiar meaning applied today, both for the highly valued collectibles built back in the days of quarter-a-gallon gas and their current high-tech offspring that now require small fortunes to fill up.

But was the 1964 GTO really Detroit's original muscle car? Other GM milestones set the stage for Pontiac's groundbreaking performance machine, including a long-forgotten

potent package that Buick introduced in 1936. That year, the guys from Flint planted the big, heavy Roadmaster's powerful straight-eight engine into the lighter, shorter Special chassis, with the results named "Century" because this car was capable of soaring nearly up to the then-hallowed 100-mile-per-hour stratosphere.

General Motors' history-making engineers followed that with their trend-setting overhead-valve V-8 models in 1949. Of high-winding, short-stroke design, Cadillac's 160-horsepower

The SS 396 superseded the GTO atop the high-performance pack in 1969 while reaching its production zenith at about 86,000.

Above
Pontiac's GTO kicked off the modern muscle car era with a bang in 1964. The "Goat" not only established a first-year new-model sales record for Pontiac that year, it also helped establish a new annual production standard for the GM division in June 1964. At far left is Pontiac General Manager Elliot "Pete" Estes, the man who made sure the GTO made it past corporate killjoys and into production.

Police needed it... Olds built it... Pursuit proved it!

Put this one on your WANTED list!

OLDSMOBILE 4-4-2
4-BARREL CARBURETOR!
4-ON-THE-FLOOR!
DUAL EXHAUSTS!

Now ready to put more muscle and hustle into *your* everyday performance needs! The Olds **4-4-2** —brand new action-tailored F-85 package—delivers 310 h.p. and 355 lb.-ft. of torque from its 4-barrel Jetfire Rocket V-8! Makes life still more exciting with a floor-mounted 4-speed synchromesh transmission, track-tested Red-Line tires, dual exhausts and heavy-duty chassis components—all part of the package!* Ask for details on the all-new **4-4-2**—available in any F-85 V-8 model except station wagons. *Additional special-duty options also available at extra cost.*

GET THE FULL STORY!
See your Local Authorized Oldsmobile Quality Dealer!

GO OLDS WHERE THE ACTION IS!

OLDSMOBILE DIVISION · GENERAL MOTORS CORPORATION · QUALITY BUILDERS OF THE NINETY-EIGHT, STARFIRE, SUPER 88, DYNAMIC 88, JETSTAR I, JETSTAR 88, F-85

MOTOR TREND/JULY 1964 17

Left
Oldsmobile followed in Pontiac's tracks, rolling out its first 4-4-2 midyear in 1964. As this ad explains, those three numerals stood for four-barrel carburetor, four on the floor, and dual (as in two) exhausts.

Below
Chevrolet's take on the GTO theme, the Chevelle SS 396, appeared midyear in 1965 and by 1969 was Detroit's best-selling muscle car. *Mike Mueller*

331-cubic-inch V-8 qualified as Detroit's most powerful offering that year. Oldsmobile, meanwhile, put a similarly designed 303-cube OHV V-8 to work hauling around a lot less tonnage. With an industry-best power-to-weight ratio, the 135-horsepower Rocket 88 instantly transformed Olds into the leader of the postwar performance pack, both on the street and at the track. Olds Rockets became big winners in Bill France's newly formed National Association for Stock Car Automobile Racing (NASCAR) racing league in 1949 and 1950.

The only muscle-bound milestone of the 1950s that mattered from a common man's perspective came from Chevrolet in 1955. Triple digits on the speedometer had never come as cheaply before GM's low-priced leader introduced its all-new OHV V-8, and the so-called "Hot One" continued taxing thermometers

further each year thereafter. Optional dual four-barrel carburetors appeared atop the instantly famous small-block V-8 in 1956, and Ramjet fuel injection debuted the following year.

Chevy engineers then introduced their first big-block V-8 in 1958, and this 348-cube mill evolved into the legendary 409 three years later. Arguably, no factory hot rod was finer in 1961 than the 409-powered Impala Super Sport. But, like all other supreme high-performance haulers before it (though fun to run, most V-8 Bel Airs didn't quite compare to the 1950s' meanest machines), Chevy's new SS 409 also was a high-priced heavyweight. Few Americans got the chance to experience Detroit's rapidly advancing horsepower race prior to 1964 because they simply couldn't afford the entry fee.

Not so, as far as the first GTO was concerned, and therein lies the reasoning that

Pontiac gets credit for creating the modern muscle car. Convinced that less indeed could be more, PMD movers and shakers simply took a lightweight, midsize body shell, stuffed it full of big-car engine, threw in a bit of heavy-duty hardware and a Hurst stick on the floor, then topped it all off with a bottom line within easy reach of the baby boomer set just coming of age. Talk about good timing.

Along with being America's first mass-produced performance car, the relatively affordable GTO also helped usher in a truly new era, as various midsize muscle-bound knockoffs quickly followed in the Tiger's tracks. GM at first was racing itself, with Oldsmobile's 4-4-2 appearing late in 1964, followed by Buick's Gran Sport and Chevrolet's Chevelle SS 396 in 1965. A limited-edition, high-priced experiment in its first year, the SS 396 became a big hit in 1966,

Dream sequence—
1968 edition.

We can't think of four better ways to take that new-car gleam out of your eye and put it in your driveway instead. That's if you're the kind who thinks an automobile is something other than a set of wheels.

And if the looks aren't enough to turn a young man's fancy, think about the total combination of engineering you've got going for you.

Just for starters, you've got a parcel of V-8's . . . each one a super sophisticate with tachs available to keep you aware of the numbers. For transmissions, take your pick of automatics like Turbo Hydra-Matic, Super Turbine and Powerglide (if you're the clutchless fan); or a choice of all-

synch 3- and 4-speed manuals, if you're the kind of guy who wants to do it yourself. Match these to a raft of axle-ratio options and you've got a power train ready to do just about any job you want it to do.

Then consider suspensions. We've paid plenty of attention to these. And the result is that the road testers call this troupe the best handling in GM's history. And don't forget brakes. We've got hefty drums standard all around —with power discs available.

Still trying to make up your mind? Why not get down to earth with the man who sells your favorite.

The more you look, the more our mark of excellence means.

CHEVROLET · PONTIAC · OLDSMOBILE · BUICK · CADILLAC

Our dream stable: Pontiac's GTO, Chevelle SS 396 from Chevrolet, GS 400 by Buick and Oldsmobile's 4-4-2.

Above Left
By 1968 GM muscle cars were everywhere, thanks to the contributions of every division except Cadillac. From left to right: a Pontiac GTO, Chevrolet Chevelle SS 396, Buick Gran Sport, and Olds 4-4-2.

Left
Buick's midsize muscle car was the Gran Sport, introduced in 1965. Initially limited to engines no larger than 400 cubic-inches, the GS was allowed a mating with the division's 455-cubic inch big-block V-8 in 1970. The special-edition GSX also debuted that year. At right is a 1970 GSX; at left is a 1971 model done in special-order red paint. *Mike Mueller*

when it reappeared in a more practical package better suited for the mass market. Some 70,000 were sold that year, as Chevrolet emerged as Pontiac's main challenger for the top muscle car sales spot. The SS 396 superseded the GTO atop the high-performance pack in 1969 while reaching its production zenith at about 86,000.

The muscle car genre itself reached its peak in 1970 then quickly raced off into the archives. By 1972, it was essentially all over but the shouting as far as most of Detroit's short-lived hot rod legacies were concerned. GM's speed merchants, however, somehow managed to keep a few embers burning up through 1974. It would take another 10 years or so for the sparks to start flying again.

Why the quick death? Various factors contributed.

Up until 1969, the Goat was America's best-selling high-performance automobile, which early on hit the streets carrying the "supercar" banner, at least according to quick-thinking automotive journalists like David E. Davis Jr., Eric Dahlquist, and Brock Yates.

Right
GM killed off its F-body pony car platform in 2002 after so many years of success. Chevrolet's Camaro was born in 1967, and the top performance package early that year was the SS 350 (at right). An SS 396 version debuted midyear. At left is a 1994 Z28, which came standard with a 275-horse version of the Corvette's LT1 small-block V-8. *Mike Mueller*

First off, basically no one stood up to say Americans couldn't drive fast cars when the GTO took off in 1964. Furthermore, few apparently cared that cars like this red-hot Pontiac tended to burn fuel by the barrel load then spit out the byproducts with little regard to who was breathing them in. At the time, only Southern Californians knew about smog, right? And gasoline supplies supposedly were bottomless with a gallon, as mentioned, going for about 25 cents, as it had for years.

Unfortunately, the times were soon a-changin'. Federal lawmakers began taking notice of clean air issues as early as 1965. Government-mandated smog controls began noticeably cramping the muscle car's style in 1968. Horsepower continued running strong for a few more years, but then additional, even tighter,

Above left
The hottest Oldsmobiles during the 1960s and 1970s were the W-30 models, quietly introduced in very small numbers in 1966. Olds name-callers have revived this label at various times during the years since. *Mike Mueller*

Above middle
Ford had its Shelby Mustangs; General Motors had its Hurst/ Olds models, born in 1968. Hurst/Olds convertibles paced the Indianapolis 500 in 1972 and 1974. *Mike Mueller*

Above right
Considered a "gentleman's hot rod," Buick's Gran Sport grew horns when fitted with the optional Stage 1 V-8, introduced in 400-cubic-inch form in 1969. The 455 Stage 1 was offered beneath GS hoods up through 1974. *Mike Mueller*

emissions controls began strangling the life out of the beast in the early 1970s. With the further mandated use of lower-octane unleaded fuels right around the corner, automakers in 1971 were forced to make major compression concessions in their engines, effectively squeezing surviving ponies within an inch of their lives.

Congress also kicked off an especially vigorous investigation into automotive safety in 1965. Hearings conducted that summer by Senator Abraham Ribicoff, among other things, thrust East Coast lawyer Ralph Nader into the limelight. A new wave of tougher safety standards then followed. All this legislative work resulted in kinder, gentler, cleaner-running automobiles, all wearing higher price tags due to increased design costs.

The cost of owning a muscle car was heightened further after the insurance industry grew wise to the situation and began using growing accident statistics to increase their rates. By 1970, young Average Joe couldn't

afford to insure a high-performance vehicle, and the situation only grew worse as gas prices started to soar, along with insurance premiums a few years later. The Arab oil embargo of October 1973 transformed gasoline into gold overnight and basically killed off the few remaining muscle cars in the process.

Survivors into the 1970s included the Buick Stage 1, which managed to stand relatively tall up through 1974. But arguably the last great muscle car—perhaps coincidentally, perhaps not—was again a Pontiac. The Firebird Super Duty 455 was offered in small numbers in both Formula and Trans Am garb in 1973 and 1974, and this emissions-legal, low-compression, big-block bad boy somehow ran every bit as well as most performance machines built before federal controls began inhibiting horsepower. But even Pontiac engineers couldn't get around the restrictive catalytic converters that arrived in 1975 to finally hammer the muscle car's coffin closed.

Mighty lean years then followed, until

The Firebird Super Duty 455 was offered in small numbers in both Formula and Trans Am garb in 1973 and 1974

Detroit's engineering fraternity eventually developed the technology to effectively combine fuel efficiency, low contaminant counts, and horsepower. The muscle car was then reborn, with GM-designed examples again at the forefront. How long this generation survives is anyone's guess. But one thing remains relatively certain: a General Motors product will be there when Detroit's latest horsepower race reaches the finish line.

Above
Only one factory hot rod rolled uninterrupted from the original muscle car era up into recent times: Pontiac's Trans Am. Born in 1969, it appeared each year thereafter until GM retired its F-body models in 2002. From right to left: a 1969 Trans Am, 1974 Super Duty 455 model, and 1999 30th Anniversary convertible. Many consider the 1974 Super Duty to be Detroit's last great muscle car, at least as far as the original breed was concerned. *Mike Mueller*

01

Above
1962 Pontiac Grand Prix

Middle
1965 Pontiac 2+2

Right
1962 Impala SS 409

Full-Size Flyers

01

Sixties Sensations Big Chevys and Pontiacs

Big cubes in big cars sporting big price tags represented the only way to fly around Detroit before the GTO came along to change all the rules. Discounting Chevrolet's Corvette, the hottest GM machines available during the early 1960s were based on heavyweights like Pontiac's Catalina and Chevy's Impala, simply because these were the only candidates available. Multiple model lines didn't exist in the Big Three arena during the 1950s (again excusing the Corvette's presence), and when this concept fully blossomed in the next decade, it initially involved frugal compacts, mini-mobiles like Chevrolet's rear-engine Corvair.

→ Both Pontiac and Chevrolet introduced all-new overhead-valve V-8s in 1955, and the latter relied on the innovative ball-stud rocker arm design created for the former.

→ In 1957, new NASCAR rules effectively banned superchargers and multiple-carburetor setups, leaving only single four-barrel engines legal to compete on its tracks.

→ Pontiac's full-size Super Duty (SD) models were joined in 1963 by a small run of radically modified SD Tempests.

→ While the 348 V-8 was dropped as a passenger car option in 1961, it remained available for Chevrolet trucks up through 1965.

While GM's senior compacts—Buick's Special and Oldsmobile's F-85—did appear in 1961 with a little more size and a lot more prestige than the Corvair (not to mention standard V-8 power), they had no business putting on excessive muscle. Same for Pontiac's rather off-the-wall Tempest, introduced with its so-called "rope" driveshaft and a standard four-cylinder in 1961. Next to no one atop GM's executive ivory tower at the time was interested in reinventing the hot wheel anyway, so what did it matter that not one of these budding intermediates was capable (at least not without major modifications) of rushing into nearby phone booths and bursting back out in supercar guise?

While such transformations did occur soon enough, they didn't become physically possible until after the Buick-Olds-Pontiac trio was

reborn on General Motors' upsized A-body platform in 1964. Equally key was the Pontiac execs' willingness to go where no other GM division heads dared with their supposedly taboo Tiger. But that's another tale for another chapter—the next one, to be exact.

As for Detroit's high-performance history before the GTO rewrote the books, it was no coincidence that Pontiac Motor Division (PMD) also was home to some of Detroit's meanest machines during the late 1950s and early 1960s. Semon E. Knudsen simply wouldn't have it any other way. "Bunkie" to both friends and foes, Knudsen was a really big fan of fast cars, as his bosses quickly discovered after he was made PMD general manager in June 1956. "You can sell a young man's car to an old man," began his prime motto, "but you'll never sell an

old man's car to a young man." He knew full well
that speed always sells and it does so especially well to those young bucks he spoke of. So
it was that he transformed Pontiac seemingly
overnight from the staid, stoic builder of automobiles your grandpa loved into a source for
truly exciting performance.

To help build that excitement, Knudsen
hired chief engineer Elliot "Pete" Estes away
from Oldsmobile and staff engineer John De

Lorean from dying Packard. Bunkie also took
up relations with legendary speed merchant
Smokey Yunick, of Daytona Beach racing fame,
and became a close comrade of big Bill France,
who had founded the NASCAR stock car racing
circuit in 1948.

By 1957, Pontiac was a newfound force to
be reckoned with in Detroit's horsepower race.
Hot-off-the-stove high-performance hardware
that year included fuel injection (for the lim-

ited-edition Bonneville convertible) and "Tri
Power," a triple-carb induction setup Estes had
borrowed from Olds before jumping over to
Pontiac. At the same time, a new performance
parts program was under development, primarily to help make Pontiac competitive on Bill
France's tracks.

In truth, Pontiac's competition efforts had
begun just before Knudsen took over. Early in
1956, engineers Bob Holan, Bob Clift, and

Bill Aldrich teamed up with veteran Indy 500 wrenchman Lou Moore to prepare two Pontiacs for February's annual Speed Weeks trials in Daytona Beach, where one of these machines reportedly ran 132 miles per hour in practice. The duo also qualified well (third and fourth) for NASCAR's Grand National race on February 26 but fell victim early to overheating problems.

Knudsen arrived that summer and picked up where Moore's gang left off, creating an in-house engineering team that, according to noted Pontiac promotions guru Jim Wangers, was called the "Super Duty group." Team members included Malcolm McKellar, who had helped develop Pontiac's new V-8 for 1955 and then donated his name to a series of high-performance camshafts that would soon be at the heart of the division's hottest powerplants.

Among the group's earliest products was a supertough, forged NASCAR connecting rod, officially released in February 1957. Various other race-ready components soon followed, even after the Automobile Manufacturers Association (AMA) supposedly banned factory racing involvement that June. Pontiac engineers continued work on what McKellar later called their "Super Duty packages" as if nothing had changed.

Pontiac 389 Super Duty Catalina

1961 Pontiac 389 Super Duty Catalina

Model	two-door coupe w/aluminum bumpers
Wheelbase	119 inches
Curb weight	3,880 pounds
Track	62.5 inches, front and rear
Suspension	independent upper/lower A-arms, coil springs, stabilizer bar in front; control arms, coil springs in back
Steering	recirculating ball
Brakes	four-wheel drums
Engine	368-horsepower 389 cubic-inch Super Duty V-8
Bore & stroke	4.06 x 3.75 inches
Compression	10.75:1
Fuel delivery	single Carter four-barrel carburetor
Transmission	Borg Warner T-10 four-speed manual

Above

Pontiac's Catalina line featured three two-door models in 1961: a coupe, convertible, and sport sedan. Super Duty coupes and sedans were both built that year. Total production is estimated at about 25, including this coupe. A weight-saving aluminum front bumper was added to the Super Duty package in 1961. *Mike Mueller*

Left

The 1961 389 Super Duty V-8 was token-rated at 368 horsepower, whether topped by a single Carter four-barrel (shown here) or optional Tri Power. Late that year, the Super Duty V-8 was bored out to 421 cubic-inches. *Mike Mueller*

These packages at first included solid lifters, stiffer valve springs (to increase rev limits), dual exhausts, and a lumpy Iskenderian E-2 cam. The pot was sweetened even further for the stock car racing set in 1959 after Pontiac engineers created a beefed-up cylinder block for the division's latest, greatest V-8, stroked up to 389 cubic-inches from the 370 cubes displaced the year before.

In December 1959, Pontiac announced a more complete competition engine package (for 1960 models) that many enthusiasts today call the first true Super Duty V-8. Inside its four-

bolt block, the new 389 Super Duty featured a beefed, forged-steel crank and tough, forged rods. Forged pistons squeezed the mixture to a 10.75:1 ratio, and a big four-barrel carb on an aluminum intake supplied that mix. On top were special cylinder heads with large ports and big valves. In place of the aftermarket Isky cam was Pontiac's own No. 7 McKellar solid-lifter shaft. Spent gases were handled by unique, free-flowing, cast-iron manifolds that incorporated individual runners in tube-header fashion.

Offered only as an over-the-counter dealer option, the 389 Super Duty was arbitrarily rated at 348 horsepower, only 15 horses more than Pontiac's hottest regular-production street engine (with four-barrel carb) for 1960. Another 389 SD, this one fitted with Tri Power and rated at 363 horsepower, was created for drag racers, who weren't limited by National Hot Rod Association (NHRA) rules to a single carburetor like their NASCAR counterparts.

Those in the know could only laugh at Pontiac's token output ratings for these two muscle-bound mills. According to NASCAR mechanics, the new 389 SD produced at least 40 to 50 horses more than Pontiac's factory race engine from 1959. Results quickly supported their claims as Edward Glenn "Fireball" Roberts' Super Duty Pontiac surpassed 150 miles per hour during qualifying for NASCAR's second Daytona 500 in February 1960. Later, on Labor Day, part-time racer/full-time ad exec Jim Wangers copped the Super Stock title at the NHRA Nationals in Detroit at the wheel of his unbeatable Catalina. Buck Baker's SD Pontiac took NASCAR laurels at Darlington that same day, all this after Louie Unser had conquered the Pikes Peak Hillclimb in a Super Duty a few weeks before. Speed king Mickey Thompson then capped things off on September 9 at

Bonneville by running a record 406 miles per hour in his *Challenger I* salt-runner, powered by four Super Duty V-8s.

For 1961, both Super Duty V-8s—single-carb and Tri Power—were rated the same 368 horsepower. Improvements included a lumpier No. 8 McKellar cam and new cylinder heads featuring even larger ports. A lightweight aluminum Tri Power intake was new as well, and bumpers were made of aluminum at both ends to cut loose more unwanted pounds. Last, those aggressive-looking Super Duty exhaust manifolds were fitted with clever split-flow collectors incorporating twin 2-inch outlets—one to connect up to stock dual pipes, the other capped by a bolt-on cover that could be removed easily for wide-open operation.

These upgrades further solidified the Super Duty Pontiac's hold on sanctioned racing in

Above left
Pontiac's standard Grand Prix image in 1962 included special grillework front and rear. Attractive eight-lug wheels, first offered in 1960, were optional. Those lugs attached the rim to a finned aluminum brake drum. *Mike Mueller*

Above
Bucket seats and a console with floorshift were standard for the 1962 Grand Prix. Both a four-speed manual and Pontiac's Hydra-Matic automatic were options. In this case, the four-speed backs up the optional 421 Super Duty V-8. Only 16 Super Duty Grand Prix coupes were built for 1962. *Mike Mueller*

Pontiac 421 Super Duty Catalina

1962 Pontiac 421 Super Duty Catalina

All 1962 Super Duty models are fully documented due to the transfer from clandestine dealer extra to full-fledged factory option, a move that created an official paper trail.

Model	two-door coupe w/aluminum hood, fenders, and bumpers
Wheelbase	120 inches
Length	211.6 inches
Width	78.6 inches
Height	55.9 inches
Curb weight	3,800 pounds
Track	62.5 inches, front and rear
Suspension	independent upper/lower A-arms, coil springs, heavy-duty stabilizer bar in front; control arms and coil springs in back
Steering	recirculating ball
Brakes	heavy-duty 11-inch finned aluminum drums optional in front, cast-iron drums in back
Engine	405-horsepower 421-cubic-inch Super Duty V-8
Bore & stroke	4.09 x 4.00 inches
Compression	11.1:1
Fuel delivery	two Carter four-barrel carburetors (1,000 cfm total)
Transmission	Borg-Warner T-10 four-speed
Axle ratio	4.30:1 in Safe-T-Track four-pinion differential
Production	139 (another 16 Super Duty Grand Prix coupes and 24 Super Duty Catalina sedans were built in 1962)

1961. After a 1-2-3 finish at Daytona, Pontiac teams went on to win 30 of 52 NASCAR races that season. Super Duty drag racers also swept through the four top stock classes at the NHRA Nationals in September 1961.

Just prior to the NHRA Nats, Pontiac officials announced a bigger, stronger Super Duty V-8 based on a bored-out 389 block. This 421-cubic-inch monster also was grossly underrated, this time at 373 horsepower. And it was exceedingly rare. Only a dozen or so were shipped to preferred drag racers, including Arnie Beswick and Mickey Thompson, prompting NHRA officials to finally step in.

Drag racing's rules moguls previously had allowed Detroit's performance pipeline to flow unchecked, supplying select, limited-run racing parts to select, prominent racers under the guise of dealer-offered options programs. In the interest of fairness, NHRA people demanded

that manufacturers either offer these packages to Average Joe as regular production options or forget about pumping up the corporate image on NHRA quarter-miles, at least in stock classes. A new class, Factory Experimental (FX), was created for exotic factory racers that didn't qualify as production stock.

Pontiac's immediate response to the new NHRA mandate was a regular production run of 200 optional 421 SD V-8s (rated at 405 horsepower) for 1962. As for the 1961 389 Super Duty Pontiac, no one really knows how many were built. All 1962 Super Duty models are fully documented due to the transfer from clandestine dealer extra to full-fledged factory option, a move that created an official paper trail. Accordingly, of those 200 engines, 139 went into Catalina coupes, 24 into Catalina sedans, and 16 into Grand Prix sport coupes. The remaining 21 were spares for race teams.

Another 13 385-horsepower 389 Super Duty V-8s apparently also were produced that year, with seven going into Catalinas. The common estimate listed for the 1961 389 Super Duty is 25, and among these are both sporty coupes and mundane bat-wing sedans.

The 16 Grand Prix coupes among the 1962 Super Duty roll call still stick out like sore thumbs. Why anyone would want to combine such frills with so much balls-out muscle is anyone's guess. Introduced in September 1961, two months before Knudsen moved over to Chevrolet, the first Grand Prix was considered a gentleman's hot rod aimed at older, upscale customers. Exclusive trim treatments clearly set the sporty Grand Prix apart from its Catalina brethren on the outside, while bucket seats, a console, and full instrumentation were standard inside.

1962 Pontiac Grand Prix

1962 Pontiac Grand Prix

Model availability	two-door coupe
Wheelbase	120 inches
Length	211.6 inches
Width	78.6 inches
Height	55.9 inches
Curb weight	3,915 pounds
Base price	$3,490
Track	62.5 inches, front and rear
Wheels	14x6 stamped steel, std.; eight-lug rims with finned aluminum drums, optional
Tires	8.00x14 four-ply
Suspension	independent upper/lower A-arms, coils springs, stabilizer bar in front; control arms, coil springs in back
Steering	recirculating ball
Brakes	four-wheel hydraulic drums
Engine	303-horsepower 389-cubic-inch Trophy V-8
Bore & stroke	4.06 x 3.75 inches
Compression	10.25:1
Fuel delivery	single Carter four-barrel carburetor
Transmission	three-speed manual, std.; four-speed manual and Hydra-Matic automatic, optional
Axle ratio	3.42:1 w/manual transmission; 3.23:1 with automatic transmission
Production	30,195

A rocket scientist wasn't necessary to explain how the name came about. Pontiac grew famous for copping various legendary labels from the international racing scene during Knudsen's short stay. Before Grand Prix, there was Bonneville in 1957, followed by Le Mans (a deluxe, sporty version of the Tempest) in 1961.

Standard motivation for the 1962 GP was a 303-horsepower 389 "Trophy V-8." Tri Power was optional, boosting output to 348 horses. At the top of the list was the 421 Super Duty, the mean and nasty mill that had no business on the street, let alone between the fenders of a classy boulevard cruiser like the Grand Prix. Even Pontiac officials admitted this. "These [Super Duty models] are not intended for general passenger car use," read a 1962 corporate disclaimer, "and they are not supplied by Pontiac Motor Division for such purposes."

Purpose-built from air cleaner to oil pan, the 421 SD V-8 featured a beefy, four-bolt block with a forged-steel crank, 11:1-compression Mickey Thompson forged-aluminum pistons, and an 8-quart, wide-sump oil pan. Inside was an aggressive No. 10 McKellar solid-lifter cam, on top were two big Carter aluminum four-barrel (AFB) carbs totaling 1,000 cfm, and bringing up the exhaust end were those unmistakable long-branch headers with their convenient cutouts. New for 1962 were optional weight-saving aluminum versions of those headers, made of castiron in standard form.

Additional lightweight parts in 1962 included fenders, inner fenders, hood, front bumper, and radiator brackets all stamped from aluminum. The Super Duty frame featured perimeter rails that were cut out to transform rectangular tubes into channel, saving additional weight. A

customer also could have specified deletion of insulation and sound deadener, but only a handful did.

Again, the 405-horse rating for the 1962 Super Duty was a joke. Veteran *Motor Trend* road-tester Roger Huntington estimated that the true number was more like 465 after taking a wild quarter-mile ride (13.9 seconds at 107 miles per hour) in a Super Duty Catalina with Jim Wangers at the wheel. "I must say, this new 421 Pontiac is a terrific piece of automobile," he concluded. "I'm still shaking." Perhaps he should have tried the more comfortable Super Duty Grand Prix.

Inside and out, all 16 of these strange creations came equipped with typical GP plushness and pizzazz, and 14 of them rolled on Pontiac's high-profile, eight-lug wheels. Reportedly, the first SD Grand Prix off the line even featured air conditioning. All 16 had four-speeds and standard steel front ends in place of the weight-conscious aluminum pieces, which wouldn't have stood up long in a real world full of parking lot demolition derbies and lazy, fender-leaning valets.

When the 421 Super Duty V-8 rolled over into 1963, it appeared in three forms: a NASCAR-spec four-barrel version, rated at 390 horsepower; and two dual-four examples, one featuring 12:1 compression (like its single-carb little brother) and another that mashed the mix at a head-cracking 13:1 ratio. Ratings were the familiar 405 horses for the former, 410 for the latter. New for the 1963 Super Duty package was a lightweight Swiss-cheese frame, which was drilled to cut away even more pounds. At least 85 421 SD V-8s went into 1963 models (Tempest, Catalina, and Grand Prix), with maybe as many as three other cars released but not recorded. According to Pontiac man Fred Simmonds' exhaustive research, the Super Duty V-8 breakdown that year read 13 390-horsepower V-8s, 59 405-horsepower 421s, 5

410-horsepower 421s, and 11 405-horsepower Tempest renditions.

Production of 1963 Super Duty Pontiacs began in September 1962 but abruptly ended early the following year. On January 21, 1963, GM Chairman Frederic Donner and President John Gordon instructed all divisions to cease any and all racing involvement, something the AMA had supposedly decreed for every American automaker six years before.

"Ever since the AMA adopted—I think you can term it a recommendation—back in 1957, we have had a policy on our books, and we haven't had any change in it," said Donner at a February 16 press conference. Maybe so, but his officers still had no qualms about looking the other way while GM divisions boldly went racing prior to January 1963. Why stand up and salute then?

Above
Super Duty Pontiacs were built into early 1963 before General Motors executives ordered all of its divisions to cease their involvement in racing projects. This Super Duty Catalina was built rather clandestinely for racer Johnny Mauro in May 1963, making it the last of the breed. *Mike Mueller*

Above right
Pontiac created this single-carb 421 Super Duty V-8 for NASCAR tracks, where multiple carburetors were banned. Topped by a 625-cfm Carter AFB, this SD V-8 made 390 horsepower in 1963. *Mike Mueller*

Right
First seen late in 1959, the distinctive Super Duty cast-iron exhaust manifolds looked very much like aftermarket headers. They also featured twin openings, one leading to stock exhausts, the other sealed by a bolt-on cap that could've been removed for unrestricted, wide-open operation. In 1962, aluminum versions of these so-called "long-branch" manifolds were cast. *Mike Mueller*

The corporation's top brass were more or less covering their asses, probably in an effort to divert any additional attention from federal investigators who already were on GM's case concerning purported monopolistic business practices. Whatever the case, the Super Duty story came to a close, though not before a few '63 models managed to escape into the wild in February and March. One final Super Duty Catalina even rolled off the line in May.

From there, the leader of Pontiac's full-size performance pack was the 2+2, first offered in 1964 as a $291 option package for Catalina hardtops and convertibles. That price jumped to $418.54 in 1965, as the 421 V-8 was added to the 2+2 mix. In 1964, the 389 was standard, with the 421 listed as a separate option. In 1965, it was 421 cubic-inches or none at all.

Above
Pontiac's 2+2, offered from 1964 to 1967, represented the company's last shot at the full-size performance field. The 2+2 deal was an options package in 1964 and 1967; in between, it was offered as an individual model on its own. This convertible is one of 11,251 2+2 Pontiacs built for 1965. *Mike Mueller*

Left
The top 2+2 engine option in 1965 was this 421 Tri Power V-8, rated at 376 horsepower. Compression was 10.75:1. *Mike Mueller*

Above
Pontiac's big 2+2 made one last appearance as a distinct model in 1966 (shown here) then became an options package for its 1967 encore.

The leader of Pontiac's full-size performance pack was the 2+2.

Pontiac 2+2

1965 Pontiac 2+2	

Model availability	two-door coupe, two-door convertible
Wheelbase	121 inches
Length	214.6 inches
Width	79.6 inches
Height	55.2 inches
Curb weight	4,160 pounds
Price	2+2 option cost $418.54
Track (front/rear, in inches)	63/64
Wheels	optional eight-lug rims w/finned aluminum brake drums
Tires	8.55x14 rayon whitewalls
Suspension	independent upper/lower A-arms, heavy-duty coil springs, stabilizer bar in front; control arms, heavy-duty coil springs in back
Steering	recirculating ball
Brakes	four-wheel hydraulic finned drums
Engine	376-horsepower 421-cubic-inch V-8 (optional: 338-horsepower 421 V-8, std.)
Bore & stroke	4.09 x 4.00 inches
Compression	10.75:1
Fuel delivery	three Rochester two-barrel carburetors
Transmission	three-speed manual w/Hurst shifter, std; four-speed manual and Hydra-Matic automatic, optional
Axle ratio	3.42:1 w/manual transmission; 3.23:1 w/automatic
Production	11,521 (5,316 w/manual transmissions, 6,205 with automatic)

Three different High Output (HO) 421s were offered to 2+2 buyers in 1965. The base HO big-block that year featured 10.5:1 compression and a single four-barrel carb topped by a chrome low-restriction air cleaner. Output was 338 horsepower. Boosting compression to 10.75:1, trading the four-barrel for Tri Power, and adding dual straight-through mufflers resulted in the 356-horsepower version. Another 20 horses were let loose by adding three open-element air cleaners, a hotter cam, special valve-train gear, low-restriction exhaust manifolds, and a de-clutching fan.

As it had in 1964, the basic 2+2 package in 1965 also included a Hurst-shifted heavy-duty three-speed manual, bucket seats, and promi-

nent exterior identification. Underneath was a typically stiffened suspension with beefier springs and shocks and a thickened front stabilizer bar. Optional in 1965 was a four-speed manual or three-speed Turbo Hydra-Matic automatic.

After showing up for 1966 as an individual model, the 2+2 made one last appearance, again as an options package, in 1967. From there, the big-car performance field was left to another GM product, a full-size flyer also identified using superlative terminology. This time the tagline read "Super Sport."

Chevrolet's now-famous SS badge has appeared on many vehicles over the years, including trucks dating back to 1990. Nova, Chevelle,

and Camaro were treated to this simply snazzy package during the 1960s, and all three varieties still have a healthy following today. The most popular of the breed back then, though, was the original, the Impala Super Sport, unveiled midyear in 1961. Some 920,000 of these big babies hit the streets before the plug was pulled in 1969, as buyers by then apparently no longer cared so much about supersizing their sporty flights of fancy. Chevy customers in 1970 still could install the new 454 big-block V-8 beneath Impala or Caprice hoods, but it just wasn't the same. An era had ended, and an Impala SS wouldn't be seen again until the breed was briefly revived, in four-door form, from 1994 to 1996.

1961 Chevrolet Impala SS

1961 Chevrolet Impala SS

Model availability	two-door coupe
Wheelbase	119 inches
Length	209.3 inches
Width	78.4 inches
Height	55.5 inches,
Curb weight	3,480 pounds
Price	SS trim package cost $53.80; various mandatory options pushed the total price to around $3,700.
Track (front/rear, in inches)	60.3/59.3
Wheels	14x6 stamped-steel
Tires	8.00x14 four-ply with narrow whitewalls
Suspension	independent upper/lower A-arms, heavy-duty coils springs, stabilizer bar in front; four-link control arms and heavy-duty coil springs in back; heavy-duty shock absorbers
Steering	power-assisted recirculating ball
Brakes	power-assisted four-wheel hydraulic drums with sintered metallic linings
Engine	305-horsepower 348-cubic-inch V-8 (RPO 572)
	340-horsepower 348-cubic-inch V-8 (RPO 590)
	350-horsepower 348-cubic-inch V-8 (RPO 573B)
	360-horsepower 409-cubic-inch V-8 (RPO 580)
Bore & stroke	4.125 x 3.25 inches (348 V-8); 4.3125 x 3.5 inches (409 V-8)
Compression	9.5:1 (305-hp 348 V-8), 11.25:1 (340-hp and 350-hp 348 V-8s), 11.25:1 (409 V-8)
Fuel delivery	single Carter four-barrel carburetor (305-hp and 340-hp 348 V-8s), three Rochester two-barrel carburetors (350-hp 348 V-8), single Carter four-barrel carburetor (409 V-8)
Transmission	four-speed manual installed behind all engines; Powerglide automatic optional only behind 305-hp 348 V-8
Axle ratio	3.36:1 (305-hp 348 V-8 w/four-speed); 3.55:1 (305-hp 348 V-8 with Powerglide); 3.70:1 (340-hp and 350-hp 348 V-8s); 3.36:1 (409 V-8)
Production	453

Above
Chevrolet's first production Super Sport debuted early in 1961 along with the famed 409 V-8. Only 453 Impala Super Sports were built that first year, with most featuring the 348 V-8, as demonstrated in this case. Notice the absence of any engine badge on the front fender. *Mike Mueller*

Chevrolet's Super Sport kit was first announced to dealers late in January 1961, just in time to help showcase the equally new 409 V-8. A fact-filled amendment to that year's *Passenger Car Specifications* book followed in February, and color brochures officially introduced the deal to the public, though not without some confusion. According to Chevy paperwork that year, this sexy option was available for all Impala series models except the Nomad station wagon. Two-door or four, sedan, coupe, or convertible, each variety supposedly could've been tricked out in SS trim. In reality, apparently all 453 Super Sports built for 1961 featured two doors and coupe roofs. Some reports claim a few convertibles were released. But without a doubt, no SS sedans or four-doors made it into public hands.

The SS trim package on its own cost a mere $53.80, and for that tidy sum a 1961 Impala was dressed up with exclusive wheel covers and "SS" badges on the deck lid and rear quarters. Those wheel covers were adorned with triple-blade spinners intended to simulate knockoff hubs. Added inside was a Corvette-style grab bar on the dashboard's far right and a bright floor plate for the shifter in

Unfortunately, the cash register didn't stop ringing there, as various other regular production options (RPOs) were mandatory along with the 409 V-8.

four-speed models.

Unfortunately, the cash register didn't stop ringing there, as various other regular production options (RPOs) were mandatory. A 1961 Super Sport customer also had to shell out for RPO 200 (heavy-duty shock absorbers), RPOs 253 and 593 (heavy-duty springs front and rear, respectively), RPO 324 (power steering), RPO 412 (power brakes), RPO 331 (7,000-rpm tachometer), RPO 427 (padded instrument panel), RPO 686 (police car metallic brake linings), and RPO 691 (8.00x14 four-ply tires with narrow whitewalls). Available only for the Impala SS in 1961, those tires represented Chevrolet's first application of modern skinny whitewalls, and they were mounted on station-wagon rims that measured 1 inch wider than the 14x5 wheels found on other Chevy passenger cars that year.

Like its 348 forerunner, the 409 served as a powerful workhorse in Chevy truck ranks.

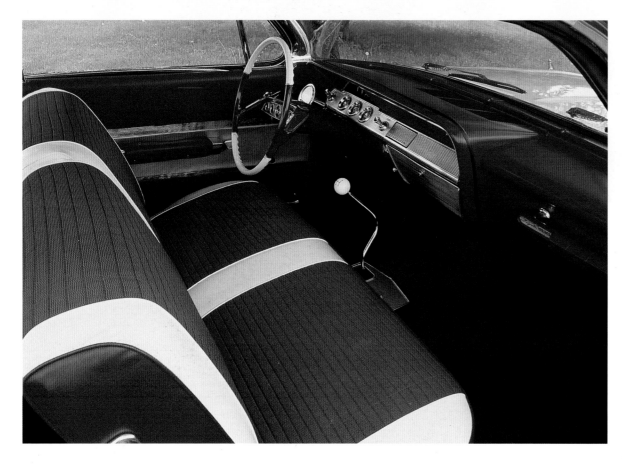

Left
A tachometer and a passenger-side grab bar were standard inside the 1961 Impala SS, as was a bright floor plate for manual transmission models. *Mike Mueller*

As for power, no small-block V-8s or sixes were even considered in keeping with this model's supersporty ideal. It was W-series big-block all the way. But despite the coincidental introduction of the Impala SS and the 409 V-8, not all Super Sports featured this famed power-plant, which also found its way into Biscaynes and Bel Airs that year. Total 409 V-8 production for 1961 is commonly listed at 142, with no breakdown known by model line. All remaining Super Sports were fitted with one of three 348-cubic-inch W engines rated at 305, 340, or 350 horsepower. Super Sport transmission choices in 1961 numbered two: a heavy-duty Corvette-type Powerglide automatic (RPO 313) or a four-speed manual (RPO 685). The Powerglide was only available behind the 305-horse 348

(RPO 572), while the 340/348 (RPO 590) and 350/348 (RPO 573B) were limited to the four-speed, which in this case relied on a 2.54:1 low gear. The 409's (RPO 580) close-ratio four-speed contained a 2.20:1 first gear.

W-series roots ran back to 1958, the year the original Impala also appeared. Chevy's first big-block V-8 initially was conceived for both car and truck duty. The contributing engineers included Richard Keinath, Fred Frincke, Denny Davis, Cal Wade, and Al Kolbe. In the automotive realm, the 348 represented Chevrolet's hottest passenger car option each year from 1958 into early 1961. All W engines featured high compression (9.5:1 or better), all relied on at least a four-barrel carburetor (no single two-barrels; no way, no how), and all had dual

exhausts. Ultimate renditions relied on solid lifters and were fed by three Rochester two-barrel carburetors.

Helping the 348 run so hot were staggered valves, made possible by the innovative ball-stud rocker arm design used originally in the new V-8s rolled out in 1955 by both Chevrolet and Pontiac. All rival V-8s at the time featured straight-line valve layouts, this because their rockers were mounted together on long shafts that spanned the length of each head. GM's ball-stud rockers allowed the W engine design team to independently position valves where they would work best. In a 348 head, intake valves were positioned up high near the intake manifold runners. Exhaust valves, in turn, were found down low, close to the exhaust manifolds. This distinctive zigzag layout translated into less passage wall area to inhibit intake and exhaust flow.

Equally distinctive were the W engine's combustion chambers. Conventional V-8 designs have long featured cylinder block decks that are perpendicular to their bores, and atop these are heads with combustion chambers machined into their undersides. Not so in the 348's case. The working face of its head was basically smooth (valves opened and closed in slight pockets) as the combustion chambers were created inside the block by sloping each cylinder bank's deck 16 degrees off

perpendicular. Pent-roofed pistons defined their own wedge-shaped squish area within their bores once they squeezed up against the flat-faced heads. This design both simplified head production and allowed the installation of really big (for the time) valves.

Chevy's base 348 V-8 was rated at 250 horsepower from 1958 to 1961. Both this four-barrel big-block and the lowest-performance triple-carb 348 (tagged at 280 horsepower during the same span) were not available for the 1961 Impala SS. Of the three 348s listed for the first Super Sport, two (RPOs 572 and 590) were topped by single four-barrel carbs. The top-dog 350-horsepower 348 featured those triple Rochesters, while the newest W engine, the 409, relied on a single Carter four-barrel to help produce 360 horsepower.

Like its 348 forerunner, the 409 served as a powerful workhorse in Chevy truck ranks. But there was nothing yeomanlike about the 409s installed on the car side of the fence. While more than one witness mistakenly considered this improved W-series big-block to be little more than an enlarged 348, it was nowhere near as simple as that. For starters, boring the 348 block represented a risky proposition—not enough iron existed between the water jacket and cylinder bore. Accordingly, the block was recast, allowing the bores to increase from 4.125 to 4.3125 inches without fear of

1963 Chevrolet Z11

1963 Chevrolet Z11

Body modifications	hood, hood catch, grille filler panel, fenders, bumpers. and bumper brackets all made of weight-saving aluminum; some cars featured deleted sound deadener, insulation and heater
Wheelbase	119 inches
Length	210.4 inches
Width	79 inches
Height	55.5 inches
Curb weight	3,405 pounds
Price	Z11 option cost $1,237
Track (front/rear, in inches)	60.3/59.3
Wheels	15x5.5 stamped-steel
Tires	6.70x15 bias ply
Suspension	independent upper/lower A-arms, heavy-duty coil springs in front; four-link control arms and heavy-duty coil springs in back; heavy-duty shock absorbers (front stabilizer bar deleted)
Steering	recirculating ball
Brakes	four-wheel hydraulic drums with sintered metallic linings and special cooling equipment for rear drums
Engine	430-horsepower 427-cubic-inch W-series V-8 with raised-port heads (2.19-inch intake valves, 1.72-inch exhaust valves) and two-part intake manifold
Bore & stroke	4.3125 x 3.65 inches
Compression	13.5:1
Fuel delivery	two Carter four-barrel carburetors with special cowl-induction air cleaner
Transmission	Borg-Warner T-10 four-speed manual
Axle ratio	4.11:1 Posi-traction
Production	57 (some sources claim 55)

Above
The supreme 409 was the Z11 rendition, built for racing only. Displacing 427 cubic-inches, thanks to a stroker crank, the Z11 featured special raised-port heads that mandated the installation of an equally special two-piece intake manifold. *Mike Mueller*

compromising the cylinder walls. At the same time, stroke was lengthened a quarter inch to 3.50, resulting in the displacement figure that fit so well into the Beach Boys' famous lyrics.

Modifications were plenty from there, so much so that swapping parts between the 348 and 409 basically was out of the question. New forged-aluminum pistons featured centered wrist pins and symmetrical valve reliefs milled straight across the piston top in pairs. Their 348 counterparts had offset wrist pins with one large intake relief and one smaller exhaust relief. This meant a 348 required two opposite sets of four pistons, each set with its own part number. All 409 pistons interchanged regardless of which cylinder bank they went into.

Connecting those pistons to a beefed-up, forged-steel crank were shortened, reinforced rods, while superior Morraine 500 steel-backed aluminum bearings replaced the 348's outdated Morraine 400 pieces. Cylinder heads closely resembled the 348 design but were specially cast to accept larger-diameter pushrods and machined on top for heavier valve springs. Valve sizes stayed the same–2.066-inch intakes, 1.720 exhausts–but the cam was a far more

aggressive solid-lifter unit. Compression was 11.25:1.

Bringing up the rear in the Super Sport 409's mandatory supporting cast was a 3.36:1 highway axle. Curiously, the 340- and 350-horsepower 348 models got more suitable (from an off-the-line perspective) 3.70:1 standard rear gears. Go figure. Fortunately, various stump-pulling cogs were available optionally, as was Posi-Traction.

Factory hot rod fans first got wind of just what Chevy had wrought in February 1961 when a white Impala coupe and red Biscayne sedan rolled into Pomona, California, and proceeded to take the NHRA's first annual Winternationals by storm. Both cars were fitted

with early-production 409 V-8s delivered direct-ly to their owners in crates just days before the Pomona drags commenced. Hastily dyno-tuned and tested for NHRA stock class competition, Don Nicholson's 409-powered Impala left the Pontiac and Ford guys gawking after a 13.19-second trial pass topping out at 109.48 miles per hour, then slammed the hammer down with a 13.59/105.88 Stock Eliminator victory over Frank Sanders' 409-urged Biscayne—this after Sanders had beaten Nicholson for the Super Stock title the day before. "Dyno" Don's 409 then went on to become a match race legend in 1961, touring the country and never once losing to a Ford.

Factory hot rod fans first got wind of just what Chevy had wrought in February 1961

Above
Chevrolet released various race-ready goodies for its full-size flyers during the summer of 1962. Among these were aluminum body parts, created to save weight on the strip. This veteran quarter-miler has those rare aluminum components. *Mike Mueller*

Left
Optional dual carburetors were first offered atop the 409 late in 1961 and then became a full-fledged RPO the following year. Advertised output for this real fine mill was 409 horsepower in 1962. It hit 425 horses in 1963.

RPO 580 grew more attractive the following year as 20 extra horses were let loose, but that wasn't all. Optional dual carburetors (RPO 587) appeared officially in factory paperwork after apparently finding their way atop a few 409s late in 1961 as an over-the-counter Service Package dealer option. Compression for this real fine mill was 11.1:1; output was 409 horsepower.

Revised RPO codes appeared in 1963 with the base 409, now rated at 400 horsepower, listed as the L31 V-8. Boosted up to 425 horses, the dual-carb 409 took on the L80 label, and a third variant, the L33, also appeared. This "police option" V-8, tagged at 340 horsepower, featured a single Rochester four-barrel, a relatively mild hydraulic cam, a softened 10:1 squeeze, and an optional Powerglide automatic transmission. The latter piece of equipment was a 409 first; all other 409s were delivered with four-speed manuals only.

This W engine trio carried on into 1964, but only the two single-carb renditions (L31 and L33) reappeared in 1965, the last year for

the 409. Another variety did appear during the 409's short run but, like Pontiac's Super Duty V-8, was never meant for the street. And just as the first 409-horsepower 409 went from clandestine dealer option late in 1961 to a full-fledged RPO in 1962, so too did this race-only rendition in 1963.

The tale began on August 1, 1962, when Chevrolet released about 20 sets of lightweight aluminum body parts (hood and inner and outer fenders) for that year's full-size models. These competition-conscious components were joined by another service package two weeks later. Along with a hotter cam, the deal included radical raised-port cylinder heads and a revised two-piece dual-carb intake created to mate up with those taller heads. The lower section of the manifold served as a valley cover, while the high-rise upper half handled fuel delivery chores. No one knows exactly how many of these tall-port 409s were installed in 1962 Chevys; common estimates claim no more than 20.

Above
The Mystery Motor Chevys took everyone (including GM corporate execs) by surprise at Daytona in February 1963, running in excess of 165 miles per hour.

Below
Key to the Mystery Motor's success was its free-breathing cylinder heads; the engine was nicknamed the porcupine-head for the manner in which its valves protruded upward in haphazard fashion.

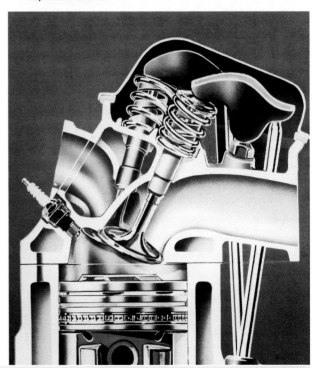

The Mk II represented a marked departure from the rather archaic W engine

Left
Originally a high-profile, high-performance machine, the Impala SS was diluted big time in 1962 as it became available with all engines, including mundane six-cylinders. Production soared thanks to this widened scope to 99,311 in 1962 and 153,271 in 1963. This 1963 SS coupe is powered by a 283 V-8. *Mike Mueller*

Below
Anyone could have walked into any Chevy dealership during the early 1960s and ordered a 409 V-8 in the model of his or her choice—hence the four-door Impala shown here. Beneath its hood is a 425-horsepower 409. *Mike Mueller*

All of these upgrades rolled over into 1963 as part of the Special Performance Equipment Package, listed under RPO Z11. Priced at $1,237, the Z11 deal added another aluminum nose (plus aluminum front and rear bumpers), a close-ratio Borg-Warner T-10 four-speed, sintered metallic brakes with special cooling gear for the rear drums, a heavy-duty Posi-Traction axle with 4.11:1 gears, and the raised-port 409, which at that time didn't actually displace 409 cubic-inches. A stroke increase to 3.65 inches translated into 427 cubes for the 1963 Z11 V-8, which also featured head-popping 13.5:1 compression and a special Cowl Induction air cleaner that helped suck in cooler, denser outside atmosphere from the high-pressure area at the base of the windshield. Chevrolet paperwork claimed the Z11 409 made 430 horsepower, but those in the know, knew better—more than 500 horses surely were present.

Reportedly, 57 Z11 Impalas were released in 1963, and more might have made it into racers' hands had GM execs not pooped on the party early that year. Killed off at the same time as the drag-racing Z11 was another 427-cube big-block that undoubtedly would have rewritten NASCAR record books, had it gotten the chance.

Above
Many Chevy fans today still feel the 1964 Impala SS was the finest of the line, especially so when fitted with the 409 V-8 like this convertible. *Mike Mueller*

Above right
A "police option" 409 V-8 appeared in 1963 and carried on up through 1965. Rated at 340 horsepower, the rather mild rendition was available with an optional Powerglide automatic. All other 409s were limited to four-speed manual installations. *Mike Mueller*

Right
Chevrolet discontinued the 409 V-8 early in 1965 as the company's new 396-cubic-inch Mk IV big-block emerged to take its place. Impala Super Sports were fitted with both old and new big-blocks that year. This convertible features the 340-horse 409. *Mike Mueller*

Primarily the work of Dick Keinath, the mean mill began taking shape in July 1962 and was originally called the Mk II V-8 after the 409 breed was tabbed Mk I. The Mk II represented a marked departure from the rather archaic W engine, resembling it only slightly on the block's bottom end. The two distant relatives also shared the same displacement total early on, before Keinath developed a stroker crank that maximized cubes to take full advantage of NASCAR's 427-cubic-inch limit. The name then became Mk IIS—"S" for stroke. This crank also was responsible for the Z11's rise in size.

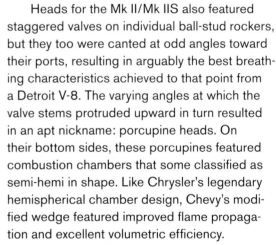

Above
Full-size Super Sport production fell to 73,932 in 1967.

Left
Impala SS sales peaked at 243,114 in 1965 and slowly eased downhill from there. This 327-powered coupe was one of 119,314 Super Sports built for 1966.

Below
Chevrolet introduced its Mk IV big-block V-8 in February 1965. Three 396 Turbo-Jet V-8s were offered: a 425-horsepower version for the Corvette, 375 horses for the new Chevelle Malibu SS 396, and 325 horses for Chevy's full-size models.

Heads for the Mk II/Mk IIS also featured staggered valves on individual ball-stud rockers, but they too were canted at odd angles toward their ports, resulting in arguably the best breathing characteristics achieved to that point from a Detroit V-8. The varying angles at which the valve stems protruded upward in turn resulted in an apt nickname: porcupine heads. On their bottom sides, these porcupines featured combustion chambers that some classified as semi-hemi in shape. Like Chrysler's legendary hemispherical chamber design, Chevy's modified wedge featured improved flame propagation and excellent volumetric efficiency.

According to Smokey Yunick, only 42 Mk IIS V-8s were manufactured, just enough to allow Chevrolet to go stock car racing in 1963. Dyno tests reportedly claimed 520 horsepower for the engine dubbed the "Mystery Motor" after it showed up that year at Daytona, where it wowed witnesses with speeds in excess of 165 miles per hour. A Mystery Motor Chevy won both 100-mile Daytona 500 qualifiers that year, but mechanical failures allowed Fords to dominate the big show. As it was, the new 427 was history even before the checkered flag dropped thanks to GM's antiracing order, issued a month before. Fortunately, the story didn't end there.

In February 1965, the Mystery Motor was reborn as Chevrolet's new Turbo-Jet Mk IV big-block, offered in 396-cube form (thanks to a smaller bore) for the midsize Chevelle SS, Corvette, and full-size models. A 375-horsepower 396 appeared for the Chevelle, a truly brutal 425-horse variation for the Corvette. Big Chevy buyers that year had two choices: the 325-horse, hydraulic-cam L35 or the Corvette's solid-lifter L78. The 409 was phased out once the 396 Turbo-Jet became available.

The Mystery Motors' original bore size was restored in 1966, though top advertised output remained at 425 horsepower for the 427 Turbo-Jet, which was listed as an Impala SS option along with its 396 little brother up through 1968. Only the 427-cube Mk IV was installed in the last of Chevrolet's original Super Sports.

A Mystery Motor Chevy won both 100-mile Daytona 500 qualifiers that year, but mechanical failures allowed Fords to dominate the big show.

1969 Chevrolet Impala SS 427

1969 Chevrolet Impala SS

Model availability	two-door coupe, two-door convertible
Wheelbase	119 inches
Length	215.9 inches
Price	RPO Z24 cost $422.35
Track (front/rear, in inches)	62.5/62.4
Wheels	15-inch stamped steel, std.; 15-inch Rally rims, optional
Tires	G70x15 redline
Suspension	independent upper/lower A-arms, heavy-duty coil springs in front; four-link control arms and heavy-duty coil springs in back; heavy-duty shock absorbers
Steering	recirculating ball
Brakes	power-assisted front discs; rear drums
Engine	390-horsepower 427-cubic-inch Mk IV V-8 w/hydraulic lifters
	425-horsepower 427-cubic-inch Mk IV V-8 w/solid lifters
Bore & stroke	4.251 x 3.76 inches
Compression	10.25:1 (390-hp 427 V-8); 11:1 (425-hp 427 V-8)
Fuel delivery	single Rochester Quadrajet four-barrel carburetor (390-hp 427 V-8); single Holley four-barrel carburetor (425-hp 427 V-8)
Transmission	heavy-duty three-speed, std.; close- and wide-ratio four-speeds, Turbo Hydra-Matic, optional
Axle ratio	3.31:1, std. w/390-hp 427 V-8 (2.73:1 w/Turbo Hydra-Matic automatic transmission)
Production	2,455

Customers snatched up 2,124 SS 427s, coupes and convertibles that first year, followed by another 1,778 in 1968.

Of course, not all Impala Super Sports built between 1961 and 1969 were real factory hot rods. After that first year, the SS trim option became available for any Impala sport coupe or convertible with any engine, be it a budget-minded six-cylinder or yeoman 283 small-block V-8. A dilution, definitely, but this repackaging also widened the car's scope, which brought buyers in by the droves. Impala SS sales soared to 99,311 in 1962, followed by 153,271 in 1963, and 185,325 in 1964. New for that latter year was full-fledged, individual model-line status for the big SS.

Impala Super Sport production peaked at 243,114 in 1965, and it was downhill from there: 119,314 in 1966, 73,932 in 1967, and 38,210 in 1968. In 1969, Chevrolet product planners chose to offer only the SS 427 Impala, introduced two years before as a top-shelf running mate for the mass-market full-size SS. Listed

under RPO Z24 in 1967, the SS 427 package included the 385-horsepower L36 427, stiffened suspension components, and redline tires on 14x6 rims. Customers snatched up 2,124 SS 427s, coupes and convertibles that first year, followed by another 1,778 in 1968. That same year, the base SS lost its honored position as a model on its own. Instead, buyers had to check off RPO Z03 to add the Super Sport imagery to their Impalas. Handwriting on the wall?

You betcha. Not only did Chevrolet roll out only the SS 427 in 1969, it did so with far less fanfare. Other than a blacked-out grille and ever-present "SS" badges, the final SS 427 image fell a bit flat compared to its forerunners. The 1967 SS 427 had its exclusive domed hood (with fake vents) and large "SS 427" cross-flag emblems. The 1968 rendition had its unique fender gills. The 1969 model, on the other hand, left most interested onlookers squinting

almost in vain while trying to make out those small "427" badges hidden atop the side-marker lights on each front fender.

But at least a decent dose of performance remained behind that understated facade. Beneath the plain hood was again the L36 big-block, rated at 390 horsepower thanks to mildly modified pistons and heads. Returning as well were heavy-duty underpinnings and wide-oval redline rubber. Power front discs were thrown in as part of the $422 deal. Popular options included either a close- or wide-ratio Muncie four-speed, a Turbo Hydra-Matic automatic, and attractive 15-inch Rally wheels with trim rings. As in 1968, the truly hot, definitely rare, 425-horse L72 427 also was available at extra cost.

Chevrolet sold 2,455 Impala SS 427s in 1969 before the book quietly closed on this boulevard brute—the last of General Motors' full-size muscle machines.

Above
Chevrolet offered its full-size Super Sport for the last time in 1969. And while both the SS 427 and simple Super Sports were seen in 1967 and 1968, only the former was around when the story came to a close. SS 427 production for that last year was 2,455. *Mike Mueller*

Right
The standard Mk IV big-block for the last of the big Super Sports was rated at 390 horsepower in 1969. *Mike Mueller*

02

Above
1964 GTO

Middle
1967 GTO

Right
1969 GTO Judge

Founding Father

02 ⋯⇢

Pontiac GTO 1964–1974

Pontiac's GTO was the hands-down leader of the high-performance pack during the 1960s and early 1970s. Counting the re-bodied 1973 rendition and downsized Ventura-based 1974 model, the complete tally was 514,793. Disregarding those last 350-powered examples still leaves a total of 507,735 big-block brutes. Sure, Chevrolet did build 577,600 Super Sport Chevelles between 1964 and 1973. But more than one-sixth of that total consisted of the lower performance small-block V-8 and frugal six-cylinder models offered in 1964 and 1965, and the 350-equipped cars of 1971–1973. From 1966, when the SS 396 went mainstream, to 1972, Chevy dealers rolled out 390,891 A-body Super Sports. GTO production during the same span was 395,127.

It took five years for the SS 396 to steal the annual muscle car sales lead away from Pontiac. By 1969, however, the GTO legend was already cast in stone, never to be knocked down. Still standing today with it is the model-year sales standard established by Pontiac's performance progenitor in 1966. The SS 396's best effort, 86,307 cars sold, came in its breakthrough year of 1969. Plymouth's Road Runner also peaked in 1969 with 84,420 beep-beeping their way into the race. Both of these figures, though certainly nothing to sneeze at, still fall well short of the 96,946 GTOs Pontiac let loose in 1966. No matter how you slice it, the Goat was king during Detroit's original muscle car era. Being the first of its breed obviously had something to do with the Tiger grabbing the early lead in the muscle car market and holding it securely with

both paws. But Pontiac Motor Division (PMD) General Manager Pete Estes and crew not only did it first, they did it right.

As David E. Davis Jr. later told *Car and Driver* in a 1975 tribute to Detroit's high-performance pioneer, the 1964 GTO "appeared on the American scene like a Methodist minister leaving a massage parlor." Although Pontiac's quick-thinkers obviously didn't invent horsepower, it was the way they packaged it that had the congregation up in arms. Both weight and price were low, image was subtle yet sure, muscle was mighty, and intentions were obvious. "The message was straight-line speed," continued Davis' retrospective review, "and it felt like losing your virginity, going into combat and tasting your first beer all in about seven seconds."

Opposite
The GTO's hottest engine option yet, Pontiac's Ram Air IV big-block, appeared for 1969. Ram Air IV hardtop production that year was 700.

Below
Pontiac's Tempest debuted with standard four-cylinder power in 1961. At the top of the Tempest lineup was the sporty Le Mans, fitted with standard bucket seats. A 1963 Le Mans convertible appears here.

And to think General Motors, top execs didn't want to see it built. They'd already done their darnedest to shut down their divisions' racing programs early in 1963, killing off Pontiac's savage 421 Super Duty cars in the process. Then along with GM's groundbreaking midsize A-body lines came a corporate mandate limiting these new-for-1964 models to no more than 330-cubic-inches, worth of engine. Talk about party-poopers.

The year before, Pontiac engineers had stuffed the 421 Super Duty V-8 into 11 little Tempests to go drag racing. Outrageously fast, for sure, but these soon-to-be-outlawed machines plainly were never meant for the street. The best a Pontiac senior compact customer could do performance-wise in 1963 was equip his upscale Le Mans with a 260-horsepower 326-cubic-inch V-8, a new Tempest option. Yes, the 326's big brother, the 389 V-8, could've

slipped right in between Tempest fenders, and engineers indeed toyed with this very idea. But they predictably found the unit-body platform, with its rear transaxle and flexible "rope" drive-shaft, to be an uncooperative patient as far as a serious horsepower transplant was concerned. Those Super Duty Tempests were radically modified beyond anything humanly possible for a regular-production application.

Fortunately, the new A-body Tempest—with

its rigid, perimeter-rail frame, conventional transmission location, and solid rear axle– was perfectly able to handle lots of horses. Unfortunately, there was the little matter of that corporate displacement limit. Leave it to Pete Estes. Without his influence at the top, the 389-powered GTO undoubtedly wouldn't have gotten past the proposal stage.

Pontiac's ever-present advertising wizard, Jim Wangers, was already at work with John De Lorean on a muscle-bound milestone before the ink on the A-body's blueprints even dried. De Lorean, Bill Collins, and crew had the engineering groundwork laid, while Wangers had his finger on the pulse of an excitable, youthful market poised to pounce on his powerful proposition. All that remained was to sneak their big-block intermediate past GM's top brass.

Well aware of the obvious roadblocks, De Lorean made an end run. New models required corporate approval, but option packages didn't. He decided to quietly create a 389 option for the Tempest and worry about the consequences later. Luckily, Estes loved the idea and made sure it didn't get shot down by those in GM's ivory tower. His clueless superiors didn't detect the options list ruse until it was too late. GTO sales were swift from the get-go, and no exec worth his severance package was going to argue against rising revenues.

Credit for the name went to De Lorean, who copped it, with nary an apology, from Enzo Ferrari. While purists cringed, the American public ate it up. Frank Bridge, Pontiac sales manager, predicted 1964 sales, at best, would reach 5,000. By the time the tire smoke cleared, 32,450 Goats had rolled out the door, a division sales record for first-year models. Even more could've been sold had the production line been able to keep up with demand. Second-year production in 1965 then soared to 75,352.

Above
Bunkie Knudsen (left) traded his Pontiac general manager position for the same roll at Chevrolet in November 1961. His chief engineer, Pete Estes (right), then kept the ball rolling after stepping into Knudsen's old shoes at Pontiac.

Right
Another of Knudsen's main men was engineer John De Lorean, hired by Pontiac along with Estes in 1956. De Lorean later replaced Estes as Pontiac general manager in July 1965.

By then GM officials–with perhaps just a bit of egg on their faces–had raised the displacement lid to 400 cubic-inches, just in time for Chevrolet to roll out its first SS 396 Chevelle in February 1965. SS 396, Gran Sport, 4-4-2– these and other legendary knockoffs from GM rivals all owed their existence to the high-performance machine that first broke the rules then made new ones for the rest of Detroit to follow.

"All this unabashed copying by Ford and the other GM divisions is the most powerful single proof of the GTO's position of leadership in this very special area of automotive marketing," concluded a *Car and Driver* 1966 Yearbook report. Told you so.

1964 GTO

1964 GTO	

Model availability	two-door coupe, hardtop and convertible
Wheelbase	115 inches
Length	203 inches
Width	73.3 inches
Height	53.5 inches (coupe)
Curb weight	3,360 pounds (convertible)
Base price	$295.90 for optional GTO package
Track (front/rear, in inches)	58
Wheels	14x6 stamped-steel
Tires	7.50x14 US Royal Tiger Paw
Suspension	independent upper/lower A-arms, coil springs, stabilizer bar in front; control arms, coil springs in back
Steering	recirculating ball
Brakes	four-wheel drums
Engine	325-horsepower 389-cubic-inch V-8, std.
Bore & stroke	4.06 x 3.75 inches
Compression	10.75:1
Fuel delivery	single 500-cfm Carter AFB four-barrel carburetor
Transmission	Hurst-shifted three-speed manual, std.
Axle ratio	3.23:1, std.
Production	32,450

Right
Pontiac temporarily revived the GTO nameplate from 2004 to 2006. Based on the Australian-sourced Holden Monaro, the 2004 Goat (shown here in drift race competition) relied on the Corvette's LS1 V-8 in 2004. The 400-horse LS2 then replaced the LS1 for the 2005 and 2006 GTOs. *Mike Mueller*

Left
Pontiac put together this custom GTO convertible for the 1964 auto show circuit.

Right
The GTO was available in three body styles for 1964: a "pillared" coupe (shown here), airy hardtop, and carefree convertible. Coupe production that year was 7,384

1964

Officially released on October 1, 1963, Pontiac's GTO debuted as an option package for Le Mans sports coupes and convertibles. A hardtop then joined the mix soon afterward. The option group included a 325-horse 389 V-8 featuring a hydraulic cam, a 500-cfm Carter AFB four-barrel, and a pair of high-compression heads borrowed from the 389's big brother, the 421. Stiffer suspension, 7.50x14 US Royal Tiger Paw redline tires, a three-speed manual with a Hurst shifter, and various dress-up items (a blacked-out grille, "GTO" identification, and twin dummy scoops on the hood) were also part of

the deal, priced at $295.90. Bucket seats were included inside, as was a padded dash.

Popular options included a Muncie four-speed, metallic brakes, a limited-slip Safe-T-Track differential, and an even hotter 348-horsepower 389 topped by three Rochester two-barrel carbs. A four-spoke wood-grained Custom Sport steering wheel, 7,000-rpm tach, and console could've been added to sex up the interior. And snazzy chrome splitter tips were available for the standard dual exhausts.

Armed with the optional 348-horse 389 and

3.90:1 gears, a 1964 GTO could trip the lights at the drag strip's far end in 14.30 seconds according to *Popular Hot Rodding*. As *Car and Driver*'s David E. Davis saw it, the new GTO "does what so many others only talk about—it really does combine brute, blasting performance with balance and stability of a superior nature."

Production breakdowns for 1964 read 7,384 coupes, 18,422 hardtops, and 6,644 convertibles. Engine production was 24,205 for the 325-horsepower 389, and 8,245 for the optional 389 Tri-Power topped by those three little air cleaners.

Left
A blacked-out grille, done in Pontiac's trademark split layout, was a standard GTO feature in 1964. So, too, were twin dummy hood scoops. *Mike Mueller*

Below left
Most gearheads were soon familiar with this badge, although many had little idea what the metric reference meant. Prior to 1967, those 6.5 liters translated into 389 cubic-inches; afterward they equaled 400 cubes. This badge was last used in 1968. *Mike Mueller*

Below
Total production of 1964 GTOs was 32,450, including 6,644 convertibles. The twin split exhaust tips seen here were optional. *Mike Mueller*

Above left
This stainless-steel Custom unit (with three-eared spinner) was one of four wheel cover styles offered for the 1964 GTO. A simulated wire wheel style also was optional. *Mike Mueller*

Below left
Many sports car purists were offended when Pontiac borrowed Ferrari's famous GTO name for its 1964 midsize muscle car. *Car and Driver* fanned the flames further by pairing the two GTOs from opposite sides of the world against each other in an unforgettable road test. *Mike Mueller*

Above right
Bucket seats, a floorshift, and an engine-turned instrument panel were all standard. Eagle-eyes might notice the optional tachometer located in the far right instrument pod—don't worry, drivers in 1964 couldn't see it, either. *Mike Mueller*

Below right
The GTO's 389-cubic-inch V-8 was fitted with cylinder heads borrowed from Pontiac's 421 big-block. When topped with the division's famed "Tri Power" triple-carb option, the 389 produced 348 horsepower. *Mike Mueller*

1965 GTO

1965 GTO

Model availability	two-door coupe, hardtop and convertible
Wheelbase	115 inches
Length	206.1 inches
Width	73.4 inches
Height	53.6 inches (convertible)
Weight	3,700 pounds (convertible)
Base price	$295.90 for optional GTO package
Track (front/rear, in inches)	58
Wheels	14x6 stamped-steel
Tires	7.75x14 US Royal Tiger Paw
Suspension	independent upper/lower A-arms, coil springs, stabilizer bar in front; control arms, coil springs in back
Steering	recirculating ball
Brakes	four-wheel drums
Engine	335-horsepower 389-cubic-inch V-8, std.
Bore & stroke	4.06 x 3.75 inches
Compression	10.75:1
Fuel delivery	single 500-cfm Carter AFB four-barrel carburetor
Transmission	Hurst-shifted three-speed manual, std.
Axle ratio	3.23:1, std.
Production	75,352

A new, truly cool scoop graced the 1965 GTO's hood but was not functional, at least in most cases.

Above
Base price for a 1965 GTO convertible was $3,093. Topless production that year was 11,311.

1965

A revised Tempest body, now with stacked headlights up front and a revised taillight treatment, appeared this year, and the GTO was again available for coupes, hardtops, and convertibles by way of the options list. A new, truly cool scoop graced the 1965 GTO's hood but was not functional, at least in most cases. This same scoop would remain a GTO trademark up through 1967.

Beneath that lid were more horses as an improved intake manifold and revised cylinder heads helped increase standard output to 335 horsepower. The same improvements translated into 360 horses for the optional Tri-Power

389. Compression remained at 10.75:1 in both cases. Chrome dress-up was again standard.

New at the corners were larger 7.75x14 standard tires, and optional 14x6 Rally wheels debuted for 1965, priced at $52.72. Painted silver, the Rally rim incorporated five cooling slots and was adorned with a center cap and trim ring done in chrome.

In August 1965, dealers began offering a special pan, or "tub," that sealed the Tri-Power V-8's air cleaners to the hood's underside using a large foam gasket. On top, the GTO's previously ornamental hood was modified with replacement trim (installed by the dealer or

customer) that unblocked the scoop, allowing cooler, denser air a direct path into the hungry mouths of those three Rochester two-barrels. Although not officially recognized as such, this parts counter option kicked off Pontiac's "Ram Air" legacy.

The GTO production count for 1965 was 8,319 coupes, 55,722 hardtops, and 11,311 convertibles. The underhood tally was 54,805 335-horse 389s and 20,547 Tri-Powers. *Car Life*'s test of a 1965 triple-carb GTO produced a quarter-mile time of 14.5 seconds at 100 miles per hour. Rest to 60 miles per hour went by in a quick 5.8 seconds.

Right
The Tempest's horizontal headlights were traded for stacked units in 1965. The twin hood scoops seen on the 1964 GTO's hood were replaced by a stylish single unit the following year.

Below
The GTO received its third facelift in three years in 1966. While the stacked headlights and split grille theme carried over from 1965, it was slightly restyled with a dramatic effect. The body itself was new for 1966. *Mike Mueller*

1966 GTO

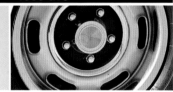

1966 GTO

Model availability	two-door coupe, hardtop and convertible
Wheelbase	115 inches
Length	206.4 inches
Width	74.4 inches
Height	53.2 inches (hardtop)
Curb weight	3,620 pounds (convertible)
Base price	$2,783 (coupe), $2,847 (hardtop), $3,082 (convertible)
Track (front/rear, in inches)	58/59
Wheels	14x6 stamped-steel
Tires	7.75x14 US Royal Tiger Paw
Suspension	independent upper/lower A-arms, coil springs, stabilizer bar in front; control arms, coil springs in back
Steering	recirculating ball
Brakes	four-wheel drums
Engine	335-horsepower 389-cubic-inch V-8, std.
Bore & stroke	4.06 x 3.75 inches
Compression	10.75:1
Fuel delivery	single Carter AFB four-barrel carburetor
Transmission	column-shifted three-speed manual, std.
Axle ratio	3.55:1, std. (3.23:1, std. w/air conditioning)
Production	96,946

1966

Taking the generic reference soon to belong to the many fully functional hood scoops used by various automakers and transforming it into the formal "Ram Air" moniker for a family of PMD performance big-blocks wasn't exactly a Pontiac idea. Not originally. This Tiger tale began in earnest in February 1966, when Pontiac engineers introduced a new 389 Tri-Power engine to go along with the dealer-offered induction tub of 1965. The XS-code big-block featured a stronger cam and stiffened valve springs, along with that functional hood. Mandatory XS options also included an M21 close-ratio four-speed, heavy-

Above
Pontiac's familiar Tri-Power option (left) was dropped after 1966, replaced by Rochester's new Quadrajet four barrel (right). Notice the corresponding Ram Air tubes in the background.

Below
Introduced for 1965, this Rally wheel returned as a snazzy option, priced at $56.80, for the 1966 GTO. *Mike Mueller*

duty fan, metallic brake linings, and a 4.33:1 limited-slip differential.

Although not labeled in any factory papers as such, the 1966 XS 389 was the division's first Ram Air V-8. Or at least it was the engine that began inspiring enthusiasts to start referring to Pontiac's top free-breathing performance mills by that name. Customers, not PMD officials, coined the term. By 1967, GTO and Firebird buyers in with the in-crowd knew that the hottest of Pontiac's newly enlarged big-blocks in 1967 was a "Ram Air 400." That reference then retroactively became "Ram Air I" once an even hotter "Ram Air II" V-8 superseded the former in March 1968.

The progression continued in 1969 with the arrival of the Ram Air III and IV 400s, the latter being the supreme rendition of the breed,

Right

Like the nose, the tail on the 1966 GTO was restyled again with the third different design in as many years. Recognizable "GTO" badging appeared on the deck lid, as it had in 1965 and 1964. Chrome exhaust tips were optional. *Mike Mueller*

at least on the street. An outrageous race-ready Ram Air V was built in small numbers but never made it into regular production, escaping instead into the wild only in crates by way of dealer parts counters.

Ram Air numbers terminology didn't begin appearing abundantly in Pontiac factory literature until 1970, when the Ram Air III 400 began receiving full coverage in shop manuals and on order forms. Previously, "Ram Air IV" factory identification had appeared in decal form on 1969 hoods. Other than that, a service bulletin sent out in February 1968 did mention the Ram Air II 400, as did a Pontiac advertisement that year. Pontiac's two new hot rods for 1969, the GTO Judge and Firebird Trans Am, both came standard with the Ram Air III 400, but each was identified by hood scoop decals that simply read "Ram Air."

In other news for 1966, the GTO graduated from options package to full-fledged model

status, and the new line featured three familiar models: hardtop, sport coupe with side-glass pillars, and convertible. Production was 73,785 for the pillarless hardtop, 10,363 for the coupe, and 12,798 for the convertible. The engine tally was 77,901 four-barrel 389s and 19,045 Tri-Powers. No official number is available for XS installations.

The 1966 GTO was also treated to its third facelift in three years. Those crisp, creased lines were traded for softer contours and clear "Coke-bottle" impressions. In back, the 1965 GTO's six-ribbed side-to-side rear grille was traded for taillights split into three individual slits on each side.

Up front, Pontiac's familiar split-grille theme, which dated back to 1959, was more fully defined in far more dramatic fashion. Those two grilles were again blacked out and a trademark "GTO" badge was once more located in the driver's-side opening, as well as on the

rear quarter panels and deck lid. A "6.5 LITRE GTO" crest was again located at the lower end of each front fender directly behind the wheel opening. This metric reference to underhood displacement was standard GTO fare from 1964 to 1968.

Popular options included the Rally Gauge cluster and the Rally clock, which fit into the far right instrument pod, but only with the standard gauge cluster. When the Rally Gauge option was added, the right-hand pod contained gauges for water and oil temperature. The remaining pods, from right to left, featured an 8,000-rpm tach, 120-mile-per-hour speedometer, and the fuel gauge/battery status light combo.

As in 1965, a two-spoke deluxe steering wheel was standard and a passenger-side grab bar was incorporated into the dash above the glove box. The same three-spoke Custom Sports wheel offered at extra cost in 1965 was a 1966 GTO option, priced at $38.44. Bucket seats (with improved padding) were again standard, although a bench seat was offered as an option for the first time. New this year, too, was a mundane column-mounted shifter for the standard three-speed manual transmission.

The optional heavy-duty three-speed and two four-speed transmissions (wide- and close-ratio) each used Hurst sticks. Pontiac's two-speed automatic transmission also came with a column shift unless a buyer anted up for the floor-mounted shifter with console. Sending torque to the transmission of choice was again the standard 335-horsepower 389 or its 360-horsepower Tri-Power running mate, which traded the small center carb used in 1965 for one that matched its two larger mates in throttle bore size.

This was the last year for optional Tri-Power as GM officials banned multicarb setups for all its products except the Corvette in 1967. The 389 was retired that year, too, replaced in 1967 by the enlarged 400-cid big-block. The familiar "6.5-LITRE" identification remained despite this displacement increase.

Above
Convertible production for 1966 was 12,798. The total figure for drop-tops, coupes, and hardtops that year, 96,946, established an all-time high for the breed. *Mike Mueller*

Left
As in 1965, bucket seats and a two-spoke deluxe steering wheel were standard GTO features in 1966. New that year was an optional bench seat. The console with floorshift also was optional—a mundane column shift was standard. *Mike Mueller*

1967 GTO

Model availability	two-door coupe, hardtop and convertible
Wheelbase	115 inches
Length	206.6 inches
Width	74.7 inches
Height	53.7 inches (hardtop)
Curb weight	3,445 pounds (hardtop)
Base price	$2,871 (coupe), $2,9357 (hardtop), $3,165 (convertible)
Track (front/rear, in inches)	58/59
Wheels	14x6 stamped-steel
Tires	F70x14 Wide Oval
Suspension	independent upper/lower A-arms, coil springs, stabilizer bar in front; control arms, coil springs in back
Steering	recirculating ball
Brakes	four-wheel drums
Engine	335-horsepower 400-cubic-inch V-8, std.
Bore & stroke	4.12 x 3.75 inches
Compression	10.75:1
Fuel delivery	single Rochester Quadrajet four-barrel carburetor
Transmission	column-shifted three-speed manual, std.
Axle ratio	3.55:1, std. (3.23:1, std. w/air conditioning)
Production	81,722

Above
The plastic egg-crate grille seen in 1966 was replaced by a sportier wire mesh layout for 1967. The chrome headlight bezels and front bumper carried over unchanged from 1966. *Mike Mueller*

Engine options included the 400 HO and 400 Ram Air, both rated at 360 horsepower.

Above
While the 1967 GTO's nose remained familiar, its tail was freshened notably. Backup lights in the bumper were standard. *Mike Mueller*

Inset
The 1967 GTO's standard 335-horse 400-cubic-inch V-8 used a louvered chrome air cleaner. The optional 400 HO was topped by a larger open-element air cleaner. *Mike Mueller*

valves springs. While the HO was available with a standard three-speed, its Ram Air brother was limited to either the four-speed manual or TH-400 automatic. "King of the Supercars!" was *Car Life*'s description for the free-breathing 1967 GTO. "The Ram Air GTO provided a level of acceleration beyond belief to anyone not accustomed to Supercars." Sixty miles per hour was reached from rest in 6.1 seconds for an automatic-equipped model. Quarter-mile performance was 14.5 seconds at 102 miles per hour. If there was one downside it was cooling, which proved especially problematic due to the Ram Air package's specified 4.33:1 rear axle. The rev counter was constantly taxed in all driving situations. Braking, on the other hand,

was superb in the *Car Life* test car thanks to Pontiac's new optional power front disc brakes, priced $104.79. "The GTO may be the eldest of the current Supercars, but it remains a worthy target for would-be competitors," concluded the *Car Life* report. "Performance brakes and styling continue to set the pace for other manufacturers." Also debuting on the 1967 options list was a set of attractive Rally II five-spoke wheels. A slightly different Rally II wheel (with different offset) was created for the disc brake option to allow extra clearance for the caliper. Optional Rally I rims carried over from 1966. Also new was a groovy optional hood-mounted tachometer, a dealer-installed feature prior to April 1, 1967. A factory option from then on, this flashy

tach featured white lettering on a steel-blue background, the same as interior instruments. Redline was at 5,100 rpm and the maximum reading was 8,000 revs.

Production by body style was 65,176 hardtops, 7,029 coupes, and 9,517 convertibles. Engine breakdowns read 64,177 standard 400s, 2,967 two-barrel V-8s, 13,827 400 HO big-blocks, and 751 Ram Air renditions.

Above
Nineteen-sixty seven was the last year three GTO body styles were offered. Convertible production that year was 9,517. *Mike Mueller*

Left
Optional five-spoke Rally II wheels were new for the 1967 GTO. The Rally I rims offered in 1965 and 1966 rolled on into 1967 too. *Mike Mueller*

Far left
Hurst introduced its Dual Gate automatic transmission shifter in 1964. The Dual Gate allowed both conventional automatic operation and manual shifts. It became a GTO option in 1967 along with the new three-speed Turbo Hydra-Matic transmission. *Mike Mueller*

1968 GTO

1968 GTO	

Model availability	two-door hardtop and convertible
Wheelbase	112 inches
Length	200.7 inches
Width	74.8 inches
Height	52.2 inches (hardtop)
Shipping weight	3,506 pounds (hardtop)
Base price	$3,101 (hardtop),
	$3,327 (convertible)
Track (front/rear, in inches)	60
Wheels	14x6 stamped-steel
Tires	G77x14 US Royal
Suspension	independent upper/lower A-arms, coil springs, stabilizer bar in front; control arms, coil springs in back
Steering	recirculating ball
Brakes	four-wheel drums
Engine	350-horsepower 400-cubic-inch V-8, std.
Bore & stroke	4.12 x 3.75 inches
Compression	10.75:1
Fuel delivery	single Rochester Quadrajet four-barrel carburetor
Transmission	Hurst-shifted three-speed manual, std.
Axle ratio	3.55:1, std. (3.23:1, std. w/air conditioning)
Production	87,684

1968

A totally fresh, sensationally contoured "Coke bottle" body appeared this year with trend-setting hideaway windshield wipers, optional headlights that also could be hidden away, and an innovative energy-absorbing Endura front bumper. Color-keyed to the body, this steel-backed synthetic bumper bounced back into shape after low-speed impacts. An optional chrome unit was available for those who simply couldn't warm up to the new monochromatic look. Rear bumpers remained traditionally chromed on all models.

Below
A shapely Coke-bottle body was new for midsize Pontiacs in 1968, as was an energy-absorbing chromatic Endura nose. New, too, that year were hidden wipers and optional hideaway headlights. The Le Mans' chrome bumper also was optional for the 1968 GTO. *Mike Mueller*

Honored with *Motor Trend* magazine's Car of the Year award, the latest GTO was now available only in hardtop and convertible forms. Either could've been dressed up with an optional hood-mounted 8,000-rpm tachometer, which appeared in three styles during the year. Notably lower physically than the 1967 unit, the first style for 1968 used the same coloring but a higher 5,200-rpm redline. Longer incremental lines and a smaller "RPM" label appeared in mid-December 1967. A third tach, with a 5,500-rpm redline, later appeared for the Ram II 400 only.

Both the base 400 and optional (at no extra cost) two-barrel V-8 received slight power boosts for 1968, up to 350 and 265 horsepower, respectively. Both the HO and Ram Air big-block options rolled over from 1967. Revised heads with round instead of D-shaped ports keyed the March 1968 switch to production of the Ram Air II 400, rated at 366 horses for GTOs and 340 for their Firebird counterparts. Like the original Ram Air V-8, the Ram Air II used a Quadrajet four-barrel carburetor. Total Ram Air production (both I and II) for 1968 was 1,054, consisting of 757 hardtops with manual transmissions, 183 hardtops with automatics, 92 convertibles with manual transmissions, and 22 convertibles with automatics.

All Ram Air V-8s this year were backed by either a four-speed or Turbo Hydra-Matic 400. A Hurst floorshift returned as standard fare for the base three-speed manual—no more three-on-the-trees—but a column shifter did remain standard for the TH-400 automatic.

The total 1968 GTO breakdown by body style was 77,704 hardtops and 9,980 convertibles. The non–Ram Air engine counts were 72,793 for the base V-8, 3,273 for the two-barrel 400 (still backed by an automatic only), and 10,564 for the HO.

A totally fresh, sensationally contoured "Coke bottle" body appeared this year.

Above
Dual hood scoops reappeared on the GTO's hood for 1968, and they again were not functional in standard form. *Mike Mueller*

Rear bumpers remained traditionally chromed on all models.

Left
Chrome exhaust extensions were optional in 1968. Both the Rally I and Rally II (shown here) wheels returned as options that year. *Mike Mueller*

Above
An optional hood-mounted tachometer became a GTO option in 1967. A slightly revised unit appeared as an extra-cost addition in 1969. The maximum reading in both cases was 8,000 rpm. *Mike Mueller*

Upper right
Standard beneath a 1968 GTO's hood was a 350-horsepower 400 big-block V-8. Compression was 10.75:1. *Mike Mueller*

Right
A completely redesigned instrument panel (again with a simulated woodgrain appliqué) graced the 1968 GTO interior. *Mike Mueller*

1969 GTO

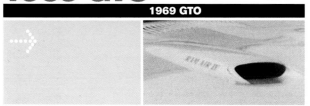

1969 GTO	
Model availability	two-door hardtop and convertible
Wheelbase	112 inches
Length	201.5 inches
Width	75 inches
Height	52 inches (hardtop)
Curb weight	3,735 pounds (hardtop)
Base price	$3,156 (hardtop), $3,382 (convertible)
Track (front/rear, in inches)	60
Wheels	14x6 stamped-steel
Tires	G78x14 redline
Suspension	independent upper/lower A-arms, coil springs, stabilizer bar in front; control arms, coil springs in back
Steering	recirculating ball
Brakes	four-wheel drums
Engine	350-horsepower 400-cubic-inch V-8, std.
Bore & stroke	4.12 x 3.75 inches
Compression	10.75:1
Fuel delivery	single Rochester Quadrajet four-barrel carburetor
Transmission	Hurst-shifted three-speed manual, std.
Axle ratio	3.55:1, std. (3.23:1, std. w/air conditioning)
Production	72,287 (includes Judge)

Standard power carried over from 1968, as did the no-cost economizer V-8 option.

Below
Revised grillework once again set the latest GTO apart from its forerunners in 1969. Optional hideaway headlights rolled over from 1969.

1969

Minor trim changes marked the 1969 GTO's arrival. Perhaps most noticeable was the deletion of side vent windows. Optional Rally I wheels were dropped this year, and standard tires were G78x14 redlines. Fiberglass-belted G70 rubber was optional.

Standard power carried over from 1968, as did the no-cost economizer V-8 option. The optional HO was dropped, superseded by the new Ram Air III V-8, fitted with D-port heads, a Power Flex fan, and free-flowing "long-branch" cast-iron exhaust manifolds. Advertised output for the Ram Air III was the same as the Ram

Air II: 366 horsepower. As mentioned, Ram Air III GTOs and Firebirds in 1969 were identified with hood decals that only read "Ram Air."

A more specific "Ram Air IV" decal announced the arrival of the latest, greatest Pontiac performance V-8, one of the original muscle car era's meanest monster mills. Conservatively rated at 370 horsepower (345 in Firebird form), the Ram Air IV 400 featured a heavy-duty four-bolt block; exceptionally free-breathing heads with huge, round ports; revamped exhaust manifolds; an enlarged Rochester Quadrajet four-barrel carb on a special aluminum intake (in place of the Ram Air III's cast-iron piece); and a serious cam with a 0.520-inch lift and 308 degrees of intake duration, 320 on the exhaust side. Overlap was a hefty 87 degrees, making for a race-car-like idle that, according to *Car Life*, was "a rough, rolling

bark, music to the driver's ears and a warning to people in the next lane."

Air conditioning was understandably not available with the Ram Air IV. Mandatory equipment included a heavy-duty radiator and a limited-slip differential containing either 3.90:1 or 4.33:1 gears. Ram Air IV V-8s made their way into 700 GTO hardtops in 1969: 549 with four-speeds and 151 with automatics. The convertible count was 59: 45 with four-speeds, 14 with automatics.

The Ram Air III tally read 8,129 hardtops, and 362 convertibles. Base V-8 production was 54,776 hardtops and 6,800 convertibles, while the two-barrel 400 went into 1,246 hardtops and 215 convertibles. The total GTO body count was 64,851 hardtops and 7,436 convertibles.

1969 Judge

1969 Judge

Model availability	two-door hardtop and convertible
Wheelbase	112 inches
Length	201.5 inches
Width	75 inches
Height	52 inches (hardtop)
Curb weight	3,735 pounds (hardtop)
Base price	$337 for Judge package
Track (front/rear, in inches)	60
Wheels	14x6 Rally II w/o trim rings
Tires	G70x14 Wide Tread fiberglass-belted
Suspension	independent upper/lower A-arms, coil springs, stabilizer bar in front; control arms, coil springs in back
Steering	recirculating ball
Brakes	four-wheel drums
Engine	366-horsepower 400-cubic-inch Ram Air III V-8, std.
Bore & stroke	4.12 x 3.75 inches
Compression	10.75:1
Fuel delivery	single Rochester Quadrajet four-barrel carburetor
Transmission	Hurst-shifted three-speed manual, std.
Axle ratio	3.55:1, std. (3.23:1, std. w/air conditioning)
Production	6,833

1969 Judge

The concept today is commonly known as "biggest bang for the buck." The idea was the same back in the late 1960s: give a muscle car buyer the most performance possible for the least amount of cash. Plymouth's Road Runner, introduced for 1968, was the best at this trick then, explaining why it ranked second in Detroit's high-performance sales race—behind the SS 396, well ahead of the former leader, GTO—in 1969. Ford tried to match the Road Runner that year with its no-nonsense Fairlane Cobra, and Pontiac too planned a rival for 1969. But the latter's end product ended up being far from a plain Jane.

John De Lorean's cost-cutters initially envisioned a very mundane machine: a revision of the existing, somewhat overglamorous GTO that would bring back warm memories of those first singularly focused Goats of 1964. Early discussions mentioned a 350 HO small-block, one exterior paint choice on perhaps a bargain-basement pillared coupe, and even rubber floor mats in place of carpet. So much for the plans of mice, men, or otherwise.

Announced in December 1968, the GTO "Judge" was by no means a bare-bones package. The car's funny name—a spoof of the then-popular gag line, "here comes da Judge," borrowed from Rowan and Martin's hit television show, *Laugh-In*—right off the bat guaranteed that next to no one could miss this machine in a crowd. Radioactive Carousel Red paint (on early cars; other shades became available

Right
New for 1969 was the Judge, offered in hardtop or convertible forms. Production was 6,725 for the former, only 108 for the latter. *Mike Mueller*

Inset
Pontiac borrowed the name from the gag line, "here comes da Judge," then popularized by television comedians Dan Rowan and Dick Martin. *Mike Mueller*

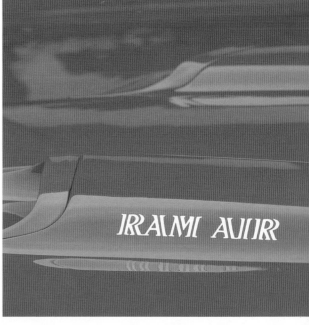

Above
This decal identified the Judge's standard Ram Air III V-8. Installing the optional Ram Air IV 400 added the appropriate Roman numerals to the Judge's twin functional hood scoops. *Mike Mueller*

Upper left
Judge production began in January 1969. The first 2,000 or so examples off the line were all painted Carousel Red. All GTO shades were eventually offered. *Mike Mueller*

Left
The Judge's rear wing measured 60 inches wide and required a deck lid support to hold up the extra weight whenever the trunk was opened. *Mike Mueller*

later in the run), splashy striping and decals, a blacked-out grille, and a high-flying wing on the deck lid further contradicted any thoughts about this car keeping it simple. On the other hand, the Judge's standard Rally II wheels did come without trim rings. Such a deal.

At least standard performance was no joke. Along with those trimless Rally rims, the Judge's equipment list included G70 rubber, a typically stiffened suspension, and a trendy Hurst shifter, in this case fitted with a unique T-handle. Standard power came from Pontiac's proven Ram Air III big-block, backed by a three-speed

manual. All this for a reasonable $337 atop a GTO coupe or convertible's bottom line–though the Judge might have looked expensive, it really wasn't. In base form, that is.

Customers with a greater need for speed and a few more dollars to spend could have opted for the hairy 370-horse Ram Air IV 400, priced at $390, and backed it up with the $195 four-speed. Such decisions, of course, would have led a buyer away from the no-nonsense ideal. When *Car Life* tested a Ram Air IV GTO Judge in 1969, the car's fully loaded sticker read $4,439–not exactly what anyone would've considered a steal. But either way, expensively optioned or bone-stock, the Judge had no problem turning heads in 1969. Pontiac sold 6,833 of them that first year, including 108 convertibles.

Right
Both automatic trans and four-speed judges were built in 1969.
Mike Mueller

Inset
This glove box emblem began showing up inside the 1969 Judge after the first 2,000 or so examples were built. *Mike Mueller*

Below right
The 366-horse Ram Air III 400 big-block (shown here) was standard for the 1969 Judge. Pontiac's 370-horse Ram Air IV 400 was optional. *Mike Mueller*

Below
Rally II wheels, sans trim rings, were standard for the Judge in 1969. *Mike Mueller*

1970 GTO

1970 GTO	
Model availability	two-door hardtop and convertible
Wheelbase	112 inches
Length	202.9 inches
Width	76.7 inches
Height	52.3 inches (hardtop)
Curb weight	3,830 pounds (hardtop)
Base price	$3,267 (hardtop), $3,492 (convertible)
Track (front/rear, in inches)	61/60
Wheels	14x6 stamped-steel
Tires	G70x14 fiberglass-belted
Suspension	independent upper/lower A-arms, coil springs, stabilizer bar in front; control arms, coil springs and stabilizer bar in back
Steering	recirculating ball
Brakes	four-wheel drums
Engine	350-horsepower 400-cubic-inch V-8, std.
Bore & stroke	4.12 x 3.75 inches
Compression	10.25:1
Fuel delivery	single Rochester Quadrajet four-barrel carburetor
Transmission	Hurst-shifted three-speed manual, std.
Axle ratio	3.55:1, std. (3.23:1, std. w/air conditioning)
Production	40,149 (includes Judge)

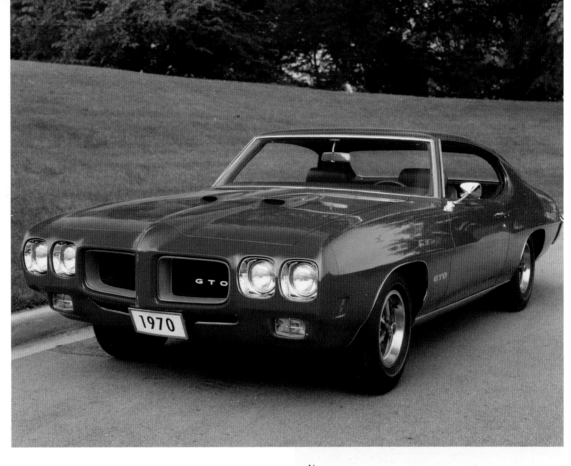

Above
Advertisements called the 1970 GTO "The Humbler." A minor restyle deep-sixed the optional hideaway headlights seen in 1968 and 1969.

1970

Here comes da Judge again in 1970, this time with a standard front chin spoiler in most cases. The option price didn't change, and the Ram Air III remained the base V-8. Total production was 3,629 hardtops and only 168 convertibles.

A minor restyle of the base Le Mans this year did away with the hidden headlight possibility, and chrome quad exhaust tips were made standard equipment. The Endura front bumper carried over from 1969. New mechanicals included a thicker front stabilizer bar, a standard rear stabilizer bar (measuring 0.875-inch in diameter), and optional variable-ratio power steering.

Another new option, Vacuum Operated Exhaust (VOE), was briefly offered for the 1970 GTO. Controlled by an under dash knob, the VOE system reduced exhaust backpressure, increasing horsepower in the process. Of course, it also raised the exhaust note, along with the ire of upper-office killjoys, who cancelled it in January 1970.

The 1970 GTO engine lineup rolled over from 1969, save for minor compression cuts and one trade-off. Gone was the two-barrel 400, replaced by Pontiac's biggest big-block yet, the 455-cid V-8, rated at 360 horsepower. Although certainly torquey (a whopping 500 lb-ft), the L75 455 was not as hot as it looked on paper as its long stroke inhibited high rpm operation. Ram Air induction equipment was included with the L75 V-8, and compression was 10:1. New squeezes were 10.25:1 for the base 400 and 10.5:1 for the Ram Air III and IV options.

The base V-8, Ram Air III 400, and 455 all were backed by a three-speed manual in standard form. The optional four-speed and Turbo Hydra-Matic 400 automatic were again the only choices behind the Ram Air IV.

Production totals were 30,556 standard 400 V-8s (27,496 hardtops, 3,060 convertibles), 4,146 L75 455s (3,747 hardtops, 399 convertibles), and 4,644 Ram Air IIIs (4,356 hardtops, 288 convertibles). Ram Air IV installations numbered 767 hardtops (140 with four-speeds, 627 with automatics) and 37 convertibles (24 with four-speeds, 13 with automatics).

Discounting Judge models, Pontiac built 32,737 GTO hardtops and 3,615 convertibles for 1970.

Here comes da Judge again in 1970, this time with a standard front chin spoiler in most cases.

1971 GTO

1971 GTO	
Model availability	two-door hardtop and convertible
Wheelbase	112 inches
Length	202.3 inches
Width	76.7 inches
Height	52.6 inches (hardtop)
Shipping weight	3,619 pounds (hardtop)
Base price	$3,446 (hardtop), $3,676 (convertible)
Track (front/rear, in inches)	61/60
Wheels	14x6 stamped-steel
Tires	G70x14 fiberglass-belted
Suspension	independent upper/lower A-arms, coil springs, stabilizer bar in front; control arms, coil springs and stabilizer bar in back
Steering	recirculating ball
Brakes	four-wheel drums
Engine	300-horsepower 400-cubic-inch V-8, std.
Bore & stroke	4.12 x 3.75 inches
Compression	8.2:1
Fuel delivery	single Quadrajet (Rochester or Carter) four-barrel carburetor
Transmission	Hurst-shifted three-speed manual, std.
Axle ratio	3.55:1, std. (3.23:1, std. w/air conditioning)
Production	10,532 (includes Judge)

Right
Only 661 GTO convertibles were built for 1971. Base price was $3,676. After 1971, no more topless GTOs were offered.

1971

The GTO total for 1971 fell to 10,532, including 9,497 hardtops and 661 convertibles. Included were a mere 374 Judge models (357 hardtops, 17 convertibles), the last of this high-profile breed. A mildly revised nose and new hood (with more dramatic scoops moved up toward its leading edge) appeared for the 1971 GTO.

Declining numbers said it all: the muscle car era was rapidly winding down as horsepower, too, began fading into the sunset. Industrywide compression cuts were mostly responsible for the power outage. In GTO terms, the base L78 400 V-8 now featured a humble 8.2:1 squeeze. Advertised output was 300 horsepower, 255 by Detroit's new net rating system. Fortunately, the proud Ram Air V-8s didn't survive to see this indignation. In the Ram Air III and IV options' place for 1971 was the L75 455, which featured 8.4:1 compression. Available only with the Turbo Hydra-Matic automatic, the L75 produced 325 gross horsepower, 260 net horsepower.

The top performance option this year was the LS5 455 HO, which also relied on 8.4:1 compression. Rated at 335 horsepower (310 net), the HO featured round-port heads and

free-flowing exhaust manifolds similar to those used previously by the Ram Air IV. An aluminum intake was included, too, and Ram Air induction was optional. A three-speed stick was standard behind both the base 400 and 455 HO. All 1971 Judges featured the HO big-block.

HO installations numbered 888 in 1971 hardtops (476 manuals, 412 automatics) and 48 in convertibles (21 manuals, 27 automatics). The L75 455 count was 534 hardtops and 43 convertibles. The base 400 V-8 went into 8,432 hardtops (2,011 manuals, 6,421 automatics) and 587 convertibles (79 manuals, 508 automatics).

New on the 1971 options list were snazzy honeycomb wheels, available in both 14x7 and 15x7 sizes. Both these honeycombs returned in 1972 but with different center caps. A red Pontiac crest was added the second time around. The optional five-spoke Rally II wheel was offered in two sizes for 1971, in this case 14x6 and 15x7. The two Rally II rims carried over into 1972 as well, with the 14-incher expanding to 7 inches wide.

Below
The Judge presided one last time in 1971. Production was
357 hardtops, 17 convertibles. *Mike Mueller*

Above
An appropriate decal went on at the ends of the 1971 Judge's rear wing. Other 455 HO GTOs wore such identification on their front fenders. *Mike Mueller*

Above left
The GTO's typical interior was again standard inside the Judge, as were a Hurst T-handle shifter and "Judge" glove box emblem. *Mike Mueller*

Left
The 455 HO big-block, rated at 335 horsepower, was the only engine available for the 1971 GTO Judge. *Mike Mueller*

1972 GTO

1972 GTO	

Model availability	two-door coupe and hardtop
Wheelbase	112 inches
Length	202.3 inches
Width	76.7 inches
Height	52.6 inches (hardtop)
Base price	$353.88 for GTO package
Track (front/rear, in inches)	61/60
Wheels	14x6 stamped-steel
Tires	G70x14 fiberglass-belted
Suspension	independent upper/lower A-arms, coil springs, stabilizer bar in front; control arms, coil springs and stabilizer bar in back
Steering	recirculating ball
Brakes	four-wheel drums
Engine	250-horsepower 400-cubic-inch V-8, std.
Bore & stroke	4.12 x 3.75 inches
Compression	8.2:1
Fuel delivery	single Quadrajet (Rochester or Carter) four-barrel carburetor
Transmission	Hurst-shifted three-speed manual, std.
Axle ratio	3.44:1, std. (3.23:1, std. w/air conditioning)
Production	5,807

Above
A new standard steering wheel appeared for the GTO interior in 1972. *Mike Mueller*

Below
The ever-present Ram Air hood remained a GTO option in 1972, for either the 400 or 455 big-blocks. *Mike Mueller*

Above
Standard power for the 1972 GTO came from the L78 400, rated at 250 horsepower. Options included the 250-horse L75 455 and the 300-horse 455 HO. *Mike Mueller*

1972

GTO production dropped to an all-time low of 5,807 for 1972. Now available by way of a $353.88 option package for Le Mans coupes and hardtops only, the 1972 GTO was available with the same three big-blocks: the base L78 400, L75 455, or LS5 455 HO. Net output ratings were 250, 250, and 300 horsepower, respectively. A three-speed manual was standard behind the L78 400, while an automatic again was the only choice with the L75 455. Either a four-speed or TH-400 was available for the 455 HO. Optional Ram Air induction also was listed for the HO and 400.

The familiar Endura nose was again part of the deal, but bucket seats no longer were. The basic Le Mans interior, with a mundane bench in front, was standard for the 1972 GTO. Adding the optional Le Mans Sport interior brought along Strato buckets and padded door panels. An optional ducktail spoiler was initially considered for 1972 but only a couple of such installations are known. Much more common was a dealer-installed rear wing reminiscent of the 1969–1971 Judge's standard spoiler.

Total 1972 GTO production by body style was 5,673 hardtops and only 134 coupes. HO V-8s went into 635 hardtops (310 four-speeds, 325 automatics) and 10 coupes (3 four-speeds, 7 automatics). L75 installations numbered 238: 235 hardtops, 5 coupes. Another 4,803 hardtops featured the base V-8 (3,284 automatics, 1,519 manuals), compared to only 119 coupes (60 automatics, 59 manuals).

Above
GTO sales fell to an all-time low of 5,807 in 1972. Only coupes and hardtops were offered that year.

Right
Production of GTO hardtops (shown here) in 1972 was 5,673. Only 134 coupes were built that year. *Mike Mueller*

A three-speed manual was standard behind the L78 400, while an automatic again was the only choice with the L75 455.

1973 GTO

1973 GTO

Model availability	two-door coupe and sport coupe
Wheelbase	112 inches
Length	207.4 inches
Width	77.7 inches
Height	52.9 inches
Base price	$368 for GTO package
Wheels	15x7 stamped-steel
Tires	G60x15 fiberglass-belted
Suspension	independent upper/lower A-arms, coil springs, stabilizer bar in front; control arms, coil springs and stabilizer bar in back
Steering	recirculating ball
Brakes	four-wheel drums
Engine	230-horsepower 400-cubic-inch V-8, std.
Bore & stroke	4.12 x 3.75 inches
Compression	8:1
Fuel delivery	single Rochester Quadrajet four-barrel carburetor
Transmission	Hurst-shifted three-speed manual, std.
Axle ratio	3.44:1, std. (3.23:1, std. w/air conditioning)
Production	4,806

Below
A totally new Le Mans body served as base for the 1973 GTO. Two body styles were offered: the coupe (with exposed rear quarter glass) and the sport (or Colonnade) coupe. That latter (shown here) used the Grand Am's rear quarter window louvers. Bright hubcaps (without trim rings) were standard.

1973

An all-time low came this year as only 4,806 GTOs were built, now based on a totally restyled Le Mans body that no longer was available in a traditional pillarless hardtop form. The base Le Mans coupe featured a major roof pillar behind each door (the better to protect occupants in rollover crashes), followed by large, triangular rear-quarter glass. Pontiac's new Le Mans Colonnade coupe added the Grand Am's stylish louvers to those windows. The GTO option, priced at $368 in 1973, was available for both models. The breakdown was 4,312 Colonnade sport coupes and 494 standard coupes.

A new notchback bench seat (that looked a little like buckets) with head restraints was standard inside. A split bench and Strato buckets were optional. Two NACA-duct hood scoops were standard outside, as were 15x7 stamped steel wheels shod in G60 tires. "Baby moon" hubcaps were included with these rims, but adding bright trim rings required spending a few extra bucks. Honeycomb and Rally II wheel options appeared again and could've been wrapped up in raised-white-letter G60 tires supplied by Firestone, Goodyear, or Uniroyal.

Standard chassis features included 9.5-inch drum brakes and a heavy-duty suspension once more featuring both front and rear stabilizer bars. Power front disc brakes (with 11-inch rotors) were optional.

Although Pontiac's truly tough 455 Super Duty V-8 was initially considered a 1973 Le Mans option, it appeared only for the Firebird this year. Standard for the 1973 GTO was a 230-horsepower 400 backed by a three-speed manual. A Hurst-shifted four-speed and the TH-400 automatic remained on the options list. The only optional engine was a 250-horsepower 455 limited to Turbo Hydra-Matic applications only. Both GTO engines featured 8:1 compression in 1973.

Base L78 V-8 production for 1973 was 4,262: 3,793 Colonnade coupes (2,867 automatics, 926 manuals) and 469 base coupes (282 automatics, 187 manuals). The L75 455 count was 529 Colonnade coupes, 25 base coupes.

A new notchback bench seat
(that looked a little like buckets) with
head restraints was standard inside.

Below
Pontiac's last GTO (until 2004) was based on the compact Ventura platform. Beneath that Trans Am–style shaker hood scoop was a 350-cubic-inch small-block V-8 rated at 200 horsepower.

1974 GTO

1974 GTO

Model availability	two-door coupe and hatchback
Wheelbase	111 inches
Length	199.4 inches
Width	72.5 inches
Height	52.2 inches (hardtop)
Base price	GTO package ranged from $414 to $452 depending on body style and trim level application
Track (front/rear, in inches)	59.9
Wheels	14x6 Rally II
Tires	F78x14 radial
Suspension	independent upper/lower A-arms, coil springs, stabilizer bar in front; solid axle, parallel leaf springs and stabilizer bar in back
Steering	recirculating ball
Brakes	four-wheel drums
Engine	200-horsepower 350-cubic-inch V-8
Bore & stroke	3.88 x 3.53 inches
Compression	7.62:1
Fuel delivery	single Rochester Quadrajet four-barrel carburetor
Transmission	Hurst-shifted three-speed manual, std.
Axle ratio	3.08:1
Production	7,058

Right
The 1974 GTO was available either as a conventional coupe or hatchback. Coupes outnumbered hatchbacks 5,335 to 1,723 that year.

1974

Pontiac's last GTO was based on the compact Ventura, initially introduced in March 1970 using a familiar Chevrolet platform. When *Cars* magazine road testers got their hands on a 1974 GTO, they called it "one of the better looking Chevy Novas we had seen in a long time."

The GTO option this year carried various price tags depending on application. This deal was available for the Ventura coupe or hatchback, both bodies in turn being offered with or without Custom accoutrements. Bright exterior trim and an upscale front bench seat were included in the Custom package. Strato buckets were optional. Prices were $452 for the coupe, $426 for the Custom coupe, $440 for the hatchback, and $414 for the Custom hatchback.

Included in the GTO option was a special blacked-out grille, Trans Am–style shaker hood scoop, typical exterior identification, front and rear stabilizer bars (measuring 0.812 inch and 0.562 inch, respectively), 14x6 Rally II wheels without trim rings, E70x14 tires, a floorshift three-speed manual transmission, and a single-muffler exhaust system incorporating dual tailpipes that exited directly behind the rear wheels. Chrome splitter exhaust tips were optional. Drum brakes again were standard; front discs were optional.

Also on the options list was the Radial Tuned Suspension, consisting of special shocks, revised spring rates, suspension ride restrictors, larger grommets for the stabilizer bars, and FR78x14 steel-belted radial tires featuring either white sidewalls or white letter-

ing. An RTS-equipped GTO also came with an appropriate badge on its glove box door.

Only one engine was offered, a 350-cubic-inch small-block V-8 (L76) featuring a Quadrajet four-barrel carburetor and unleaded-friendly 7.62:1 compression. Output was 200 horsepower. According to the *Cars* road test of a four-speed 1974 GTO, these rather mild-looking ponies could run from rest to 60 miles per hour in 7.7 seconds and lope down the quarter-mile in 15.72 clicks, finishing at 88 miles per hour.

Rather cool results, but not too bad for the time considering that real performance was about as hard to find then as gruntled postal workers are now.

Total production for the 1974 GTO was 7,058: 1,723 hatchbacks, 5,335 coupes. Manual transmission applications numbered 3,174 (687 hatchbacks, 2,487 coupes), while the count for the automatic alternative was 3,884 (1,036 hatchbacks, 2,848 coupes).

Above
Pontiac tried the midsize muscle thing again in 1977 with its Can Am, based on the Le Mans sport coupe. Offered only in Cameo White, the Can Am was powered by the T/A 6.6-liter (400-cubic-inch) V-8, rated at 180 horsepower in this application. Only 1,377 of these one-hit wonders were built.

03

Above
1966 4-4-2 W-30

Middle
1967 4-4-2

Right
1970 4-4-2 W-30

Numbers Game

03 ·····➤

Oldsmobile 4-4-2 1964–1972

Among the Buick-Olds-Pontiac triumvirate, only Oldsmobile attempted to transform General Motors' senior compact into a real performance machine during this unit-body breed's short run from 1961 to 1963. Typical image enhancements came first. In May 1961, the upscale Cutlass coupe joined the new F-85 line, which featured GM's innovative 215-cid aluminum V-8 in all applications. Along with extra trim, the pricier Cutlass came standard with bucket seats inside–sporty, for sure. Yet Jack Wolfram, Olds general manager since 1951, wanted more punch behind the prestige. He asked veteran engine man Gil Burrell if a truly hot F-85 was possible. Burrell's initial answer was no, the model's all-aluminum V-8 simply couldn't be muscled up enough using simple, available bolt-on components.

Then Burrell recalled earlier turbocharging experiments performed in GM engineering labs between 1953 and 1956, all of which basically ended in failure. This time Olds engineers went one step further, combining turbo technology with clever alcohol-injection (called the Turbo Rocket Fluid system), resulting in a promising V-8 able to produce, somewhat amazingly, 1 horsepower per cubic-inch. This 215-horsepower 215-cube engine then became the heart of the new Jetfire coupe, introduced in April 1962 at the New York International Auto Show.

At the time, only Chevrolet's Corvair Spyder relied on turbocharging to make its presence felt among Detroit's jet-set. But unlike the turbo Corvair, which inspired a polite following and stuck around up through 1966, the Jetfire coupe didn't make near as much noise, though

Oldsmobile did build 3,765 in 1962 and another 5,842 the following year.

Such high-tech wizardry wasn't required anyway once a bigger, midsize F-85 arrived for 1964, now rolling on a conventional full frame able to easily handle more engine. In place of the cost-conscious, lightweight Rockette V-8 was another new powerplant, made conventionally of cast iron that displaced 330 cubic-inches. New, too, was a decent dose of performance potential, put into play easily enough after typical no-fuss upgrades like more cam, more compression, more carb. For the garden-variety 1964 F-85, the 330 V-8 produced 230 horsepower using a two-barrel carburetor, a 9.0:1 squeeze, and a single exhaust pipe. A few simple parts swaps–like, say, a switch to a four-barrel carburetor and twin mufflers–quickly

Opposite
An Olds Cutlass first appeared, as a Motorama showcar, in 1954. Named after a twin-engine Chance-Vought jet fighter, it featured a sleek reinforced plastic body that measured only 51.5 inches from road to roof.

Left
Oldsmobile was a major player in Detroit's unbridled horsepower race during the 1950s, introducing its hot-to-trot J-2 triple-carb option in 1957. Output for the 371-cubic-inch J-2 V-8 that year was 277 horsepower. The 1958 rendition, shown here, produced 312 horses.

upped the output ante with little fuss or muss, and at the same time also inspired a new Olds nameplate.

GM's second midsize muscle car showed up in April 1964 wearing a badge not everyone understood, even after early magazine ads explained it in full. No, the tag didn't read "Four-Forty-Two." Those three numbers didn't denote engine displacement, as many casual observers still unknowingly assume to this day. The proper pronunciation was "Four-Four-Two," as in four-barrel, four-on-the-floor, and dual exhausts. Who cared that three-speed manuals and automatic transmissions soon found their way into Oldsmobile's performance equation after the 4-4-2 made the scene? The moniker remained the same for years and no one ever complained.

Any need for explanation promptly faded as the 4-4-2 quickly established itself among Detroit's high-performance elite. A healthy 345-horsepower 400-cubic-inch big-block became part of the deal in 1965, after which time it was onward and upward in exciting fashion.

Clearly the good Olds guys already had tried to buff-up the F-85 prior to 1964, but the reasoning behind the muscular 4-4-2's midyear launch that year was even more apparent. "Pontiac had been tremendously successful with the GTO," said former Olds public relations man Jim Williams later in an interview with veteran automotive writer Jan Norbye. "And the 4-4-2 [represented] a way to attract people to a [similar] product for those who were inclined to buy an Oldsmobile but would otherwise have gone to Pontiac."

According to Harold Metzel, who went from chief engineer to general manager after Jack Wolfram retired in June 1964, the original 4-4-2 was "the most alert performer in Oldsmobile's entire model lineup, with three outstanding dimensions of performance: responsiveness, handling, and road sense." As Williams told it, veteran engineer John Beltz "wanted a street machine, not a hot rod." Thus overall balance, instead of brute force, became the priority.

Power came from a 310-horse rendition of the gold-painted 330 Rocket V-8, and even more ponies were on the way soon enough. But the real key to the first 4-4-2's success was its chassis. All parts typically were heavy-duty, including a hefty anti-sway bar up front. Not so familiar, however, was the car's standard rear anti-sway bar, a road-hugging feature that had appeared earlier on American Motors' Rebel in 1957 and Chevrolet's Corvette beginning in 1960. As they always do, Oldsmobile's rear stabilizer reduced body lean, which in turn helped keep more rubber on the road for increased sureness in the corners. "Although the car still basically understeers, it is within much more manageable bounds," commented *Car Life*'s critics. "There is, in our judgment, hardly a better handling passenger sedan produced in this country."

A quieter, more refined kind of performer compared to its corporate cousin from Pontiac, Oldsmobile's 4-4-2 also was the product of a kinder, gentler promotional effort. "Olds never put the kind of push behind the 4-4-2 that Pontiac gave the GTO," continued Williams. That fact, combined with its midyear status, greatly inhibited 1964 sales. Only 2,999 were built, all with Chevy-sourced Muncie four-speed gearboxes as advertised.

Above
Oldsmobile's "senior compact," the F-85, debuted in the fall of 1960 as a 1961 model. In May 1961 the Cutlass two-door sports coupe appeared as the flagship of the F-85 line. Extra trim and sporty bucket seats were standard.

Upper right
Olds introduced its turbocharged Jetfire sports coupe in April 1962. Production that year was 3,765, followed by 5,842 more for 1962.

Right
A clever alcohol-injection system, which in Olds terms used "Turbo-Rocket Fluid," allowed the Jetfire's 215-cubic-inch aluminum V-8 to mate high compression (10.25:1) with forced induction—the two normally do not work well together. Advertised output for this innovative mill was 215 horsepower.

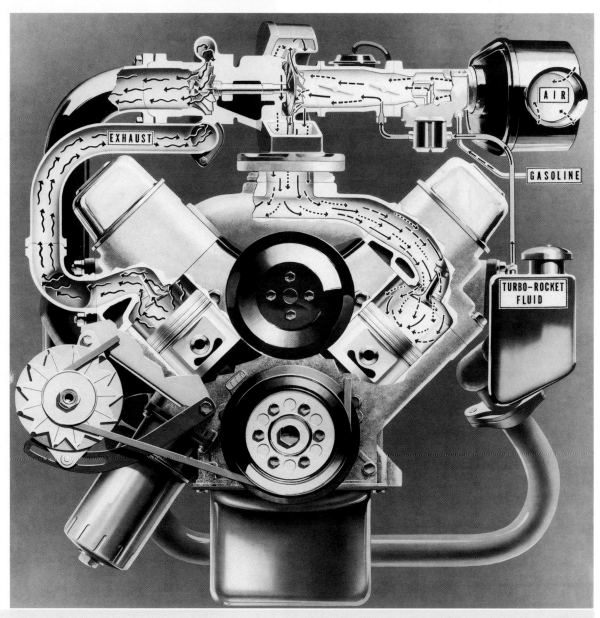

1964 4-4-2

1964 4-4-2

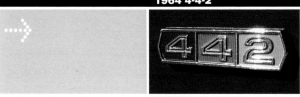

Model availability	F-85 two-door club coupe and four-door sedan, F-85 Deluxe four-door sedan; Cutlass two-door sports coupe, Holiday hardtop coupe and convertible
Wheelbase	115 inches
Length	203 inches
Weight	3,770 pounds
Base price	B09 package cost $285
Track (front/rear, in inches)	58
Wheels	14x6 stamped steel
Tires	7.50x14 US Royal Tiger Paw
Suspension	Independent upper/lower A-arms, coil springs and stabilizer bar in front; solid axle, control arms, coil springs and stabilizer bar in back
Steering	recirculating ball
Brakes	9.5-inch drums, front and rear
Engine	310-horsepower 330-cubic-inch V-8
Bore & stroke	3.93 x 3.38 inches
Compression	10.25:1
Fuel delivery	single four-barrel carburetor
Transmission	four-speed Muncie manual
Production	2,999, all body styles

1964

Unlike their Pontiac counterparts, Olds execs didn't have to break any corporate rules to rush their midsize muscle car to market in spring 1964; that 330-cube V-8 fit nicely within GM's initial displacement limit for its midsize models. It wasn't the company's big 394-cid monster mill, but it was a start, those 310 horses representing 20 more than the Cutlass' standard 330 V-8 offered. Making that increase possible was a slightly hotter cam. Compression, at 10.25:1, stayed the same. Setting the 4-4-2's V-8 apart at a glance was a dual-snorkel air cleaner in place of the Cutlass' single-inlet unit.

Like the GTO, Oldsmobile's original muscle car emerged by way of a special options group. Priced at $285, the "police apprehender pursuit package," option code B09, was offered for any V-8 F-85 models except station wagons. "Put this one on your wanted list," wailed the 67-year-old company's first ads for the new 4-4-2. "Police needed it, Olds built it, pursuit proved it!" As mentioned, the exclusive 310-horse 330 V-8, four-speed manual transmission, and cop suspension all were included in this deal. Spring rates were 120 lb-in in front, 144 in back, compared to 95/109 for the standard F-85 underpinnings.

Left
This customized Cutlass convertible made the auto show rounds in 1964.

"While such figures seem too high, the fact is that extremely good riding and handling qualities result," claimed *Car Life*. "Shock absorber valving has 50 percent greater restriction and there is no question [that] the 4-4-2 is well sprung and adequately damped." Sway bar diameters were 0.875-inch out back (the same size as the F-85's standard front stabilizer) and a hefty 0.937 at the nose.

Below
As the second "4" in the name implied, a Muncie four-speed gearbox with floorshift was standard for all 4-4-2s in 1964. The bucket seats and console with tach seen here were optional. *Mike Mueller*

Above
Oldsmobile's response to Pontiac's GTO came midyear in 1964. Production of the first 4-4-2 was a meager 2,999, including 10 four-door sedans. *Mike Mueller*

Car Life testers managed a 0-to-60 run of 7.4 seconds in a 1964 Cutlass 4-4-2 hardtop. The quarter-mile time was 15.6 seconds at 89 miles per hour. No speed records, mind you, but again a decent start.

Available as it was for all Olds models, and being born of a cop car heritage, the first 4-4-2 showed up in some cases with more than two doors. Reportedly three F-85 four-door sedans and seven (some sources say eight) F-85 Deluxe four-door sedans were built. Another 148 F-85 club coupes, 563 Cutlass sport coupes, 1,842 Cutlass Holiday coupes, and 436 Cutlass convertibles also received the 4-4-2 treatment.

Right
This badge appeared on a wide array of Olds models during the 1960s. From 1964 to 1966, the division's midsize lineup was broken down into three trim levels: F-85 Standard, F-85 Deluxe, and Cutlass. The pillared two-door F-85 (called a club coupe) and three Cutlass bodies (pillared coupe, Holiday coupe, and convertible) were available with the 4-4-2 package prior to 1966. Oldsmobile used the Holiday designation for its airy hardtop rooflines. *Mike Mueller*

Left
The first 4-4-2 featured a gold-painted 310-horsepower 330-cubic-inch V-8 topped by—you guessed it—a four-barrel carburetor beneath a dual-snorkel air cleaner, which should be orange. The chrome treatments seen here are owner-made customizations. *Mike Mueller*

1965 4-4-2

Olds ⟨442⟩
New package
of instant action:
Color it cool!

Total 4-4-2 production jumped to 25,003 in 1965, including 3,468 convertibles. A new standard engine, a 400-cubic-inch big-block V-8, also debuted that year. *Mike Mueller*

1965

Sales jumped to 25,003 for the second-edition 4-4-2, which again was offered as a special options group for the F-85 club coupe, Cutlass sport coupe, Cutlass Holiday coupe, and Cutlass convertible. No four-doors were produced this time around. Production tallies read 1,087, 5,713, 14,735, and 3,468, respectively. A standard three-speed manual and optional Jetaway automatic joined the preferred four-speed stick this year.

The biggest news, though, involved the debut of a bigger, better power source, a 400-cubic-inch big-block, a little brother to the 425-cid V-8 also introduced that year for Oldsmobile's full-size

Right
A three-speed manual transmission became standard for the 4-4-2 in 1965, and a Jetaway automatic appeared on the options list. Production of 4-4-2 Holiday hardtops (shown here) that year was 14,735. *Mike Mueller*

1965 4-4-2	
Model availability	two-door F-85 club coupe; two-door Cutlass sports coupe, Holiday hardtop and convertible
Wheelbase	115 inches
Length	204.5 inches
Width	74.5 inches
Height	54 inches
Weight	3,770 pounds
Base price	4-4-2 package cost $190.45 for F-85, $156.02 for Cutlass
Track (front/rear, in inches)	58
Wheels	14x6 stamped steel
Tires	7.75x14 redline
Suspension	Independent upper/lower A-arms, coil springs and stabilizer bar in front; solid axle, control arms, coil springs and stabilizer bar in back
Steering	recirculating ball
Brakes	9.5-inch drums, front and rear
Engine	340-horsepower 400-cubic-inch V-8
Bore & stroke	4.00 x 3.975
Compression	10.25:1
Fuel delivery	single four-barrel carburetor
Transmission	three-speed manual, std.
Axle ratio	3.55:1, std. w/manual trans; 3.23:1 w/optional automatic
Production	25,003, all body styles

lineup. Both shared the same forged steel crank (with a 3.975-inch stroke), but the 400 relied on a 4.00-inch bore, compared to 4.125 for the 425. Compression again was 10.25:1, and a Rochester four-barrel and dual exhausts were expectedly present and accounted for.

"This engine gargles and gurgles at idle, thanks to its dual multi-pinch tailpipes, in a manner suggesting a fire in the belly about to be spewed forth," explained a *Car Life* report. "It oozes out 345 bhp without trying, hinting of things to come if this big engine/little car kick lasts." Calling the new 400 "a sweetheart," *Car and Driver* reported a 15.0-second quarter-mile for a four-speed 4-4-2. Rest to 60 miles per hour required a reasonably scant 5.5 seconds. "Keep your eye on Oldsmobile," concluded the *C/D* test crew. "They may surprise us … not to mention their competition."

Above
The availability of an optional automatic transmission forced Olds promotional people to redefine their 4-4-2 code in 1965. It was retranslated as 400-cid V-8, four-barrel carb, and dual exhausts that year. *Mike Mueller*

Left
Based on Oldsmobile's 425-cubic-inch big-block, the 1965 4-4-2's 400-cubic-inch V-8 produced 345 horsepower. Compression was 10.25:1. A chromed air-cleaner was correct that year. *Mike Mueller*

The biggest news, though, involved the debut of a bigger, better power source, a 400-cubic-inch big-block

1966 4-4-2

1966

A radically restyled, considerably larger F-85 body appeared this year, and standard power rose slightly to 350 horses for the 1966 4-4-2 package, now found under option code L78, priced at $186.41. Adding the mandatory heavy-duty clutch in front of either the M14 three-speed or Hurst-shifted four-speeds (the M20 wide-ratio or M21 close-ratio) required additional cash, as did the available special-duty Jetaway automatic. L78 availability expanded to five models this year as the F-85 Deluxe Holiday coupe entered the fray.

Below
A totally restyled F-85 body appeared for 1966, as did Oldsmobile's first four-door Cutlass and a new Holiday hardtop in the F-85 Deluxe line. Total 4-4-2 production that year was 21,997, including 14,735 Cutlass Holiday coupes (shown here).

Model availability	two-door F-85 club coupe and Deluxe Holiday hardtop; two-door Cutlass sports coupe, Holiday hardtop and convertible
Wheelbase	115 inches
Length	204.2 inches
Width	75.4 inches
Height	53.6 inches
Shipping weight	3,454 pounds (F-85 club coupe), 3,502 pounds (F-85 Deluxe Holiday hardtop), 3,506 pounds (Cutlass sports coupe), 3,523 pounds (Cutlass Holiday hardtop), 3,629 pounds (Cutlass convertible)
Base price	4-4-2 package cost $186.41 for F-85, $151.61 for Cutlass
Track (front/rear, in inches)	58/59
Wheels	14x6 stamped steel
Tires	7.75x14 redline
Suspension	Independent upper/lower A-arms, coil springs and stabilizer bar in front; solid axle, control arms, coil springs and stabilizer bar in back
Steering	recirculating ball
Brakes	9.5-inch drums, front and rear
Engine	350-horsepower 400-cubic-inch V-8, std.
Bore & stroke	4.00 x 3.975
Compression	10.5:1
Fuel delivery	single four-barrel carburetor
Transmission	three-speed manual, std
Axle ratio	3.23:1
Production	21,997, all body styles

Right
The Cutlass Holiday coupe again could've been fitted with 4-4-2 gear in 1966, as demonstrated here. The F-85 club coupe, Cutlass sports coupe, and Cutlass convertible variations all carried over from 1965 too. New for 1966 was an F-85 Deluxe Holiday coupe 4-4-2.

New too was an optional engine, announced in an Olds marketing bulletin on November 24, 1965. Available only for the 4-4-2, this L69 400 V-8 was topped by three Rochester two-barrel carburetors wearing small, foam-wrapped "maximum-flow" air filters. Beneath those Rochesters was a unique intake manifold featuring a clever trick drag racers would immediately appreciate: an adjustable baffle that closed off the heat crossover passage that normally enhanced engine warm-up during typical operation. Closing this baffle meant everyday cold starts would suffer, but it also kept the fuel/air mixture inside the manifold cooler longer. A cooler mixture is denser, and a denser mixture generates more horses on the top end—just what was needed to beat the other Saturday-night warriors through those lights a quarter-mile away down the strip.

L69 production in 1966 was 2,129, all with four-speeds, this even though factory paperwork listed the three-speed stick as a possible transmission choice. The same papers claimed the triple-carb V-8 was available only for the Holiday coupe, but all five 4-4-2 models were so equipped. Breakdown production counts were 157 F-85 club coupes, 178 F-85 Deluxe Holiday coupes, 383 Cutlass coupes, 1,171 Cutlass Holiday hardtop coupes, and 240 Cutlass convertibles. Advertised L69 output was 360 horsepower, a typically token figure. A *Motor Trend* road test resulted in a sensational 13.8-second quarter-mile burst for an L69 Cutlass hardtop modified with headers and slicks.

Total 4-4-2 production for 1966 was 21,997: 647 F-85 club coupes, 1,217 F-85 Deluxe Holiday coupes, 3,787 Cutlass coupes, 13,493 Cutlass Holiday coupes, and 2,853 Cutlass convertibles.

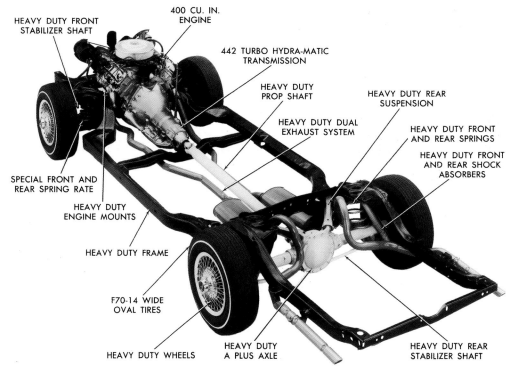

HEAVY DUTY FRONT STABILIZER SHAFT

400 CU. IN. ENGINE

442 TURBO HYDRA-MATIC TRANSMISSION

HEAVY DUTY PROP SHAFT

HEAVY DUTY REAR SUSPENSION

HEAVY DUTY DUAL EXHAUST SYSTEM

HEAVY DUTY FRONT AND REAR SPRINGS

HEAVY DUTY FRONT AND REAR SHOCK ABSORBERS

SPECIAL FRONT AND REAR SPRING RATE

HEAVY DUTY ENGINE MOUNTS

HEAVY DUTY FRAME

F70-14 WIDE OVAL TIRES

HEAVY DUTY WHEELS

HEAVY DUTY A PLUS AXLE

HEAVY DUTY REAR STABILIZER SHAFT

Opposite page, middle
All 4-4-2s were typically treated to various chassis upgrades, including a rear stabilizer bar. A 1966 4-4-2 bare chassis is exposed here.

Opposite page, bottom
An open-element air cleaner appeared in 1966 for manual-trans 4-4-2s. A chromed single-snorkel air-cleaner continued to top the L78 400 V-8 in automatic transmission applications. L78 output went up slightly to 350 horsepower that year.

A cooler mixture is denser, and a denser mixture generates more horses on the top end—just what was needed to beat the other Saturday-night warriors through those lights a quarter-mile away down the strip.

Beneath those Rochesters was a unique intake manifold featuring a clever trick drag racers would immediately appreciate: an adjustable baffle that closed off the heat crossover passage that normally enhanced engine warm-up during typical operation.

Below
The L69 intake incorporated a competition-conscious adjustable baffle that closed off the heat crossover passage to keep the fuel/air mixture cooler inside the manifold. A cooler mixture is denser, and a denser mixture translates into more power. Opening the baffle was as simple as removing four bolts and turning this plate 90 degrees either way, which allowed the crossover passage to typically enhance engine warm-up during normal operation by heating up the mixture.

1966 W-30

1966 W-30

Even harder to find in 1966 was Oldsmobile's first "W-machine," the 4-4-2 W-30. Introduced rather obscurely late in the year, the W-30 was targeted directly at drag racers, thus its almost secretive release and limited production. Only 54 factory-built W-30s were made for 1966, followed by 502 more in 1967. An unknown number of "Track-Pak" 4-4-2s are also known for both years, these cars featuring a dealer-installed W-30 package.

Available only with the L69 V-8, the W-30 deal included ram-air ductwork that fed cooler, denser outside air into those three Rochesters via two large plastic scoops situated in the openings in the front bumpers. These openings were normally reserved for turn signals, which were relocated inboard of each scoop for W-30 cars. These purposeful pieces of black plastic protruded slightly out from the bumper, inspiring more than one wisecrack about resemblances to Hoover vacuum sweepers. On top of that, the flexible ductwork beneath the hood looked like something stolen from the wife's dryer.

Allowing room for that ductwork to run alongside the L69 meant that the battery had to be relocated to the trunk—a fortunate turn considering that's just where drag racers put theirs for improved weight transfer to the rear wheels during hard acceleration. A unique chrome two-piece air cleaner (called a shroud) was also included. W-30 valve covers and the oil filler cap were chromed as well in 1966. Additional special equipment included a four-bladed fan without a clutch, a heavy-duty three-core radiator, and a close-ratio four-speed manual transmission. A unique high-lift, long-duration cam (with high-tension chrome vanadium steel valve springs and dampers) was stuffed inside an L69 400 ordered with the W-30 option. Though both this cam and the cool-air equipment obviously enhanced power potential, no output rating change was listed.

Production breakdowns for the 1966 4-4-2 W-30 included 25 F-85 club coupes, 8 F-85 Deluxe Holiday coupes, 5 Cutlass coupes, and 16 Cutlass Holiday coupes. Combining the W-30 equipment with a convertible was not possible.

Model availability	two-door F-85 club coupe and Deluxe Holiday hardtop; two-door Cutlass sports coupe and Holiday hardtop
Wheelbase	115 inches
Length	204.2 inches
Width	75.4 inches
Height	53.6 inches
Track (front/rear, in inches)	58/59
Wheels	14x6 stamped steel
Tires	7.75x14 redline
Suspension	Independent upper/lower A-arms, coil springs and stabilizer bar in front; solid axle, control arms, coil springs and stabilizer bar in back
Steering	recirculating ball
Brakes	9.5-inch drums, front and rear
Engine	360-horsepower 400-cubic-inch L69 V-8
Bore & stroke	4.00 x 3.975
Compression	10.5:1
Fuel delivery	three Rochester two-barrel carburetors
Transmission	four-speed manual
Axle ratio	4.11:1
Production	54

Oldsmobile's first "W-machine" appeared clandestinely in 1966. Only 54 of these W-30 models were built that year, including 25 F-85 club coupes, shown here. The incorrect F-85 Deluxe trim on this club coupe was installed by the dealer who originally sold the car. *Mike Mueller*

Above
A close-ratio four-speed manual transmission was included in the W-30 package in 1966. A bench seat was standard 4-4-2 fare that year. *Mike Mueller*

Below
The L69 triple-carb 400 was included with the W-30 package in 1966. Fitted with a special cam and air-induction plumbing, the first W-30 V-8 was conservatively rated at 360 horsepower. *Mike Mueller*

Above
The first W-30's air ducts were mounted inside the bumper where turn signals normally resided on garden-variety F-85 models. Those lamps were moved inboard to make room for the plastic intakes. *Mike Mueller*

Below
The battery on W-30 cars in 1966 and 1967 was relocated to the trunk. *Mike Mueller*

Above
First used in 1966 (only for a four-door hardtop midsize Olds), the Cutlass Supreme name reappeared for the company's top-shelf intermediate lineup in 1967. Various deluxe treatments were standard for Cutlass Supreme models, available in both two-door and four-door forms. The 4-4-2 package that year was limited to Cutlass Supreme applications. Production of 1967 4-4-2 Holiday coupes (shown here) was 16,998. This hardtop also is one of only 502 1967 W-30 models built. *Mike Mueller*

Left
A slight restyle for the F-85 nose in 1967 meant different ductwork was required to feed the W-30 V-8. Split intakes were located between the headlights that year. *Mike Mueller*

1967 4-4-2

1967 4-4-2

Model availability	two-door Cutlass Supreme sports coupe, Holiday hardtop and convertible
Wheelbase	115 inches
Length	204.2 inches
Width	76 inches
Height	53.8 inches
Shipping weight	3,452 pounds (Cutlass sports coupe), 3,489 pounds (Cutlass Holiday hardtop), 3,575 pounds (Cutlass convertible)
Base price	4-4-2 package cost $185.
Track (front/rear, in inches)	58/59
Wheels	14x6 stamped steel
Tires	F70x14 redline Wide Tread
Suspension	Independent upper/lower A-arms, coil springs and stabilizer bar in front; solid axle, control arms, coil springs and stabilizer bar in back
Steering	recirculating ball
Brakes	9.5-inch drums, front and rear
Engine	350-horsepower 400-cubic-inch V-8, std.
Bore & stroke	4.00 x 3.975
Compression	10.5:1
Fuel delivery	single four-barrel carburetor
Transmission	three-speed manual, std
Axle ratio	3.23:1
Production	24,827, all body styles

1967

The L78 4-4-2 Performance Package was limited to Cutlass Supreme models (sport coupe, Holiday hardtop, and convertible) this year, and simulated louvers appeared on the 4-4-2 hood. Being based on the Cutlass Supreme, the 1967 4-4-2 also featured Strato buckets seats as a no-cost option. Trading them for a conventional bench earned the buyer a $68 credit.

The 350-horse 400 big-block remained the star of the show, but the optional automatic was now the Turbo Hydra-Matic. Apparently the new L66 Turnpike Cruising option could've been combined with the L78 package to create a more fuel-efficient 4-4-2. Included in the L66 deal was a two-barrel-fed 300-horse 400 V-8 and the Turbo Hydra-Matic automatic. Total 1967 4-4-2 production was 24,827: 4,750 sport coupes, 16,998 Holiday coupes, and 3,079 convertibles.

Of the 502 W-30s built for 1967, 129 were sport coupes and 373 were Holiday coupes. Officially known as the "Outside Air Induction" (OAI) option, the W-30 package was revised this year as a GM upper-office edict banned multiple carburetor setups in midsize applications after 1966. Thus a single four-barrel replaced those three Rochesters. Also helping set the 1967 W-30 apart were new weight-saving inner fender wells made of red plastic.

The air intakes up front were new, too, due to styling changes that required the use of a "split" scoop located between the 1967

Above
GM executives banned triple-carb induction setups for all its divisions' models, save for Chevrolet's Corvette, in 1967. Thus that year's W-30 V-8 was topped by a single Rochester four-barrel. Similar air-induction plumbing carried over from 1966. New for the 1967 W-30 was an optional Turbo Hydra-Matic automatic transmission. *Mike Mueller*

Above
Production of 4-4-2 convertibles in 1967 was 3,079. The total count for all three body styles was 24,827 that year. *Mike Mueller*

Right
The 4-4-2 was made supreme in 1967 by adding optional bucket seats and a console. *Mike Mueller*

Below
As in 1966, no W-30 convertibles were built for 1967. W-30 production breakdown that year was 129 pillared coupes (shown here) and 373 Holiday hardtops. *Mike Mueller*

Cutlass' revised dual headlamps. Featuring two openings each—one above the turn signal, one below—these smaller scoops did not stand out in a crowd as much as the 1966 design.

A pair of Air Injection Reactor (AIR) cylinder heads, introduced as part of the K19 option (designed to meet California's tough emission standards), also were added to the 1967 W-30. Note that the heads were included but the AIR air-pump plumbing was not. This meant that the air-injection ports in the AIR heads, located just behind the spark plugs, had to be plugged for the W-30 application. An optional automatic, the new Turbo Hydra-Matic, became available for the second-edition W-30 too.

Heavy-duty valvetrain gear, a lumpier cam, enhanced cooling, and all that air-induction plumbing were again all part of the W-30 deal in 1968.

1968 4-4-2

1968 4-4-2	
Model availability	two-door Cutlass coupe, hardtop and convertible
Wheelbase	112 inches
Length	201.6 inches
Width	76.2 inches
Height	52.8 inches
Shipping weight	3,450 pounds (pillared coupe), 3,470 pounds (hardtop), 3,540 pounds (convertible)
Base price	$3,087 (coupe), $3,150 (hardtop), $3,341 (convertible)
Track (front/rear, in inches)	59
Wheels	14x6 stamped steel
Tires	F70x14 redline Wide Oval
Suspension	independent unequal A-arms with heavy-duty coil springs and stabilizer bar in front; solid axle with control arms, heavy-duty coil springs and stabilizer bar in back
Steering	recirculating ball
Brakes	9.5-inch drums, front and rear
Engine	325-horsepower 400-cubic-inch V-8 (w/automatic transmission); 350-horsepower 400-cubic-inch V-8 (w/manual transmission)
Bore & stroke	3.87 x 4.25 inches
Compression	10.5:1
Fuel delivery	single four-barrel carburetor
Transmission	three-speed manual
Production	36,587, all body styles

1968

Another restyled Cutlass body appeared at the same time the 4-4-2 finally was promoted into its own individual model series. Consisting again of a sport coupe, hardtop, and convertible, all featured standard Strato bucket seats. Production counts were 4,726, 26,719, and 5,142, respectively. The 36,587 grand total was an all-time high for Oldsmobile's midsize muscle car.

A 350-horse 400 V-8 remained standard fare for the 1968 4-4-2, but this was a new engine derived from Oldsmobile's equally new

455-cid big-block. The latest 4-4-2 V-8 used the 455's cast-iron crank (with its lengthy 4.25-inch stroke) combined with a downsized 3.87-inch bore to stay right at GM's 400-cube limit. A tame 325-horse Rocket V-8 was used when the optional Turbo Hydra-Matic automatic was ordered.

The forced-air W-30 option carried over into 1968 and remained at 360 horsepower. Still listed was the Turnpike Cruising package, now featuring a 290-horsepower 400. W-30 production for 1968 was 1,911: 170 convert-

ibles, 315 coupes, and 1,426 hardtops. All featured the new W-36 Rally stripe, which ran vertically on each front fender directly behind the wheel opening. These paint stripes were optional for other 4-4-2 models.

Another W-machine debuted this year, perhaps to help fool those damned insurance agents who were rapidly making it all but impossible for Average Joe to insure a big-block muscle car. The "Ram Rod 350" 1968 Olds featured the 350-cid W-31 V-8 force-fed by the same ram-air ductwork used by the W-30 big-

Above
Another restyled F-85 body appeared for 1968. The air-induction ducts for the 4-4-2's W-30 package went below the front bumper that year. The latest W-30 400 V-8 was again conservatively rated at 360 horsepower.

Right
The 4-4-2 became the flagship of the F-85 line in 1968 and again was offered only as three top-shelf Cutlass models: a pillared coupe, Holiday hardtop, and Cutlass Supreme convertible. Notice the vertical Rally stripe on the fender. This new feature was included on W-30 models and was optional on other 1968 4-4-2s.

block. Output was 325 horses for this hot little small-block. Running separately from the high-profile 4-4-2, Oldsmobile's W-31 Cutlasses and F-85s were quietly offered up through 1970. When *Hot Rod* magazine's Steve Kelley tried one on for size that year, he couldn't believe the way the small-block Ram Rod left the line much like its big-block brother. "On first tryouts," he wrote, "most of the group figured the 350-inch W-31 for the 455." W-31 production for 1968 was 742.

1969 4-4-2

Top
The horizontal taillights used in 1968 were replaced by vertical units for the 1969 F-85 line. Dual exhaust tips again tucked nicely into the 1969 4-4-2's rear bumper, as they had for the first time in 1968.

Above
Freshened styling front and rear set the 1969 4-4-2 apart from its 1968 predecessor. The Holiday hardtop (shown here) was once again the most popular 4-4-2 model that year. Production was 22,560.

1969

Dr. Oldsmobile, the mythical ruler of the Olds performance realm, even unleashed a detuned version of the W-30 for 1969, undoubtedly as another sacrifice to the gods of insurance surcharges. Still fed by those two air intakes mounted beneath the front bumper, the W-32 used a less-aggressive cam and was rated 10 horsepower less than the W-30 at 350 horses. The W-32 400 was offered for only one year, probably because it found only 297 buyers in 1969.

Standard 4-4-2 output again amounted to 350 or 325 horses, depending on transmission choice. New for the W-30 were barely noticeable fender decals, the first exterior identification for the big-block W-machine. W-30 production for 1969 was 1,389: 1,097 hardtops, 171 coupes, and 121 convertibles.

Total 4-4-2 production was 29,839, including 2,984 coupes, 4,295 convertibles, and 22,560 hardtops. The count for the 1969 W-31 small-block was 913: 212 F-85 club coupes, 26 Cutlass convertibles, 106 Cutlass coupes, and 569 Cutlass hardtops.

Dr. Oldsmobile, the division's "mod, mod scientist," began making appearances in ads and at auto shows in 1969.

W 30

Above
All that induction plumbing, with its bumper-mounted intake ducts, appeared one last time for the W-30 package in 1969. D-code cylinder heads (top) were new that year. Total 1969 W-30 production was 1,389.

Right
Dr. Oldsmobile, the division's "mod, mod scientist," began making appearances in ads and at auto shows in 1969. The good doctor's various "zany assistants" were Elephant Engine Ernie, Hy Spy, Esses Fernhill, Shifty Sidney, and Wind Tunnel Waldo.

W 32

Above
The small-block W-31 option appeared in 1968 for F-85/Cutlass customers who didn't need the 4-4-2's big-block muscle—or couldn't stomach its price tag. The heart of the W-31 Olds was the Ram Rod 350 V-8, rated at 325 horsepower. A 1969 W-31 Cutlass Supreme poses here on an auto show stage.

Top right
Oldsmobile's W-32 big-block featured a less aggressive cam to make 10 less horsepower than the W-30 400 in 1969. Both the W-32 and the W-31 small-block used the W-30's air-induction equipment.

Right
Offered for 1969 only, the W-32 option attracted less attention from insurance agents compared to its meaner W-30 cousin. Total W-32 production that year was a mere 297: 25 coupes, 247 Holiday hardtops, and 25 Cutlass Supreme convertibles.

1970 4-4-2

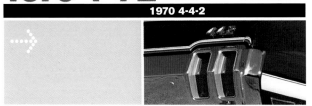

1970 4-4-2

Model availability	two-door Cutlass coupe, hardtop and convertible
Wheelbase	112 inches
Length	203.2 inches
Width	76.2 inches
Height	52.8 inches
Shipping weight	3,801 pounds (pillared coupe), 3,817 pounds (hardtop), 3,844 pounds (convertible)
Base price	$3,312 (coupe), $3,376 (hardtop), $3,567 (convertible)
Track (front/rear, in inches)	59
Wheels	14x7 stamped steel
Tires	G70x14
Suspension	independent unequal A-arms with heavy-duty coil springs and stabilizer bar in front; solid axle with control arms, heavy-duty coil springs and stabilizer bar in back
Steering	recirculating ball
Brakes	9.5-inch drums, front and rear
Engine	365-horsepower 455-cubic-inch V-8
Bore & stroke	4.125 x 4.250 inches
Compression	10.5:1
Fuel delivery	single Quadrajet four-barrel carburetor
Transmission	three-speed manual
Axle ratio	3.08:1
Production	19,332, all body styles

New for the W-30 package was a second 455 rated at 370 horsepower.

1970

All that forced-air ductwork was deleted for 1970 and replaced by the W-25 fiberglass hood with two gaping scoops located at its leading edge. A special air cleaner sealed up with the hood's underside, allowing outside air a direct passage into the 4-4-2's ever-present four-barrel. The W-25 lid was included in the W-30 and W-31 deals. It was a $158 option on other 4-4-2s. A high-profile fiberglass rear wing, priced at $73.72, also debuted on the 4-4-2's option list in 1970. New too for the big- and small-block W-machines were reasonably visible metal fender badges. This was the last year for the small-block W-31, still rated at 325 horsepower.

Production was 1,352: 207 F-85 coupes, 116 Cutlass coupes, and 1,029 Cutlass hardtops.

GM dropped its 400-cid limit in 1970, opening the door for Oldsmobile's biggest big-block, the 455, to make its way down into midsize ranks. Standard for the 1970 4-4-2 was a 365-horse 455 V-8. Total production was 19,330: 1,688 coupes, 2,933 convertibles, and 14,709 hardtops.

New for the W-30 package was a second 455 rated at 370 horsepower. Optional air conditioning and power brakes also were made available with the W-30 for the first time in 1970. Production was 3,100: 264 convertibles, 262 coupes, and 2,574 hardtops.

A 4-4-2 convertible paced the Indianapolis 500 in 1970, resulting in a requisite run of pace car replicas, identified on the options list by the Y-74 code. Included in this deal were the W-25 hood and the typical striping and decals. Both Cutlass and 4-4-2 Y-74 convertibles were built, with the latter coming only with the 365-horsepower 455. The W-30 455 was not available. Some of the Cutlass pace car replicas featured 350 small-block V-8s. Total pace car production was 626: 268 4-4-2s and 358 Cutlasses.

Oldsmobile's truly big 455-cubic-inch big-block V-8 became standard for the 4-4-2 in 1970. Notice the optional vinyl roof on this 1970 4-4-2 Holiday hardtop.

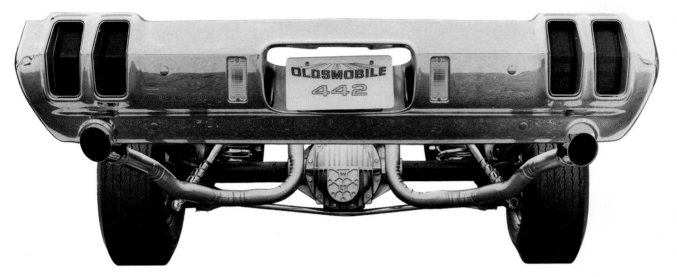

Left
A rear stabilizer bar and dual exhausts (still exiting through the rear bumper's lower edge) were again standard beneath the 4-4-2 in 1970. New that year was the W-27 aluminum axle cover, which looked cool and kept differential fluid temperatures down. The dealer-installed W-27 option cost $57.57.

Below
The 1970 4-4-2 was again available in coupe, hardtop, and convertible forms. This 4-4-2 is one of 14,711 Holiday hardtops built for 1970. The total count was 19,332. Notice the rear wing, a new option that year. *Mike Mueller*

Left
A new fiberglass hood with twin functional scoops appeared in 1970 to do away with the cumbersome ductwork previously included in the W-30 package. This W-25 hood was standard for the 1970 W-30, optional for other 4-4-2s. The 1970 4-4-2 shown here is one of 2,572 W-30 hardtops built that year. The total W-30 count was 3,100. *Mike Mueller*

Below, left
Bucket seats became standard inside a 4-4-2 in 1968. Options on this 1970 W-30 hardtop include Oldsmobile's attractive four-spoke steering wheel and a full console. *Mike Mueller*

Below
The 455-cubic-inch W-30 V-8 was rated at 370 horsepower in 1970. Notice the special air cleaner that now allowed outside air to rush into the carburetor through the W-25 hood's twin scoops. The red plastic fender wells became W-30 trademarks in 1967. *Mike Mueller*

1970 Rallye 350

1970 Rallye 350

Model availability	two-door F-85 sports coupe; two-door Cutlass coupe and Holiday hardtop (all done in monochromatic Sebring Yellow finishes)
Wheelbase	112 inches
Length	203.2 inches
Width	76.2 inches
Height	52.8 inches
Curb weight	3,745 pounds
Base price	$3,253
Track (front/rear, in inches)	59
Wheels	14x7 Super Stock II (painted Sebring Yellow)
Tires	G70x14
Suspension	independent unequal A-arms with heavy-duty coil springs and stabilizer bar in front; solid axle with control arms, heavy-duty coil springs and stabilizer bar in back
Steering	recirculating ball
Brakes	9.5-inch drums, front and rear
Engine	310-horsepower 350-cubic-inch V-8
Bore & stroke	4.057 x 4.385 inches
Compression	10.25:1
Fuel delivery	single four-barrel carburetor
Transmission	three-speed manual
Axle ratio	3.23:1
Production	3,547

1970 Rallye 350

The good Dr. Oldsmobile tried his hand at small-block performance again in 1970, this time in far-from-quiet fashion. For starters, the new Rallye 350 came in only one screaming shade: Sebring Yellow. The wheels were also yellow, as were the bumpers, thanks to a urethane coating. Contrasting black striping, a blacked-out grille, W-25 ram-air hood, and an optional rear wing helped turn heads even farther. "It's Wurlitzer heavy," was *Car Life*'s description for this package, listed under the W-45 option code.

That wasn't necessarily a bad thing. "Beneath that gaudy paint and wing lurk bargains in performance and handling," continued the *Car Life* review. The Rallye 350 came standard with the FE2 heavy-duty suspension, and power was supplied by a 310-horsepower 350 four-barrel V-8.

"Its 350 V-8, combined with a specially designed suspension system, provides a fine combination of effortless performance and smooth handling for a beautiful driving experience," said newly promoted General Manager John Beltz in February 1970. "In addition, it is competitively priced in the industry's intermediate market, available in Oldsmobile's lowest priced F-85 sports coupe body style, as well as in the Cutlass coupe and hardtop coupe."

Total production for this one-hit wonder was 3,547: 1,020 F-85 club coupes, 160 coupes, and 2,367 Holiday hardtops.

With its monochromatic yellow finish, the Rallye 350 simply couldn't be missed in 1970. Creating one of these high-profile machines was a matter of ordering Oldsmobile's W-45 Appearance Package, which was available that year only for F-85 club coupes, Cutlass pillared coupes (shown here), and Cutlass Holiday hardtops. *Mike Mueller*

Sebring Yellow was the only exterior finish available for the 1970 Rally 350, and this shade carried over to the urethane-coated bumpers and mandatory 7-inch-wide Super Stock II wheels.

Right
The W-45 option was priced at $157.98 in 1970. Black and orange decals were included in this deal, as were the W-25 functional hood, FE-2 Rallye suspension, D-35 sport mirrors, and W-35 rear deck wing. *Mike Mueller*

Below
The only available engine for the 1970 Rallye 350 was Oldsmobile's L74 small-block V-8, rated at 310 horsepower. *Mike Mueller*

Below, right
Oldsmobile's cool Custom-Sport steering wheel (N-34) was standard inside the Rally 350. So was a mundane bench seat. Options appearing here include air conditioning, power steering, power brakes, and an 8-track stereo. *Mike Mueller*

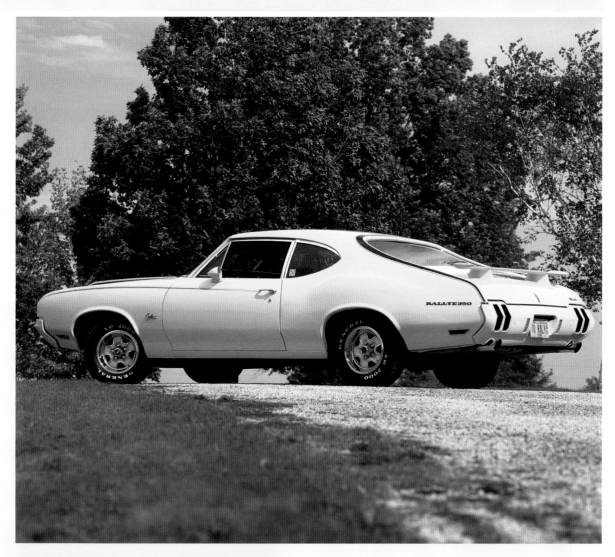

1971 4-4-2

Model availability	two-door Cutlass hardtop and convertible
Wheelbase	112 inches
Length	203.5 inches
Width	76.2 inches
Height	52.9 inches
Shipping weight	3,835 pounds (hardtop), 3,792 (convertible)
Base price	$3,551 (hardtop), $3,742 (convertible)
Track (front/rear, in inches)	59
Wheels	14x7 stamped steel
Tires	G70x14
Suspension	independent unequal A-arms with heavy-duty coil springs and stabilizer bar in front; solid axle with control arms, heavy-duty coil springs and stabilizer bar in back
Steering	recirculating ball
Brakes	9.5-inch drums, front and rear
Engine	270-horsepower 455-cubic-inch V-8
Bore & stroke	4.125 x 4.250 inches
Compression	8.5:1
Fuel delivery	single Quadrajet four-barrel carburetor
Transmission	three-speed manual
Production	7,589, all body styles

Above

Olds engineers began developing hemi-head V-8s during the 1960s to compete with Chrysler's 426 Hemi. Various experimental engines were built, some with four-valve heads and overhead cams. This conventional pushrod 455 Hemi was originally planned for regular production in 1970 but was cancelled due to changing attitudes around Detroit toward high-performance vehicles.

Opposite page

A 4-4-2 convertible was chosen to pace the Indianapolis 500 in May 1970. A pace car replica package, option code Y-74, was offered for both Cutlass and 4-4-2 convertibles that year.

1971

This was the last year for a stand-alone 4-4-2 model series, and only two varieties were offered: a Holiday hardtop and Cutlass Supreme convertible. Production was 6,285 for the former, 1,304 for the latter. Gone were the small-block W-31 and the high-profile Rallye 350. The W-30 remained, but those darned compression cuts helped drop its output to 300 horsepower. The 4-4-2's standard 455 V-8 was rated at 270 horses this year. W-30 production totaled 920: 810 hardtops and 110 convertibles.

Left
The 4-4-2 stood tall as a model line all its own for the last time in 1971. Only two body styles were offered that year: hardtop and convertible. Drop-top production was 1,304. *Mike Mueller*

Below left
Strato buckets were again standard in 1971. Options included the four-spoke Custom-Sport steering wheel, a console, and the ever-present Hurst Dual Gate automatic transmission shifter. *Mike Mueller*

Below
Advertised output for the W-30 455 V-8 in 1971 was down to 300 horsepower, thanks mostly to the same compression cut made in all GM V-8s that year. Red plastic fenderwells were once more included in the W-30 deal. *Mike Mueller*

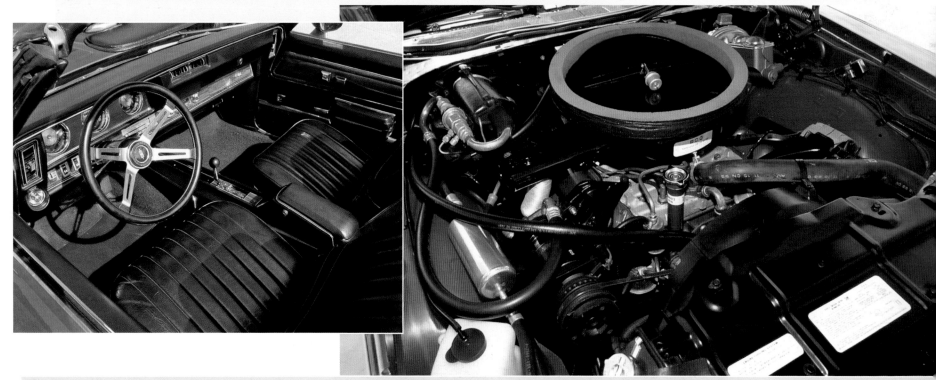

1972 4-4-2

1972

The 4-4-2 became available in 1972 by way of the 4-4-2 W29 Appearance and Handling Package, available for the Cutlass and Cutlass Supreme. The L32 350 small-block, topped by a two-barrel carburetor, was now standard, net-rated at 160 horsepower. A 180-horsepower 350 (L34) was optional, as was the L75 455 and W-30 big-block, both rated the same as in 1971.

Total 4-4-2 production for 1972, big-block or small, was 9,715: 751 Cutlass hardtops, 123 Cutlass S sport coupes, 7,800 Cutlass S hardtops, and 1,041 Cutlass Supreme convertibles. The total W-30 count was 772.

Both the 4-4-2 and W-30 continued into 1973, now based on Oldsmobile's revamped midsize platform, but these still-attractive machines paled in comparison to their predecessors as far as real performance was concerned.

Model availability	two-door Cutlass hardtop; two-door Cutlass S club coupe, hardtop and convertible
Wheelbase	112 inches
Length	203.6 inches
Width	76.2 inches
Height	52.9 inches
Price	4-4-2 package ranged from $71 to $150 depending on model/body style application
Track (front/rear, in inches)	59
Wheels	14x7 stamped steel
Tires	G70x14
Suspension	independent unequal A-arms with heavy-duty coil springs and stabilizer bar in front; solid axle with control arms, heavy-duty coil springs and stabilizer bar in back
Steering	recirculating ball
Brakes	9.5-inch drums, front and rear
Engine	160-horsepower 350-cubic-inch L32 V-8, std.
Bore & stroke	4.057x 3.385 inches
Compression	8.5:1
Fuel delivery	single four-barrel carburetor
Transmission	three-speed manual
Production	9,845, all body styles

Above
Ordering a 4-4-2 in 1972 required checking off the same option code, W-29, used in 1967. A 350 small-block V-8 was standard for the 1972 W-29 package, which was available for four body styles: Cutlass hardtop, Cutlass S club coupe and hardtop, and Cutlass Supreme convertible.

Left
An attractively restyled Cutlass body appeared as a base for Oldsmobile's 4-4-2 in 1973. Production that year was 9,797. Oldsmobile's original 4-4-2 legacy carried on up through 1980. Those three numbers returned from 1985 to 1988 and 1990 to 1991.

04

Above
1963 Nova SS

Middle
1966 Nova SS L79

Right
1969 Nova SS396

A Super Star Is Born

04

Chevrolet Nova SS 1964–1971

Americans really didn't know they needed smaller, cheaper automobiles before Chevrolet and Ford rolled out all-new compacts a half century ago. But boy did we want 'em once the Corvair and Falcon appeared–so much so that Chevy product planners wasted no time creating a second little car to help meet the growing need. A decision was made to add a fourth model to the Bowtie lineup just two months after the air-cooled Corvair was introduced on October 2, 1959. This new compact went from drawing board to reality in a scant 18 months, making it one of the quickest development sagas in General Motors' storied history. New-for-1962 Chevy II models started rolling off the assembly line in August 1961.

Like the car itself, the name too came about in rapid-fire fashion. Most rumors around Detroit in 1961 had the new compact wearing the Nova badge, which had been glowing brightly around the division's experimental studios dating back to 1955. But even most blind men noticed that Nova didn't begin with a C, the prerequisite for Chevy model names during the 1960s. With no other more imaginative candidates in the running, Chevy II plainly and simply emerged to take Nova's place almost at the last minute. No one needed to grieve for the N-word, though. The Nova tag was saved for a top-shelf Chevy II subseries. It then became the sole identity for the entire line when Chevy II was dropped after 1968.

The first Chevy II shared none of its structure with any other GM product when it made

its public debut on September 29, 1961. Its conservatively styled, yet crisp, three-box unibody shell featured an isolated subframe up front (bolted to the body in 14 places) and a rear suspension consisting of a typical live axle held in place by single-leaf springs called Mono Plates. Measuring 5 feet in length, each Mono Plate was rolled from high-strength chromium-steel bar stock and used rubber bushing mounts at both ends to insulate the unitized body from road shocks. Advantages also included less unsprung weight (one strong leaf weighed less than a typical stack of steel leaves), lower manufacturing costs (one single leaf was simpler than many clamped together), and improved rust resistance (those stacked leaves always trapped moisture in between them).

→ The new-for-1962 Chevy II was Chevrolet's second model to use unitized body/frame construction. The Corvair, introduced two years earlier, was the first.

→ An over-the-counter V-8 swap kit (offered by Chevrolet) appeared for the Chevy II early in 1962.

→ Chevrolet's hottest factory-delivered compact in 1962 was the new Corvair Spyder, powered by a 150-horsepower turbocharged six-cylinder.

→ In 1963, the Nova became the second Chevrolet to join the Super Sport fraternity. The Nova SS legacy ran up through 1976.

→ The first Nova Super Sport ended up being the most popular of the series; production for 1963 hit 42,432.

→ A convertible Nova SS was offered for one year only: 1963.

→ Both the Nova sport coupe and Super Sport models initially failed to return for 1964 but were reinstated midyear by popular demand.

→ A factory-installed optional V-8 was introduced in 1964.

→ The Chevy II name was used for the last time in 1968.

→ The Nova SS 396 was built from 1968 to 1970.

→ The Rally Nova was offered for two years: 1971 and 1972.

→ Chevrolet's original Nova retired after 1979.

Opposite
The Chevy II debuted for 1962 as a slight step up from Chevrolet's truly compact Corvair. Top of the line in Chevy II ranks was the deluxe Nova rendition, offered only with six-cylinder power. A convertible was only available in the Nova group.

But even most blind men noticed that Nova didn't begin with a C, the prerequisite for Chevy model names during the 1960s.

Right
The Chevy II's base engine in 1962 was a budget-conscious 153-cubic-inch four-cylinder, rated at 90 horsepower.

Below
The Chevy II became the second Chevrolet model to wear the SS badge in 1963. Six-cylinder power was the only choice for Nova Super Sport buyers that year.

Below right
An enlarged six-cylinder became a Nova option in 1964. Displacement was 230-cubic-inches; output was 155 horsepower.

Powering the first Chevy II was another exclusive, an all-new inline four-cylinder, Chevrolet's first four-holer since 1928. This frugal mini-motor displaced a meager 153 cubic-inches and produced 90 horsepower. An equally new 120-horsepower six-cylinder (that shared various internal components with its smaller running mate) was optional for the Chevy II, standard for the top-line Nova.

Setting the 1962 Nova further apart from its plain-Jane brethren were extra trim, upgraded upholstery, and larger tires. Two-door sport coupe and convertible models also were exclusive to the high-grade line. Veteran *Mechanix*

Illustrated road-tester Tom McCahill drove the Nova ragtop and came away quite happy. "With a little hopping up, a stick shift and its low price, it should sell like a cold beer on a hot Fourth of July."

Chevrolet began handling hop-up chores the following year, when the popular Chevy II returned looking basically the same save for a few trim updates and some interior freshening. New in 1963 was a Nova Super Sport, offered with or without a roof. Extending the SS touch into compact ranks clearly was a no-brainer (kinda like selling icy suds during sizzling summer afternoons), especially after market reac-

tions in 1962 had demonstrated an interesting trend: Of the 326,607 Chevy IIs sold that first year, 59,741 were upscale Nova sport coupes, 23,741 were carefree Nova convertibles. Apparently not all Chevy II buyers minded doling out a few more bucks for a little added flair.

Above
A convertible Nova Super Sport was offered for one year only: 1963. All others were sport coupes or sedans. *Mike Mueller*

Inset
The compact Super Sport legacy began in 1963 and ended 13 years later. *Mike Mueller*

Adding the SS package (RPO Z03) in 1963 required an extra $161. Unlike the first full-size Super Sport deal two years before, the new Z03 option was all show, no go. It simply dressed things up inside and out, beginning with "Nova SS" emblems on the deck lid and both rear quarters, special body-side moldings with silver inserts, and a bright insert added to the cove panel in back. Bigger 14-inch wheels (13-inchers were standard for the Chevy II) were a mandatory option for the 1963 Nova SS, and those rims were hidden with the same spinner wheel covers seen on that year's Impala Super Sport.

Interior additions included all-vinyl upholstery, bucket seats, "SS" identification on the steering wheel, "Nova SS" on the glove box, an electric clock, and bright instrument-panel trim. Real gauges for oil, electrics, and water temperature replaced the Chevy II's idiot lights within that panel. Powerglide-equipped Nova Super Sports were further adorned with a floorshift surrounded by a bright dress-up plate. Base three-speed examples used a yeoman column shift.

Like all 1963 Novas, the SS was available with only one power source, the purely practical 120-horse 194-cube six. Customers who

noticed that the Chevy II engine bay had been designed all along to accept the Bowtie small-block could've swapped in the 283- or 327-cube V-8 with relative ease beneath the nearest shade tree. Or they could have paid big bucks to have their local dealer install Chevrolet's own V-8 conversion kit—the going rate was $1,500 *plus* labor, or more than half of what an entire Chevy II cost. Few opted for this expensive transformation, meaning nearly all early Nova Super Sports struggled to get out of their own way.

No, Chevy's latest SS obviously wasn't a muscle car. But it was a start.

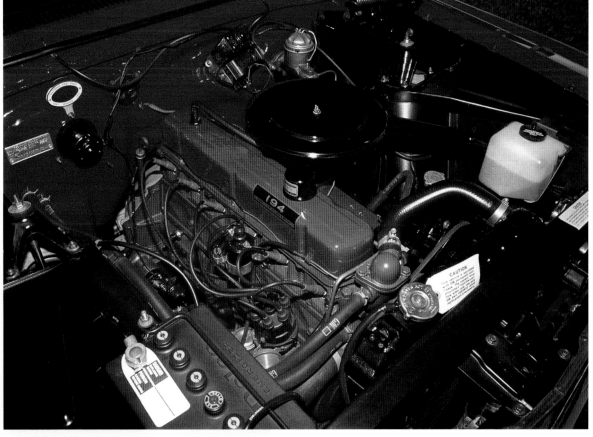

Above
The first Nova SS was all show, no go, with only one overhead-valve six-cylinder engine made available beneath its hood in 1963. Standard dress-up items included a bright tail panel and various SS identification. *Mike Mueller*

Above right
Standard inside the 1963 Nova SS were bucket seats, a deluxe steering wheel, and extra instrumentation. *Mike Mueller*

Right
The only engine offered beneath the 1963 Nova SS hood was a 194-cubic-inch six-cylinder rated at 120 horsepower. *Mike Mueller*

Like all 1963 Novas, the SS was available with only one power source, the purely practical 120-horse 194-cube six.

1964 Nova SS

1964 Nova SS

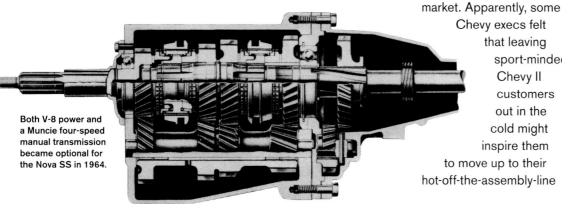

Model availability	two-door sport coupe
Wheelbase	110 inches
Length	183 inches
Width	70.8 inches
Height	55 inches
Curb weight	2,675 pounds
Base price	$2,433
Track (front/rear, in inches)	56.8/56.3
Wheels	14-inch stamped-steel
Tires	6.50x14 two-ply
Suspension	independent upper A-arms, lower controls arms, coil springs and stabilizer bar in front; multi-leaf springs, solid axle in back
Steering	recirculating ball (power assist optional)
Brakes	four-wheel hydraulic drum
Engine	120-horsepower 194-cubic-inch inline six-cylinder, std. 155-horsepower 230-cubic-inch inline six-cylinder, optional 195-horsepower 283-cubic-inch V-8, optional
Bore & stroke	3.563 x 3.25 inches, 194 six; 3.875 x 3.25 inches, 230 six; 3.875 x 3.00 inches, 283 V-8
Compression	8.5:1, six-cylinder; 9.25:1, 283 V-8
Fuel delivery	one-barrel carburetor, six-cylinder; two-barrel carburetor, 283 V-8
Transmission	three-speed manual, std.; four-speed manual and Powerglide automatic, optional
Axle ratio	3.08:1
Production	10,576

Both V-8 power and a Muncie four-speed manual transmission became optional for the Nova SS in 1964.

Chevrolet was more than happy to announce the introduction of an optional, factory-installed V-8 for the 1964 Nova

1964

Chevrolet management amazingly opted to drop the Nova sport coupe and convertible after 1963 despite healthy sales: nearly 87,500 for the closed model, 24,800 for its topless running mate. With the departure of these two class acts so too went the Super Sport, which had found 42,432 homes in 1963.

Countering this bad news was the introduction of the Chevy II's first optional, factory-direct V-8, a 195-horsepower 283-cubic-inch small-block (RPO L32) that, according to *Motor Trend*'s Bob McVay, "takes the Chevy II out of the ho-hum category and makes it fun to drive." Acceleration wasn't mind-boggling, but at least it showed progress, certainly so in comparison to the wimpy 194-cube six-cylinder, as well as the new optional 230-cubic-inch six.

Furthermore, ample performance potential obviously was present, what with all the hot parts then available from Chevrolet for its various small-block V-8s. Swapping out the L32's two-barrel carburetor for the new midsize Chevelle's 220-horse L77 283's four-barrel was just a start. Truly inspired home mechanics might've also considered trading the 283 for the 327 V-8, a mighty-mouse motor that was then making 300 horses in top form for both the Chevelle and Impala.

It was the Chevelle's debut that reportedly influenced the decision to cut the Nova Super Sport loose after only one year on the market. Apparently, some Chevy execs felt that leaving sport-minded Chevy II customers out in the cold might inspire them to move up to their hot-off-the-assembly-line

A 283-CU.-IN. V8 NEVER FOUND A HAPPIER HOME—We slung a big 195-hp 283-cubic-inch V8* into the Chevy II Nova Sport Coupe and now you'd think it was born that way.

This is the same Chevy II that spent a couple of happy years building up a following as one of the most wholesome things since brown bread. The one down-to-earth American car you wouldn't mind bringing home to mother or showing off to your friends. And the last car in the world you'd ever accuse of being pretentious. In short, a regular darb.

Now, with that V8 up front, Chevy II spends most of its time doing impressions of performance types. Give it a 4-speed all-synchro shift* and it's very close to being just that. After all, it started out with certain advantages: taut suspension, trim size, no-nonsense construction.

Is this any way for a nice, quiet, sturdy, sensible, unpretentious car like Chevy II to behave? Strangely enough, yes. Despite its new vigor, it's still a nice, quiet, sturdy, sensible, unpretentious car. With sharper teeth. Grrr. **CHEVY II NOVA** CHEVROLET

Chevrolet Division of General Motors, Detroit, Michigan   *Optional at extra cost

intermediate. But hot-headed compact buyers would have none of it. Their complaints forced Chevrolet officials to bring back the Nova sport coupe and SS early in the 1964 run, with the Super Sport listed as the new flagship model series. The convertible, unfortunately, was never seen again.

All features, including the standard 194-cubic-inch six, carried over for the 1964 Super Sport. The only notable upgrades involved the deletion of the Nova's body-side trim spear and relocation of the "Nova SS" badges from the quarter panels to the front fenders. Chevrolet's bigger, better 230-cube six-cylinder was optional, but who cared when the 283 V-8 was also waiting there on the RPO list? Price for the L32 small-block was $107. An optional Muncie four-speed (priced at $188) for the warmly welcomed V-8 was also new in 1964.

Along with the 283 came bigger, and it was hoped, better brakes. Front drums went from 9 inches in diameter to 9.5 and from 2.25 inches wide to 2.5. Rear drums measured 9.5x2 inches, compared to the 9x1.75 units used previously. Clutch, transmission, and rear axle also were beefed, and all V-8 Chevy IIs received larger 14x5 wheels.

After moving from the rear quarter panel to the front fender for 1964, "Nova SS" script returned to the tail the following year. The strongest engine option for the 1965 Nova SS was the L74 327 small-block, rated at 300 horsepower.

1965 Nova SS

Model availability	two-door sport coupe
Wheelbase	110 inches
Length	183 inches
Width	70.8 inches
Height	55 inches
Curb weight	2,690 pounds
Base price	$2,381
Track (front/rear, in inches)	56.8/56.3
Wheels	14-inch stamped-steel
Tires	6.50x14 two-ply
Suspension	independent upper A-arms, lower control arms, coil springs and stabilizer bar in front; multi-leaf springs, solid axle in back
Steering	recirculating ball (power assist optional)
Brakes	four-wheel hydraulic drum
Engine	120-horsepower 194-cubic-inch inline six-cylinder, std. 140-horsepower 230-cubic-inch inline six-cylinder, optional 195-horsepower 283-cubic-inch V-8, optional 220-horsepower 283-cubic-inch V-8, optional 250-horsepower 327-cubic-inch V-8, optional 300-horsepower 327-cubic-inch V-8, optional
Bore & stroke	3.563 x 3.25 inches, 194 six; 3.875 x 3.25 inches, 230 six; 3.875 x 3.00 inches, 283 V-8; 4.00 x 3.25 inches, 327 V-8
Compression	8.5:1, six-cylinder; 9.25:1, 283 V-8; 10:1, 327 V-8
Fuel delivery	one-barrel carburetor, six-cylinder; two-barrel carburetor, 195-hp 283 V-8; four-barrel carburetor, 220-hp 283 and 327 V-8
Transmission	three-speed manual, std.; four-speed manual and Powerglide automatic, optional
Axle ratio	3.08:1, std. w/six and 283 V-8; 3.07:1 std. w/327 V-8
Production	9,100

1965

A shortened run for the 1964 Nova SS helped drop production to 10,576. The count fell even further in 1965 to 9,100, probably due to the Chevelle's cut into the Chevy II's pie, working in concert with the Nova's rapidly aging facade. Unchanged for four years, the compact's body plainly looked old beyond its years compared to the still-fresh Chevelle, not to mention the Corvair and full-size Chevys, cars featuring markedly attractive total makeovers in 1965.

Save for a new grille and more roaming badges ("Nova SS" returned to the rear quarters), next to nothing changed as far as the top-shelf Chevy II series was concerned—at least nothing in the image department. Making really big news, though, beneath the 1965 Super

Sport's hood were even more power choices. Chevy officials went so far as to segregate that year's SS models into two separate subseries, specially coded for the six and V-8, to help keep things in order. The 194 six was again standard for the former, with the 230 six optional. The L32 283 two-barrel small-block was standard for the latter, joined midyear by the optional 220-horse L77 with its four-barrel carb and dual exhausts.

More notable were two optional 327s, both of which featured four-barrel carburetors and 10:1 compression. The L30 327 produced 250 horsepower, while its L74 brother made 300. Production reportedly was only 320 for the L30 and 319 for the L74.

1966 Nova SS

1966 Nova SS

Model availability	two-door sport coupe
Wheelbase	110 inches
Length	183 inches
Width	71.3 inches
Height	53.8 inches
Curb weight	3,140 (w/V-8)
Base price	$2,430
Track (front/rear, in inches)	56.8/56.3
Wheels	14-inch stamped-steel
Suspension	independent upper A-arms, lower control arms, coil springs and stabilizer bar in front; multi-leaf springs, solid axle in back
Steering	recirculating ball (power assist optional)
Brakes	four-wheel hydraulic drum
Engine	120-horsepower 194-cubic-inch inline six-cylinder, std. 140-horsepower 230-cubic-inch inline six-cylinder, optional 195-horsepower 283-cubic-inch V-8, optional 220-horsepower 283-cubic-inch V-8, optional 275-horsepower 327-cubic-inch V-8, optional 350-horsepower 327-cubic-inch V-8, optional
Bore & stroke	3.563 x 3.25 inches, 194 six; 3.875 x 3.25 inches, 230 six; 3.875 x 3.00 inches, 283 V-8; 4.00 x 3.25 inches, 327 V-8
Compression	8.5:1, six-cylinder; 9.25:1, 283 V-8; 10.25:1, 275-hp 327 V-8; 11:1, 350-hp 327 V-8
Fuel delivery	one-barrel carburetor, six-cylinder; two-barrel carburetor, 195-hp 283 V-8; four-barrel carburetor, 220-hp 283 and 327 V-8
Transmission	three-speed manual, std.; four-speed manual and Powerglide automatic, optional
Production	20,986

Freshened styling enhanced Nova SS appeal in 1966, as did the optional L79 V-8, a 327-cubic-inch small-block first seen in Corvette ranks in 1965. *Mike Mueller*

1966

A squeaky-clean restyle arrived in 1966, while basic structure and powertrain features rolled over from the 1962–1965 Chevy II. Modernized lines were crisp, and the 1966 new semi-fastback shape fit right in with Detroit's latest fad. "Style-wise, the Nova SS isn't likely to win any design laurels, but neither is it a bad-looking car," wrote *Motor Trend*'s Steve Kelly in trivializing tribute. Overall, the latest body also looked bigger even though basic chassis dimensions hadn't changed.

The engine lineup also stayed the same; that is, until a buyer reached the optional 327 V-8s. The L30 327 went from 250 horsepower to 275 in 1966, while the 300-horse L74 was deleted in favor of the groundbreaking L79. Introduced for Corvettes in 1965, this seriously strong small-block relied on a Holley four-barrel on an aluminum intake, big-valve heads, and 11:1 compression to produce more than 1 horsepower per cubic-inch—350 to be exact.

In the little Nova SS, those ponies helped create one of Detroit's greatest street sleepers of all time—who would have ever guessed a compact could be so big and bad? Rest to 60 miles per hour required only 7.2 seconds, according to a *Car Life* road test that also produced a 15.1-second quarter-mile. Breaking into the 14s was simply a matter of replacing those skinny standard treads with some real meat out back.

The L79's appearance signaled a coming of age for the Nova Super Sport, as it finally could claim full-fledged muscle car status. And at about $3,600, it represented one of the biggest bangs for the buck in 1966. Its diminutive nature was a plus, while its hydraulically cammed heart was both nasty and nice. "Unlike some samples from the Supercar spectrum, [the L79 Nova] maintains a gentleness along with its fierce performance potential; its power/weight ratio is second to none and it is definitely better balanced than most," concluded *Car Life*'s critics.

Chevrolet sold 5,481 350-horsepower Chevy IIs in 1966, of which perhaps as many as 300 were low-buck, lightweight sedans—just the kind of machine a serious racer would want to take to a dragstrip. Reportedly, a mere six L79 compacts were built for 1967 before this killer combo was quietly killed off.

Above
Transmission choices behind the L79 327 in 1966 numbered two: a close- or wide-ratio four-speed manual. *Mike Mueller*

Right
The L79 327 made 350 horsepower, more than enough muscle to transform the compact Chevy II into a certified street sleeper. *Mike Mueller*

The L79's appearance signaled a coming of age for the Nova Super Sport, as it finally could claim full-fledged muscle car status.

Right
Notice the opposed twin snorkels on the 1966 Nova's L79 V-8. In Chevelle applications, these intakes were angled diagonally toward the headlight areas. Beneath that bright air cleaner was a Holley four-barrel carburetor. *Mike Mueller*

Lower right
Nova SS identification appeared in the grille for the first time in 1966. *Mike Mueller*

Below
SS identification returned to its familiar location in 1966. *Mike Mueller*

1967 Nova SS

1967 Nova SS

Super Sport

Model availability	two-door sport coupe
Wheelbase	110 inches
Length	183 inches
Width	71.3 inches
Height	53.8 inches
Curb weight	2,690 pounds (w/six-cylinder)
Base price	$2,467
Track (front/rear, in inches)	56.8/56.3
Wheels	14-inch stamped-steel
Suspension	independent upper A-arms, lower control arms, coil springs and stabilizer bar in front; multi-leaf springs, solid axle in back
Steering	recirculating ball (power assist optional)
Brakes	four-wheel hydraulic drum, std.; front discs optional
Engine	120-horsepower 194-cubic-inch inline six-cylinder, std. 155-horsepower 250-cubic-inch inline six-cylinder, optional 195-horsepower 283-cubic-inch V-8, optional 275-horsepower 327-cubic-inch V-8, optional 325-horsepower 327-cubic-inch V-8, optional (very few released early in year)
Bore & stroke	3.563 x 3.25 inches, 194 six; 3.875 x 3.25 inches, 230 six; 3.875 x 3.00 inches, 283 V-8; 4.00 x 3.25 inches, 327 V-8
Compression	8.5:1, six-cylinder; 9.25:1, 283 V-8; 10.25:1, 275-hp 327 V-8; 11:1, 325-hp 327 V-8
Fuel delivery	one-barrel carburetor, six-cylinder; two-barrel carburetor, 195-hp 283 V-8; four-barrel carburetor, 327 V-8
Transmission	three-speed manual, std.; four-speed manual and Powerglide automatic, optional
Production	10,069

1967

After selling 20,986 Nova Super Sports in 1966, Chevrolet managed to move 10,069 more the following year, all of them looking essentially identical to their predecessors. With the L79 (down-rated to 325 horsepower for 1967) dropped early on, it was left to the 275-horse 327 to carry the load—and just like that the Nova SS again found itself lost well back in Detroit's high-performance pack.

V-8s dominated Super Sport production in 1967; the total count was 8,213.

The 195-horsepower 283 small-block carried over for one last year as the Nova's standard V-8, but the 220-horsepower L77 did not return. Other mechanical news of note came in the brake department, where a safety-conscious dual-circuit master cylinder became standard and optional front discs appeared for the first time. Included with those disc brakes were attractive 14-inch Rally wheels, soon to become Chevy muscle car trademarks.

Above
Optional front disc brakes debuted for the 1967 Nova, and included with these stoppers was a set of attractive Rally wheels. *Mike Mueller*

Top right
The same stacked script showed up on both the 1966 and 1967 Nova Super Sport quarter panels. *Mike Mueller*

Right
The badge on the tail of the 1966 Super Sport Nova simply read "SS." In 1967, the name was lengthened to Nova SS. *Mike Mueller*

Opposite page
No notable exterior changes marked the arrival of the latest Nova SS in 1967. Total production that year was 8,213. *Mike Mueller*

Overall, the 1968 Chevy II was longer, taller, and notably heavier than its forerunner.

Below left
Only a handful of L79 installations were performed early in 1967 before the option was cancelled. Output that time around was 325 horsepower. *Mike Mueller*

Below right
The L79 V-8's Holley four-barrel carburetor was mounted on an aluminum intake in 1966 and 1967. *Mike Mueller*

A bigger, better, more beautiful Chevy II body debuted for 1968, and the Super Sport reappeared that year, this time with a 350-cubic-inch V-8 as standard equipment. New, too, for 1968 was the truly bad SS 396 rendition.

1968 Nova SS

1968 Nova SS

Model availability	two-door sedan
Wheelbase	111 inches
Length	187.7 inches
Width	70.5 inches
Height	54.1 inches
Curb weight	3,400 pounds (w/350 V-8)
Base price	$2,367 (for V-8 two-door sedan)
Track (front/rear, in inches)	59/58.9
Wheels	14-inch stamped-steel
Tires	E70x14 Uniroyal Tiger Paw
Suspension	independent upper A-arms, lower control arms, heavy-duty coil springs and stabilizer bar in front; multi-leaf springs, solid axle in back
Steering	recirculating ball (power assist optional)
Brakes	four-wheel hydraulic drum
Engine	295-horsepower 350-cubic-inch V-8, std.
	350-horsepower 396-cubic-inch V-8, optional
	375-horsepower 396-cubic-inch V-8, optional
Bore & stroke	4.00 x 3.25 inches, 350 V-8; 4.094 x 3.76 inches, 396 V-8
Compression	10.25:1, 350 V-8 and 350-hp 396 V-8; 11:1, 375-hp 396 V-8
Fuel delivery	four-barrel carburetor
Transmission	three-speed manual, std.; four-speed manual and Powerglide automatic, optional
Axle ratio	3.55:1
Production	5,571

1968

A second modernizing restyle appeared in 1968, supported by a nicely revamped unitized foundation that the latest Chevy II shared with its year-old Camaro cousin. Though curbside kibitzers liked to claim that the new Nova was little more than a Camaro in disguise, in truth it was the other way around. Engineers had this platform in the works already when Chevrolet's pony car project was kicked off; it was the Camaro that did the borrowing before appearing one year earlier than the updated Chevy II.

The bolt-on subframe design, front suspension, cowl structure, and Mono Plate rear springs more or less carried over between the two, as did standard staggered rear shock absorbers. Reserved for the Camaro's hotter optional V-8s in 1967, these shocks were bias mounted—the passenger-side unit in front of the axle, its opposite mate behind—to prevent dangerous wheel hop brought on during hard acceleration. All 1968 Novas fitted with optional engines also received stronger multi-leaf springs in back to limit unwanted axle windup whenever pedal met metal.

Overall, the 1968 Chevy II was longer, taller, and notably heavier than its forerunner. Wheelbase was stretched a click to 111 inches, while track went up markedly: from 56.8 inches to 59 in front and from 56.3 to 58.9 in back. Body style choices, on the other hand, were cut back to just two sedans—one with two doors, the other four—as the stylish sport coupe (not

to mention the yeoman station wagon) joined its convertible ancestor in the archives, also never to return.

Also notable that year was the complete merging of nameplates, as all models were simply called Chevy II Novas. Even the Super Sport wore Chevy II identification (above the grille) in 1968, something earlier renditions didn't do, in keeping with their elite image. With a top-line Nova series no longer present, the body styles were now segregated rather plainly by engine choice: prefix code 111 for four-cylinder models, 113 for the sixes, and 114 for the V-8s. Body style codes were 69 for the four-door, 27 for the two-door.

Replacing the retired 283 as the Nova's standard V-8 in 1968 was Chevrolet's new 307-cubic-inch Turbo-Fire engine, created by bolting a 327 crank into a 283 block. This mild-mannered motor was one of the few small-blocks never to see a high-performance transformation. Topped by a two-barrel carburetor, it produced a polite 200 horsepower.

More to leadfoots' liking was the optional L79 327, which apparently reappeared midyear in 1968. Again rated at 325 horsepower, this rather mysterious mill differed from earlier renditions in that it used a Quadrajet four-barrel carb (topped by a Corvette-style open-element air cleaner) on a cast-iron intake. But still a certified screamer, it was capable of blasting a 1968 Chevy II (with sticky slicks bolted on in back) through the quarter-mile in a sensational 14.6

seconds, according to a *Hot Rod* magazine road test.

Few L79 V-8s found their way into Novas in 1968, the last year for the 327 in Chevy II ranks. None were bolted into 1968 Super Sports, as the latest SS at first was limited to one power source when it went on sale on September 21 that year. Sixes were no longer offered either as Chevrolet's 350-cubic-inch Turbo-Fire small-block, introduced the previous year exclusively

The porcupine-head nickname for Chevrolet's Mk IV big-block V-8 came from its canted, staggered valves, which splayed out in all directions, kinda like a . . . well, you know. Mk IV big-block power became optional for the Nova SS in 1968.

as a Camaro SS option, became standard fare for the car called "Chevy II much" in company advertisements. With no less than 295 horses now at the ready, the Nova SS was once more worthy of nomination to the muscle car class. "You'll second the motion," added those ads.

The latest in a long line of bulked-up small-blocks, the 1967 Camaro's 350 Turbo-Fire wasn't simply the product of a little boring or stroking, as had been basically the case both when the original 265 morphed into the 283 in 1957 and the 283 evolved into the 327 five years later. Stretching the 265/283's 3.00-inch stroke to 3.25 inches was no big deal, and a little extra iron had to be cast into the cylinder walls to allow ample room for the 327's 4.00-inch bores. Job done.

To make the 1967's 350-cubic-inches, engineers combined the existing 4.00-inch bore with a new 3.48 stroke. And with more power potential present thanks to its added displacement, the 350 required some significant lower-end reinforcement to help hold things together

under duress. Most notable were beefier connecting rods and a tougher crank with enlarged journals: 2.45 inches for the main bearings, 2.10 for the rods. Crank journals for the 265/283/327 trio measured 2.30 inches (mains) and 2.00 (rods). Extra counterweights were required to balance the new crank, and that added material, working in concert with the heavier shaft's longer throws, meant that the 350's block had to be modified to allow ample room for everything to rotate. Extra webbing and thicker bulkheads also were cast into the block for added durability.

Even more support came in 1968. From 1955 to 1967, all Chevy small-blocks relied on two-bolt caps to hold the crank's five main bearings in place. Beginning the next year, all high-performance small-blocks with 4.00-inch bores (save for the 327) received stronger four-bolt main caps for the three inner bearings. And these four-bolt blocks were recast with extra iron in their inner bulkheads to allow all those bolts to torque up tight.

No longer an individual model, the 1968 Nova SS, like its Camaro counterpart, was created by checking off its exclusive engine code: RPO L48. Priced at $210.65, this package added 14x6 wheels wearing E70 redline rubber and a tidy collection of dress-up items: simulated air intakes on the hood, "Super Sport" block letters along the front fenders' lower edges, blacked-out grille and rear deck panel, and "SS" badges at both ends and on the steering wheel. The deal didn't include bucket seats, standard

equipment on all earlier Nova Super Sports, but they were optional, along with a console and gauge package.

The star of the show was the 295-horse 350, which brought along with it heavy-duty springs, radiator, and clutch, as well as a high-performance starter motor. A three-speed stick was standard behind the L48 small-block; options included a heavy-duty three-speed, close-(M21) or wide-ratio (M20) four-speeds, and the Powerglide automatic.

As attractive as this new Nova SS was, few buyers took note in 1968, and fewer got wind of an even meaner rendition released later that year. Just as the L48 small-block carried over from the Camaro, so too did the 396-cubic-inch Mk IV big-block, also introduced for the Super Sport pony car in 1967. First seen beneath Corvette, Chevelle, and full-size Chevy hoods in 1965, the 396 Turbo-Jet V-8 was offered in two forms for the 1968 Nova SS: the 350-horsepower L34 and 375-horsepower L78. For more on these big bullies, see Section 5, the Chevelle SS story.

With a hydraulic cam and Rochester four-barrel carb, the L34 appeared rather tame in comparison to the L78, which used solid lifters and was fed by a big 800-cfm Holley four-barrel. The heavy-duty M13 three-speed manual was standard behind both big-blocks. Optional for the L34 were the M20 and M21 Muncie four-speeds and the Powerglide or Turbo Hydra-Matic automatics. No automatics were offered behind the brutal L78, but two top-shelf four-speeds were: the M21 and the super-heavy-duty M22 "Rock Crusher," nicknamed for its noisy, gnarly gears.

Talk about a sleeper. The new big-block Nova gave away its presence only by way of supersmall "396" lettering included along with the side marker light on each front fender. Most unsuspecting stoplight challengers never knew what had hit them after a tangle with one

1968 COPO 9738

1968 COPCO 9738

Model availability	two-door sedan
Wheelbase	111 inches
Length	187.7 inches
Width	70.5 inches
Height	54.1 inches
Price	$3,591.12 (on Gibb Chevrolet lot in LaHarpe, Illinois)
Track (front/rear, in inches)	59/58.9
Wheels	14x6 stamped-steel
Tires	Firestone E70 Wide Ovals
Suspension	independent upper A-arms, lower control arms, heavy-duty coil springs and stabilizer bar in front; multi-leaf springs, solid axle in back
Steering	recirculating ball
Brakes	four-wheel hydraulic drums w/power assist
Engine	375-horsepower 396-cubic-inch L78 V-8 (some converted to 427 V-8s by Chevy dealer Dick Harrell)
Bore & stroke	4.094 x 3.76 inches
Compression	11:1
Fuel delivery	four-barrel carburetor
Transmission	Turbo Hydra-Matic 400 automatic
Axle ratio	4.10:1 Posi-Traction
Production	50 (about 20 were Dick Harrell 427 conversions)

Vince Piggins was the main man behind various supposedly taboo Chevrolet performance projects during the 1960s, including the Camaro Z/28. He freely used the COPO paper trail to deliver Corvette-powered Chevelles and Camaros to dealers such as Don Yenko in 1969. The COPO Novas of 1968 were his work as well.

of these very rare, totally unassuming beasts. Reportedly, production was a mere 234 for the L34, 667 for the L78.

"All docile and innocent . . . the vestal virgin image pales slightly when you turn on the engine," went *Car and Driver*'s lead-in for its road test of a 375-horsepower 1968 Nova SS. Published performance stats were 5.9 seconds for the 0–60 run, 14.5 seconds at 101.1 miles per hour for the quarter-mile.

1968 COPO

While official Chevrolet paperwork didn't list an available automatic transmission option for the L78 Nova SS 396 when it appeared in April 1968, 50 such packages were put together for Chevy dealer Fred Gibb using the clandestine COPO pipeline. COPO was short for Central Office Production Order, a special-request procedure typically used by fleet buyers to circumvent corporate red tape. If a commercial-vehicle customer desired an unlisted combination of off-the-shelf parts, a COPO represented just

the ticket—it didn't require upper-management approval, only a go-ahead from the guys in engineering who would be handling the job.

COPOs came in especially handy for performance product guru Vince Piggins, whose job during the 1960s was to promote Chevy performance any way he could despite various limitations imposed by corporate execs. Remember, Chevrolet wasn't supposed to be in racing, per that infamous decree sent down from GM's ivory tower early in 1963. Yet there was the competition-conscious Camaro Z/28 dashing about SCCA tracks four years later. The Z/28 was Piggins' baby, and so too were the legendary COPO Camaros and Chevelles built in 1969 with Corvette-sourced 427-ci big-block V-8s—combinations that supposedly were taboo prior to 1970 per GM's 400-cube limit for V-8s going into its divisions' pony cars and midsized models.

Fast-thinking dealers like Fred Gibb became regular callers to Piggins' office 40 years back. Opened in LaHarpe, Illinois, in 1947, Gibb Chevrolet was home to various COPO creations, thanks to its owner's drag racing ventures, which began after his top salesman bought a Z/28 in 1967 and started campaigning it as *Little Hoss*. In 1968, *Little Hoss* won an American Hot Rod Association (AHRA) stock-class world championship. Early that summer, Gibb took note of the fact that drag racing's automatic-trans Super Stock classes were strangely devoid of capable Chevys, thanks in part to the absence of an auto-box option for the hot, new 375-horse SS Nova. He then contacted Piggins, who concocted COPO number 9738, which added Chevrolet's superior Turbo Hydra-Matic 400 automatic into the L78 Nova mix.

Above
Illinois Chevrolet dealer Fred Gibb used Chevrolet's clandestine COPO pipeline in 1968 to produce 50 automatic-equipped L78 Novas for super-stock drag racing competition. All of these COPO 9738 cars featured painted steel wheels, power drum brakes, 4.10:1 Posi-Traction gears, and a heavy-duty radiator. Aftermarket additions seen here include traction bars and headers. *copyright Geoff Stunkard, quartermilestones.com*

NHRA rules required a minimum run of 50 cars to allow said models to legally compete in its stock classes, thus the logic behind Gibb Chevrolet's order. All 50 COPO 9738 Novas were built during the first two weeks of July 1968, and all featured the same equipment: joining the L78 396 and TH 400 trans were a heavy-duty radiator, 4.10:1 Posi-Traction differential, painted 14x6 steel wheels, power-assisted drum brakes, bucket seats, and a floorshift with console. The radio was deleted, and two interior colors were specified: black or blue. Exterior finishes were Fathom Blue, Grecian Green, Matador Red, and Tripoli Turquoise. Gibb kept one COPO Nova to race himself and sold the rest; the price on his LaHarpe lot was $3,592.12.

The plot thickened further after some 20 or so COPO 9738 cars ended up in the hands of veteran drag racer Dick Harrell, who operated a Chevrolet dealership network based out of Kansas City, Missouri. Known as "Mr. Chevrolet," Harrell was the AHRA Driver of the Year in 1969, and he also was responsible for helping develop 427 Camaro conversions for both Yenko Chevrolet in Pennsylvania and Nickey Chevrolet in Chicago. Harrell applied this same approach to the COPO Novas he acquired, trading the L78s for 450-horse 427s backed by competition-prepped automatics. Additional equipment varied, with some featuring Jardine headers, Chevy Rally wheels, M&H slicks, traction bars, and fiberglass hoods with Corvette-style stingers. Cragar mags also ap-

peared. The typical price for a Harrell Nova was about $4,400.

Yenko Chevrolet, Nickey Chevrolet, and Baldwin/Motion Performance also offered 427 Novas, with Baldwin/Motion later making truly wild 454 big-block swaps. Unlike Yenko's Super Car Chevelles and Camaros, which began life in 1969 as factory-equipped 427 COPO models, its S/C Nova that year was a swap job performed in the Pennsylvania dealership's shop.

The plot thickened further after some 20 or so COPO 9738 cars ended up in the hands of veteran drag racer Dick Harrell.

1969 Nova SS

1969 Nova SS

Model availability	two-door sedan
Wheelbase	111 inches
Length	187.7 inches
Width	70.5 inches
Height	54.1 inches
Weight	3,373 pounds (SS 396)
Track (front/rear, in inches)	59/58.9
Wheels	14-inch stamped-steel
Tires	E70x14 Uniroyal Tiger Paw
Suspension	independent upper A-arms, lower control arms, heavy-duty coil springs and stabilizer bar in front; multi-leaf springs, solid axle in back
Steering	recirculating ball (power assist optional)
Brakes	front disc, rear drums, std.
Engine	300-horsepower 350-cubic-inch V-8, std. 350-horsepower 396-cubic-inch V-8, optional 375-horsepower 396-cubic-inch V-8, optional
Bore & stroke	4.00 x 3.25 inches, 350 V-8; 4.094 x 3.76 inches, 396 V-8
Compression	10.25:1, 350 V-8 and 350-hp 396 V-8; 11:1, 375-hp 396 V-8
Fuel delivery	four-barrel carburetor
Transmission	three-speed manual, std.; four-speed manual, Powerglide automatic, and Turbo Hyrdra-Matic automatic optional
Production	17,654

1969

Only the Nova name carried over from 1968 as the painfully plain Chevy II tag finally fell by the wayside at year's end. After rolling out only 5,571 1968 Nova Super Sports, Chevrolet followed that with 17,654 in 1969, all, as in 1967, showing next to no changes at a glance. Most notable were the simulated louvers added to the front fenders. The latest Super Sport package

was listed under RPO Z26 and included front disc brakes, which didn't necessarily guarantee the installation of Rally wheels as in the past. Joining those Rally rims on the 1969 options list were the same 14x7 five-spoke sport wheels seen on that year's Camaros and Chevelle Super Sports.

Various optional Turbo Hydra-Matic auto-

matic transmissions were also new. The TH 350 automatic was offered behind the standard 350 small-block, boosted in 1969 to 300 horsepower. The TH 400 was available behind the 350-horse 396, and a specially equipped version of this transmission was listed for the top-dog L78 big-block. L78 production for 1969 was 5,262. The figure for its L34 running mate was 1,947.

After rolling out only 5,571 1968 Nova Super Sports, Chevrolet followed that with 17,654 in 1969.

Opposite page
A blacked-out grille was again standard for the Nova SS in 1969. This model is one of 5,262 Super Sports built that year with the truly hot L78 396-cubic-inch big-block V-8. *Mike Mueller*

Right
Total Nova Super Sport production for 1969 was 17,654. Once again, no notable changes were made that year. *Mike Mueller*

Above
The L78 396 V-8 produced 375 horsepower for Chevelles, Camaros, and Nova Super Sports. Solid lifters and 11:1 compression were included inside the L78. *Mike Mueller*

Left
The Nova's Rally wheel was restyled for 1968, as a larger center cap replaced the small unit seen in 1967. *Mike Mueller*

Joining those Rally rims on the 1969 options list were the same 14x7 five-spoke sport wheels seen on that year's Camaro and Chevelle Super Sports.

Above
Simulated hood vents became part of the Super Sport package in 1968. *Mike Mueller*

Right
A big 800-cfm Holley four-barrel shot the juice to Chevrolet's L78 big-block V-8. *Mike Mueller*

Below right
The only outward clue to a Nova SS 396's presence was this small badge incorporated into the side marker light on each front fender. No fair! *Mike Mueller*

Below
Fake fender louvers set the 1969 Nova SS apart from its 1968 forerunner. They were removed in 1971. *Mike Mueller*

1970 Nova SS

1970 Nova SS

Model availability	two-door sedan
Wheelbase	111 inches
Length	187.7 inches
Width	70.5 inches
Height	54.1 inches
Weight	3,515 pounds (w/350 V-8)
Base price	$2,793 (w/350 V-8)
Track (front/rear, in inches)	59/58.9
Wheels	14-inch stamped-steel
Tires	E70x14 Uniroyal Tiger Paw
Suspension	independent upper A-arms, lower control arms, heavy-duty coil springs and stabilizer bar in front; multi-leaf springs, solid axle in back
Steering	recirculating ball (power assist optional)
Brakes	front disc, rear drums, std.
Engine	300-horsepower 350-cubic-inch V-8, std. 350-horsepower 402 cubic-inch V-8, optional 375-horsepower 402 cubic-inch V-8, optional
Bore & stroke	4.00 x 3.25 inches, 350 V-8; 4.126 x 3.76 inches, 402 V-8
Compression	10.25:1, 350 V-8 and 350-hp 402 V-8; 11:1, 375-hp 402 V-8
Fuel delivery	four-barrel carburetor
Transmission	three-speed manual, std.; four-speed manual, Powerglide automatic, and Turbo Hyrdra-Matic automatic optional
Axle ratio	3.07:1 (w/350 V-8)
Production	19,558

Above
Revised taillights set the 1970 Nova apart from its forerunners. A new grille also appeared up front. Chevy's 300-horse L48 small-block remained the Nova SS's base engine that year.

Right
The Nova SS 396 made one final appearance in 1970. Two big-blocks remained available that year: the 350-horsepower L34 and 375-horsepower L78.

1970

Revised taillights and a new grille represented the easiest way to identify a 1970 Nova SS, which found 19,558 buyers that year. The Z26 deal rolled over unchanged, at least on paper. Chevrolet's latest Mk IV big-block was bored out slightly from 4.094 inches to 4.126, upping the cubic-inch count to 402 for 1970. All labels, however, still read "396 Turbo-Jet." Why displace the boat, right?

The 300-horse L48 small-block remained the base V-8 for the 1970 Super Sport, and the two 402-cube big-blocks still produced 350 and 375 horses, respectively. Unfortunately, this was the last year for the L34 and L78 in Nova SS ranks, as Chevrolet's compact performance legacy began its final downturn.

Above
The Nova Super Sport's base small-block, the L48 350 V-8, was bumped up to 300 horsepower in 1969 and stayed at that level for 1970.

Right
By 1970, the mouse motor's cylinder block was as tough as it got thanks to various upgrades performed since 1967. Most notable were the four-bolt main bearing caps applied in 1968.

IMPROVED 307-327-350 CU. IN. V-8 CYLINDER BLOCK

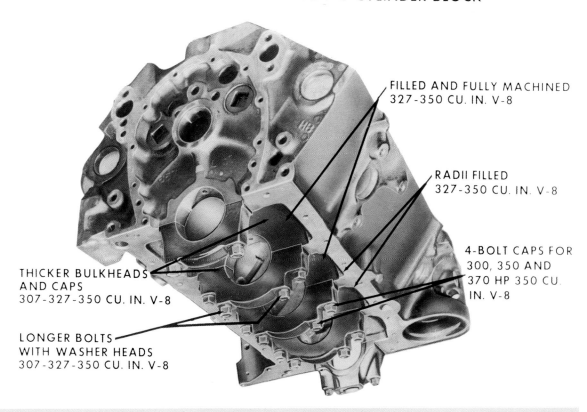

FILLED AND FULLY MACHINED
327-350 CU. IN. V-8

RADII FILLED
327-350 CU. IN. V-8

4-BOLT CAPS FOR
300, 350 AND
370 HP 350 CU.
IN. V-8

THICKER BULKHEADS
AND CAPS
307-327-350 CU. IN. V-8

LONGER BOLTS
WITH WASHER HEADS
307-327-350 CU. IN. V-8

1970 Yenko Deuce

1970 Yenko Deuce

Model availability	two-door sedan
Wheelbase	111 inches
Length	187.7 inches
Width	70.5 inches
Height	54.1 inches
Weight	3,515 pounds
Base price	$4,395
Track (front/rear, in inches)	59/58.9
Wheels	14x7 SS five-spokes
Tires	E70x14 Uniroyal Tiger Paw
Suspension	independent upper A-arms, lower controls arms, heavy-duty coil springs and stabilizer bar in front; multi-leaf springs, solid axle in back
Steering	recirculating ball (power assist optional)
Brakes	power-assisted front discs, rear drums
Engine	360-horsepower 350-cubic-inch LT-1 V-8
Bore & stroke	4.00 x 3.25 inches
Compression	11:1
Fuel delivery	four-barrel carburetor
Transmission	close-ratio four-speed manual, std.; Turbo Hydra-Matic automatic, optional
Axle ratio	4.10:1 Posi-Traction
Production	176 (two other non-Yenko COPO 9010 LT-1 Novas were delivered to Canada)

1970 Yenko Deuce

Don Yenko's Chevy dealership in Canonsburg, Pennsylvania, planted only a few dozen 427 big-blocks into SS 396 Nova bodies in 1969, basically because the combo was just too nasty for public consumption. Stuffing 450 horses beneath those compact hoods translated into some seriously surreal performance, like rest to 60 miles per hour in something like 4 seconds. Even Yenko himself later called his 427 Nova "a real beast. It was almost lethal," he added. "In retrospect, this probably wasn't the safest car in the world."

So Yenko Chevrolet came back in 1970 with a less-explosive Nova. Soaring insurance costs had transformed his S/C Chevelles and Camaros from tough sells into nearly impossible transactions, leaving him little choice but to send these two mean machines into the archives. In their place came the small-block Yenko Deuce, a 350-equipped Nova created through yet another COPO, this one coded number 9010.

Left
Pennsylvania Chevrolet dealer Don Yenko began dropping Corvette 427 V-8s into Novas in 1969 but found the combination far too mean for the street. He then created the Yenko Deuce in 1970 using another Corvette V-8, the small-block LT-1. *Steve Statham*

Above
Chevrolet built 178 COPO 9101 1970 Novas, all fitted with the Corvette's bodacious small-block. The 350-cubic-inch LT-1 V-8 was a Corvette option from 1970 to 1972. *Steve Statham*

Right
For the 1970 Corvette, the LT-1 small-block was rated at 370 horsepower. Chevrolet's new Camaro Z28 that year was fitted with a 360-horse version of this solid-lifter V-8, and this rendition also found its way between Yenko Nova fenders. *Steve Statham*

Below
The heart of the Yenko Deuce was the Corvette's LT-1 small-block, a 350-cube V-8 rated at 370 horsepower between fiberglass fenders in 1970.

A COPO was required because the 350 V-8 in this case wasn't offered for the 1970 Nova. Standard that year for the revamped Z/28, optional for the Corvette, was the hottest small-block yet, the solid-lifter LT-1, rated at 370 horsepower for the latter, 360 for the former. (For more on this mighty-mouse motor, see Chapter 8.) The COPO 9010 deal transplanted the 360-horse LT-1 350 into brown-paper-wrapper Novas, not Super Sports, but Yenko made up for the missing imagery by adding his own trademark graphics. Additional standard features included an M21 four-speed and 4.10 Posi gears. A Hurst shifter, power front discs, five-spoke SS wheels, and a hood-mounted tach were listed as standard options. The Turbo Hydra-Matic automatic transmission also was available.

A typical Yenko Deuce started at $4,395, not a bad price considering how little it cost to operate in dangerous daily traffic. As Yenko later explained, "Insurance companies wouldn't insure a 427 Camaro, but a 350 Nova was a normal family car. All the customer had to tell his agent was that the car was a 350 Nova. It was none of the agent's concern that the 350 was the solid-lifter LT-1 Corvette motor. We built 200 of these cars and never heard a peep from the insurance companies."

In truth, the actual count was a bit lower. Apparently, Chevrolet released 178 COPO 9010 Novas in 1970, with 176 going to Yenko Chevrolet. The other two were delivered to Central Chevrolet in London, Ontario, thanks to salesman Dave Mathers, who originally ordered 10 of these rather plain-looking, certified muscle cars. The pair he did receive remains safe and sound in collectors' hands today.

1971 Nova SS

1971 Nova SS

Model availability	two-door sedan
Wheelbase	111 inches
Length	187.7 inches
Width	70.5 inches
Height	54.1 inches
Weight	2,919 pounds
Base price	$2,254 (V-8 two-door sedan)
Track (front/rear, in inches)	59/58.9
Wheels	14-inch stamped-steel
Tires	E70x14 Uniroyal Tiger Paw
Suspension	independent upper A-arms, lower control arms, coil springs and stabilizer bar in front; multi-leaf springs, solid axle in back
Steering	recirculating ball
Brakes	front disc, rear drums
Engine	270-horsepower 350-cubic-inch V-8
Bore & stroke	4.00 x 3.25 inches
Compression	8.5:1
Fuel delivery	four-barrel carburetor
Transmission	three-speed manual, std.; four-speed manual and Turbo Hyrdra-Matic 350 automatic optional
Production	7,105

1971

The fake fender louvers seen in 1969 and 1970 disappeared in 1971, and the same could be said about much of the Nova Super Sport's performance abilities. Only one engine remained, the L48 small-block, rated at 270 horsepower thanks mostly to a compression cut from 10.25:1 to 8.5:1. Though still no slouch, the L48 Nova certainly couldn't fill the treads of the retired SS 396. Gone, too, were heavy-duty front springs and the bright engine dress-up seen on previous SS V-8s. Optional transmission choices were limited to two: the wide-ratio M20 four-speed or Turbo 350 automatic. Production was 7,015.

Basically the same 350-powered Nova SS carried over into 1972 wearing a net-rated output tag of 200 horsepower. Still rather warm, that year's Super Sport attracted 12,309 buyers, a last gasp if you will. In 1973, an available six-cylinder returned to the Z26 package. The last of the breed came and went rather meekly three years later.

Above
Only one engine was available for the Nova Super Sport in 1971: the L48 350 small-block, rated at 270 horsepower. One more small-block Nova SS appeared for 1972 before the story came to a close.

Though still no slouch, the L48 Nova certainly couldn't fill the treads of the retired SS 396.

Right
A compression cut helped drop the L48 small-block V-8 to 270 horsepower in 1971, and the engine was the only choice for Nova SS buyers that year.

Below
Chevrolet introduced two low-buck fun machines in 1971, the Heavy Chevy Chevelle and Rally Nova (shown here). In base form, both offered a decent dose of performance at a lower price compared to their Super Sport counterparts.

05

Above
1965 SS396

Middle
1970 El Camino SS 454

Right
1972 Chevelle SS

Super Duper

05

Chevrolet Chevelle SS 1964–1973

In 1959, Chevrolet offered two distinct model lines, one more than any other GM division claimed. Chevy's standard passenger-car group had been joined six years prior by the two-seat Corvette, a narrowly focused sporting proposition meant more to stand tall in its own realm than to widen the scope of GM's low-priced, entry-level division. Far better suited to the latter task was the new-for-1960 Corvair, the ground breaking compact that clearly deserves credit for helping usher in the multiple-model line craze that was soon all the rage around Detroit.

By 1964, Chevrolet could brag of five widely different lines: the tiny Corvair, the less compact Chevy II/Nova, the full-size flagships (named, since 1958, Biscayne, Bel Air, and Impala), and the niche-market Corvette. Truly new was the fifth, created especially to fill the gap that had existed for two years between the close-quartered Nova (introduced for 1962) and the big Biscayne. Based on General Motors' equally new A-body platform, this machine also was meant to compete with Detroit's intermediate-class pioneer, the Fairlane, unveiled by Ford for 1962.

Formed more or less in clay by March 1962, Chevrolet's A-body image took on various identities before final transformation into sheet metal. Another clay seen a month later clearly looked like an upsized Chevy II, and a mockup

photographed in January 1963 even carried "Chevy II Nova" identification. "Indications are very strong that Chevrolet will modify the current Chevy II, making it wider and longer," predicted an August 1963 *Motor Trend* review. Mentioned, too, was the claim that the new model "might get a new name in the bargain."

Indeed, initial plans called for trading the Chevy II for the new A-body intermediate, with the thinking being another model line would surely eat into the division's proven four-tiered sales structure. Such worries, however, quickly faded, and the decision was made late in February 1963 to put a fifth choice on the menu. The Nova didn't burn out, and one month later the "Malibu" moniker made its first appearance on an A-body mockup. But, like the Nova badge, this tag too represented icing on the

→ Bunkie Knudsen left Pontiac in November 1961 to take over Chevrolet's general manager post.

→ Knudsen introduced the all-new Chevelle to the press in August 1964.

→ Last seen in 1960, the El Camino returned in a downsized A-body form in 1964.

→ Chevy's first SS 396 appeared in a limited-edition form midyear in 1965.

→ An SS 396 El Camino appeared in 1968.

→ John De Lorean moved over from Pontiac to become Chevrolet general manager in March 1969, replacing another former Pontiac man, Pete Estes.

→ The Chevelle SS 396 unseated Pontiac's GTO from the top of Detroit's muscle car sales leader board in 1969.

→ Though its standard engine was bored out to 402 cubic-inches late in 1969, the model name remained "SS 396."

→ SS 396 gear was available in the base 300 series for one year only, 1969.

→ The SS 454 joined the SS 396 for 1970.

→ The awesome LS6 V-8 was offered only for the Chevelle SS 454 in 1970 and only for the Corvette in 1971.

→ Small-block V-8s returned to the Chevelle Super Sport in 1971.

Opposite
Appropriate badges appeared on each quarter panel and at the right side of the cove panel in 1966. Some cars also apparently featured a blacked-out cove. *Mike Mueller*

cake. Per Chevy tradition, the true model name had to begin with a "C," thus came "Chevelle."

General Manager Bunkie Knudsen introduced the Chevelle to the press in August 1963. "Impressed by its clean and handsome styling, Detroit's normally undemonstrative auto reporters broke into spontaneous applause," announced a *Time* magazine report. "The only complaint about the Chevelle was that dealers couldn't get enough of them," added *Automotive News* in September.

Within three months, Chevelle was the second hottest-selling Chevy, taking up 18 percent of the company's production schedule. When the smoke cleared, the final count for the 1964 Chevelle (discounting its second-generation El Camino derivative) totaled 338,296, tops in the intermediate ranks and some 60,000 greater than that year's Ford Fairlane tally.

Along with that El Camino rendition (marketed as a truck), the Chevelle line included the base "300" series, available in two- and four-door sedan and two- and four-door station wagon forms, and the upscale Malibu, offered as a four-door sedan, two-door sport coupe or convertible, and two- or four-door station wagon. Extra trim and more standard equipment typically set the top-shelf Malibu apart from the plain-Jane Chevelle 300. Both series featured six-cylinder and V-8 lines, and, like their 1964 B-O-P A-body counterparts, all models rolled on a 115-inch wheelbase and featured coil springs at all four corners.

Above
With the midsize Chevelle's 1964 debut, Chevrolet officials could brag of five distinct model lines. Behind the Chevelle (lower left) is the compact Corvair with its rear-mounted, air-cooled engine. From left to right is the sexy Corvette, full-size Impala, and diminutive Chevy II.

Left
Initial plans called for moving the existing Nova nameplate up into GM's new intermediate A-body ranks for 1964. Chevrolet's A-body prototypes were still seen wearing "Chevy II Nova" identification as late as January 1963.

In 1968, GM's A-body platform was revised, with a new 112-inch wheelbase created for two-doors and 116 inches for four-doors, station wagons, and El Caminos. Two years later, Chevrolet introduced its classy Monte Carlo, a Chevelle-based two-door coupe that used the longer 116-inch wheelbase. Those four extra inches went into the Monte Carlo body ahead of the cowl, translating into the lengthiest hood in Chevrolet history. An SS 454 version of this long-nosed coupe was offered for both 1970 and 1971.

General Manager Bunkie Knudsen introduced the Chevelle to the press in August 1963. "Impressed by its clean and handsome styling, Detroit's normally undemonstrative auto reporters broke into spontaneous applause," announced a *Time* magazine report.

Notice how the new 1964 Chevelle (second from bottom) fit oh so nicely into the size gap that previously existed between the Chevy II (second from top) and the full-size Chevy (bottom). At the very top is the tiny Corvair.

The Chevelle lineup was split up into six-cylinder and V-8 variations in 1964. The base V-8 was Chevrolet's 283-cubic-inch small-block, rated at 195 horsepower.

Extra trim and more standard equipment typically set the top-shelf Malibu apart from the plain-Jane Chevelle 300.

A long-hood variation on the Chevrolet's A-body theme, the first Monte Carlo debuted for 1970 and also was treated to the Super Sport treatment. The Monte Carlo SS 454 was offered for 1970 and 1971. A 1971 SS 454 appears here with a 1995 Monte Carlo. *Mike Mueller*

1964 Super Sport

1964 Super Sport

Model availability	two-door Malibu hardtop or convertible (with six-cylinder and V-8 engines)
Wheelbase	115 inches
Length	193.9 inches
Width	74.6 inches
Height	54 inches
Curb weight	3,025 pounds (six-cylinder hardtop); 3,155 pounds (V-8 hardtop)
Base price	$2,538 (six-cylinder hardtop), $2,749 (six-cylinder convertible), $2,646 (V-8 hardtop), $2,857 (V-8 convertible)
Track (front/rear, in inches)	58
Wheels	14-inch stamped steel
Tires	6.50x14
Suspension	independent upper/lower A-arms, coil springs and stabilizer bar in front; solid axle, upper and lower trailing arms, and coil springs in back
Steering	recirculating ball
Brakes	four-wheel drums
Base engines	120-horsepower 194 cubic-inch inline six-cylinder 195-horsepower 283-cubic-inch V-8
Bore & stroke	3.562 x 3.25 inches (six); 3.875 x 3.00 inches (V-8)
Compression	8.5:1 (six); 9.25:1 (V-8)
Fuel delivery	single one-barrel carburetor (six); single two-barrel carburetor (V-8)
Transmission	three-speed manual
Production	76,860 (all engines and body styles)

1964

Nearly 23 percent of the 1964 Chevelle's class-leading sales total consisted of sexy Super Sports, available in Malibu hardtop or convertible forms. Standard for the Chevelle SS were bucket seats, a four-gauge instrument cluster (in place of the base model's idiot lights), a console with floorshift for Powerglide and four-speed-equipped cars, appropriate badging, and sharp SS wheelcovers.

Popular options included Chevrolet's new Muncie four-speed gearbox, metallic brake linings, heavy-duty suspension and clutch, a tachometer in place of the clock (which moved to a pod on the dash), a Posi-Traction differential, and 3.36:1 rear gears (3.08:1 were standard). Both six-holers and V-8s were available for Chevy's first midsize Super Sport, with base models featuring a 120-horsepower 194-cubic-inch straight-six. A 155-horsepower 230-cid six was optional. Only 9,775 six-cylinder Chevrolet Super Sports were sold in 1964, perhaps proving that most buyers were indeed in the market for an SS.

More than 67,000 customers chose the V-8 variety, equipped in base form with a 195-horse-power 283-cid small-block fed by a two-barrel carburetor. The strongest option early on was RPO L77, a 220-horsepower 283 topped by a Rochester four-barrel. Then along came an announcement in December 1963 that Chevrolet's 327-cid V-8 would become available between Chevelle fenders. Two were mentioned initially, the 250-horsepower L30 and its 300-horsepower L74 running mate, with the former debuting in March, the latter three months later. Production counts were 6,598 for the L30 and 1,737 for the L74.

Many critics in 1964 likened the new Chevelle's overall impression to that of the fabled '55 Chevy. SS renditions were sold with both six-cylinder and V-8 power—the cross-flags on this 1964 Super Sport's fenders signal the presence of the optional 327-cubic-inch V-8. *Mike Mueller*

Also debuting was the Corvette's smokin' L76 small-block, a 365-horsepower 327 that featured 11:1 compression and an aggressive sold-lifter cam. An L76 Chevelle was first mentioned in assembly manuals in late January 1964, and at least one prototype was built, a roaring road rocket that apparently could hold its own with any muscle machine then running. According to *Motor Trend* spies, "the 325hp GTO and 365hp Chevelle are very comparable in performance, giving 0–60 times of around six seconds flat. They're far and away the hottest of the [new intermediates] and quicker than most big cars with high-performance engines."

Full production of the 365-horse Chevelle, however, never got rolling. Why? For various reasons, not the least of which was a shortage of 327s that developed early in 1964 due to unexpected demand from full-size Chevy buyers. But, according to *Motor Trend*, "the biggest problem is that special exhaust manifolds are needed to clear the suspension in the Chevelle chassis." Apparently engineers wanted larger, better-flowing manifolds for the 300- and 365-horsepower applications, but none were ever cast. Relying on existing exhausts for the L74 clearly wasn't a problem; not so for the L76, which was killed off before it was born. According to a March 19 product update memo sent to Chevrolet dealers, the 365-horse Turbo Fire 327 had "been cancelled and will not be offered" to Chevelle customers for 1964. Nonetheless a few did fall into public hands. Two or three mysterious survivors are known to exist today.

1965 Super Sport

1965 Super Sport

Model availability	two-door Malibu hardtop or convertible (with six-cylinder and V-8 engines)
Wheelbase	115 inches
Length	196.6 inches
Width	74.6 inches
Height	52.8 inches (hardtop)
Base price	$2,539 (six-cylinder hardtop), $2,750 (six-cylinder convertible), $2,647 (V-8 hardtop), $2,858 (V-8 convertible)
Track (front/rear, in inches)	58
Wheels	14-inch stamped steel
Tires	6.95x14
Suspension	independent upper/lower A-arms, coil springs and stabilizer bar in front; solid axle, upper and lower trailing arms, and coil springs in back
Steering	recirculating ball
Brakes	four-wheel drums
Base engines	120-horsepower 194-cubic-inch inline six-cylinder
	195-horsepower 283-cubic-inch V-8
Bore & stroke	3.562 x 3.25 inches (six); 3.875 x 3.00 inches (V-8)
Compression	8.5:1 (six); 9.25:1 (V-8)
Fuel delivery	single one-barrel carburetor (six); single two-barrel carburetor (V-8)
Transmission	three-speed manual
Production	81,112 (all engines and body styles)

1965

A cleaner grille and larger taillights made up the most noticeable appearance changes for 1965. Also present was a new wraparound bumper with a more pronounced point that helped add 2.5 inches to total length. Chassis refinements also lowered the car nearly an inch, making for a more rakish profile.

The Chevelle Super Sport carried on in similar fashion, still equipped with thrifty six-cylinder power in base form. The 195-horsepower 283 remained the base V-8, while the optional L77 283 was replaced by the 250-horsepower L30 327, at least initially. Although some factory literature indicated the L77 returned in February 1965, none showed up in that year's production records. An official L30 count, on the other hand, is known: 36,261, for both Chevelles and El Caminos. The top performance option in the fall of 1964 was the 300-horsepower L74 327 with its big aluminum four-barrel 10.5:1 compression, and dual exhausts. L74 production for 1965 was 13,593.

An even hotter 327 made its way, again from the Corvette ranks, onto the Chevelle options list not long after the 1965 models appeared. One of Chevrolet's strongest carbureted small-blocks, this L79 V-8 relied on a Holley four-barrel, big-valve heads, and 11:1 compression to help make 350 horsepower, and this with polite hydraulic lifters. "It's hard to believe Chevy's out of racing," claimed *Cars* magazine's Gordon Chittenden after roasting the rear tires on an L79 Chevelle.

The A-body platform's full, perimeter-rail frame is exposed in this 1965 auto show display.

"The perfect squelch" was the label magazine ads stuck on this 350-horse screamer. "That's a potent squelch to all others who keep talking about lions, tigers and such," continued the company pitch, which obviously aimed that big-cat reference squarely at Pontiac people.

Such barbs may have been good fun, but the plain truth was no joke: the GTO remained the muscle car to beat on the streets as 1964 rolled over into 1965. Chevelle didn't have a chance until it, too, found a big-block. Patience.

Above
Restyled SS wheel covers appeared for 1965. New, too, was engine displacement identification for the front fenders' cross-flag emblems. This SS convertible is powered by the base 283-cid small-block V-8. *Mike Mueller*

Left
Standard SS interior fare carried over from 1964. Notice the optional N34 steering wheel with its simulated wood-grained rim. *Mike Mueller*

Below
The Chevelle SS's base V-8 again produced 195 horsepower for 1965. Compression for this two-barrel 283 small-block was 9.25:1. *Mike Mueller*

Left
Introduced in 1959, Chevrolet's El Camino was dropped after 1960. It then returned as part of the Chevelle family in 1964. This 1965 El Camino is powered by that year's hottest-available small-block, the L79 327 V-8. *Mike Mueller*

Below
Also borrowed from the Corvette, the L79 327 featured big-valve heads, 11:1 compression, and a Holley four-barrel carburetor. Output was 350 horsepower. *Mike Mueller*

1965 SS 396

Nothing comparable to Pontiac's 389 big-block was available for the Chevelle in 1964. The venerable 409 wouldn't do, nor would any Corvette small-block. But that didn't stop Vince Piggins, the former Hudson racing man now hawking horsepower at GM's entry-level division. In April 1963, he proposed installing the legendary Mystery Motor, still hot off its record NASCAR runs around Daytona two months prior, in the upcoming A-body Chevelle. His plan involved using a 396-cubic-inch derivative, achieved by

reducing the porcupine-head 427's bore from 4.25 inches to 4.09 while leaving the 3.76-inch bore alone. But various glitches delayed development of this package. As it was, GM already had put its 330-cid lid on its new midsize models, making Piggins' proposed combination taboo.

Then Pontiac just had to go and boil things over. Chagrined GM execs had no choice but to raise the limit to 400 cubes, in turn making a 396 Chevelle perfectly acceptable. Introduced in February 1965, this package was listed under

1965 SS 396	
Model availability	two-door Malibu hardtop and convertible
Wheelbase	115 inches
Length	196.6 inches
Width	74.6 inches
Height	52.8 inches
Shipping weight	3,565 pounds
Base price	RPO Z16 cost $1,501
Track (front/rear, in inches)	58
Wheels	14x6 stamped-steel rims fitted with mag-style deluxe wheelcovers
Tires	7.74x14 gold-stripe
Suspension	independent upper/lower A-arms, heavy-duty coil springs and stabilizer bar in front; solid axle, upper and lower trailing arms, heavy-duty coil springs and stabilizer bar in back
Steering	power-assisted recirculating ball (15.0:1 ratio)
Brakes	11-inch drums, front and rear, with power assist
Engine	375-horsepower 396-cubic-inch Turbo-Jet V-8 (L37)
Bore & stroke	4.094 x 3.76 inches
Compression	11.0:1
Fuel delivery	single Holley four-barrel carburetor
Transmission	four-speed manual
Axle ratio	3.31:1
Production	200 hardtops, one convertible

The Surfer I combo was created by Chevrolet Engineering to showcase its new 396-cid Turbo-Jet V-8 on the 1965 auto show circuit. Both the El Camino and the boat it towed featured this bodacious big-block.

RPO Z16 on factory paperwork. On the street the name soon was simply SS 396.

Beneath the first SS 396's hood was the Turbo-Jet Mk IV big-block, a hydraulic-lifter V-8 rated at 375 horsepower for the A-body application. Behind it went a heavy-duty 11-inch clutch and a Muncie four-speed. No automatic was available. Additional special equipment included a high-torque starter, 61-ampere battery, five-blade thermo-modulated viscous-drive fan, large-capacity radiator with fan shroud, dual-snorkel air cleaner, and appropriate chrome dress-up.

Only 200 Z16 Malibu SS 396 hardtops, plus one clandestine convertible, were built in 1965, all fully loaded, and all wearing a price tag fit for a king. Standard features included mag-style wheelcovers, power brakes and steering, heavy-duty suspension with stabilizer bars front and rear, 7.75x14 gold-stripe high-speed tires on 6-inch-wide wheels, padded dash with a clock mounted on top, 6,000-rpm tach, and Chevrolet's new AM/FM Multiplex stereo radio with four speakers. The total bill for RPO Z16 was $1,501.05. Add that to the $2,600 base price for a V-8 Chevelle SS in 1965 and you get the picture.

Most Z16s went to celebrities and prominent press people, all in the interest of kicking off a high-powered bloodline with a high-profile bang.

Gold-stripe tires and a blacked-out rear cove panel were just a few of the many standard features included as part of Chevrolet's first SS 396 deal, tagged RPO Z16, in 1965. Z16 production that year was 200 hardtops and 1 mysterious convertible. *Mike Mueller*

Beneath the first
SS 396's hood
was the Turbo-Jet
Mk IV big-block,
a hydraulic-lifter
V-8 rated at 375
horsepower for the
A-body application.

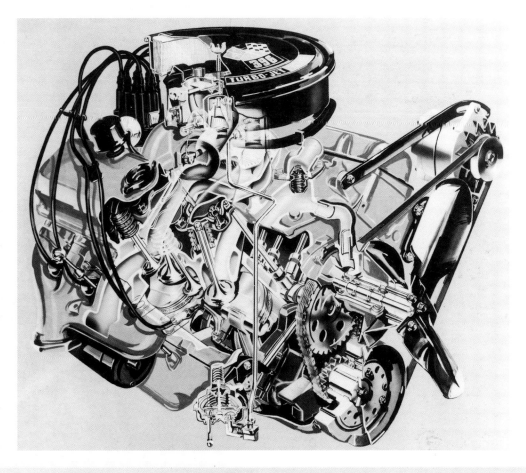

Above
Keys to the 396 Turbo-Jet's success were its free-breathing
cylinder heads, which featured canted valves actuated by
individual ball-stud rocker arms. The supreme 396 in 1965
was the Corvette's 425-horse beast.

Right
A beefier boxed convertible frame was used as a foundation
for Chevrolet's first SS 396 in 1965. Front and rear stabilizer
bars also were standard.

Most Z16s went to celebrities and prominent press people, all in the interest of kicking off a high-powered bloodline with a high-profile bang.

Top
Chrome dress-up highlighted the Z16 Chevelle's L37 big-block V-8, rated at 375 horsepower. A dual-snorkel air cleaner helped this Mk IV monster suck in needed atmosphere. *Mike Mueller*

Center
Mag-style wheel covers were standard for the Z16 Chevelle in 1965. *Mike Mueller*

Left
Fully loaded was a suitable description for the Z16 interior in 1965. Included were seat belts front and rear, a dash-mounted clock, 160-mile-per-hour speedometer, 6,000-rpm tachometer, and an AM/FM four-speaker stereo system. *Mike Mueller*

1966 SS 396

A restyled Chevelle with a mildly stated Coke-bottle body and trendy recessed rear window appeared for 1966, and the Malibu-based SS 396 returned as an individual model series all its own. No more sixes or small-blocks for the Super Sport Chevelle, it was big-block or no block at all for this midsize muscle car up until 1971.

More palatable base pricing also arrived in 1966, with an SS 396 hardtop starting at $2,776, its convertible running mate at $2,962. Cutting costs was simply a matter of also cutting both standard power and standard features. The idea, of course, was to widen the SS 396's appeal by putting it down within the reach of Average Joes everywhere. This plan worked gloriously as production soared to 72,272 for 1966.

In place of the Z16's 375-horsepower L37 396 was a more civilized standard Mk IV big-block, the 325-horsepower 396, listed as RPO L35 for El Camino applications. Gone from the standard package were the rigid convertible frame, big 11-inch full-size Chevy brakes, and rear stabilizer bar. A three-speed manual was now the base transmission, and features like the Z16's tach, fake mag wheelcovers, and bucket seats became extra-cost options. No more standard Multiplex stereo, either.

Appropriate "SS 396" badges in a blacked-out grille and on the rear cove panel, "Super Sport" rear-quarter script, and those legendary "396 Turbo Jet" cross-flags on each front fender identified the latest big-block Chevelle in 1966.

So, too, did a pair of hood bulges trimmed with nonfunctional grilles. Early brochures also showed a blacked-out rear cover, but apparently few models received this treatment. Color-accented rocker and lower rear-quarter moldings, wheel-opening trim, 7.75x14 redline tires on wide 6-inch rims, and small dog-dish hubcaps completed the deal.

If Z16-type performance was the goal, the options list was the place to shop. The Muncie four-speed was there, as were special suspension components, a Posi-Traction differential, and the L34 396, a 360-horse improvement on the L35. Both relied on 10.25:1 compression, while the hotter L34 used a lumpier cam and 585-cfm Holley four-barrel and was based on a beefier four-bolt main block.

On the top shelf was the L78 396 Turbo-Jet, rated at a familiar 375 horsepower. Making the L78 a force to be reckoned with were big-valve 427 heads, 11:1 compression, and an aluminum intake mounting a large 780-cfm Holley four-barrel. According to *Motor Trend*, "[this] engine should put the Chevelle SS right up front in the supercar market." Talk about shooting fish in a barrel.

A convertible SS 396 officially appeared in the mainstream for 1966. Production was 5,429, compared to one for 1965.

Model availability	two-door Malibu hardtop and convertible
Wheelbase	115 inches
Length	197 inches
Width	75 inches
Height	51.9 inches (hardtop), 52.8 inches (convertible)
Curb weight	3,800 pounds (hardtop)
Base price	$2,776 (hardtop), $2,962 (convertible)
Track (front/rear, in inches)	58
Wheels	14x6 stamped steel
Tires	7.75x14
Suspension	independent upper/lower A-arms, coil springs and stabilizer bar in front; solid axle, upper and lower trailing arms, and coil springs in back
Steering	recirculating ball
Brakes	four-wheel drums
Engine	325-horsepower 396-cubic-inch Turbo-Jet V-8 (L35), std.
Bore & stroke	4.094 x 3.76 inches
Compression	10.25:1
Fuel delivery	single four-barrel carburetor
Transmission	three-speed manual
Axle ratio	3.31:1
Production	72,272

The Z16's mag-style wheel covers were optional for the SS 396 in 1966. Standard were plain-Jane dog-dish hubcaps. A blacked-out grille and twin hood bulges were included in the deal. *Mike Mueller*

No more sixes or small-blocks for the Super Sport Chevelle, it was big-block or no block at all.

Above
Bucket seats and a center console (now fitted with a clock) were optional for the 1966 SS 396. *Mike Mueller*

Above right
The top power option for the 1966 SS 396 was the L78 V-8, rated at 375 horsepower. Feeding this big-block was a 780-cfm Holley four-barrel carburetor on an aluminum intake. *Mike Mueller*

Right
This cowl-induction air cleaner setup was a rare dealer option for the 1966 Chevelle SS 396. *Mike Mueller*

1967 SS 396

Model availability	two-door Malibu hardtop and convertible
Wheelbase	115 inches
Length	197 inches
Width	75 inches
Height	51.9 inches (hardtop), 52.8 inches (convertible)
Curb weight	3,800 pounds (hardtop)
Base price	$2,825 (hardtop), $3,033 (convertible)
Track (front/rear, in inches)	58
Wheels	14x6
Tires	F70x14
Suspension	independent upper/lower A-arms, coil springs and stabilizer bar in front; solid axle, upper and lower trailing arms, and coil springs in back
Steering	recirculating ball
Brakes	four-wheel drums
Engine	325-horsepower 396-cubic-inch Turbo-Jet V-8 (L35), std.
Bore & stroke	4.094 x 3.76 inches
Compression	10.25:1
Fuel delivery	single four-barrel carburetor
Transmission	three-speed manual
Axle ratio	3.31:1
Production	63,006

Above
Convertible SS 396 production for 1967 was 3,321. Shown in this factory artwork are the new Rally wheels, which were included when the equally new optional front disc brakes were ordered.

Right
Stacked "Super Sport" script and a blacked-out cove panel set the 1967 SS 396 apart from its 1966 predecessor. All Chevelles also received restyled taillights in 1967. *Mike Mueller*

1967 SS 396

A blacked-out cove treatment finally appeared for the 1967 SS 396, as did restyled simulated hood vents and reshuffled "Super Sport" script on the rear quarters. The same Chevelle body rolled over with only minor updates at its nose and tail. SS 396 mechanicals were near-complete carryovers, save for less output (350 horsepower) for the optional L34 396.

New options included GM's superb three-speed Turbo Hydra-Matic (M40) automatic transmission and power-assisted front disc brakes (J52). The J52 brakes featured 11-inch rotors and Bendix four-piston calipers. Making this option even more attractive were a set of sporty Rally wheels incorporating bright trim rings and center caps. Specially vented for the J52 application through slots in the rim center, the soon-to-be-popular Rally wheels measured the same as the stock 14x6 units. They were only available with the front disc brakes in 1967.

Above
A mundane bench seat became standard for the SS 396 in 1966. "SS" identification appeared in the steering wheel for the 1967 SS 396. New, too, that year was an optional tachometer relocated from below the dash (to the right of the steering column) to the instrument panel's far left end. *Mike Mueller*

Right
The 325-horsepower 396 Turbo-Jet was again standard for the SS 396 in 1967. The optional L34 396 was now rated at 350 horsepower, down 10 horses from 1966. *Mike Mueller*

New options included GM's superb three-speed Turbo Hydra-Matic (M40) automatic transmission.

Right
All of the SS 396's optional interior flair was made available to El Camino buyers in 1966 and 1967. Witness the bucket seats, floorshift, and deluxe console inside this 1967 model.

Opposite page
All Super Sport stuff, save for actual identification, was available for the El Camino Custom in 1966 and 1967. This 1967 El Camino not only wore the fake mag wheel covers made famous by the 1965 Z16 Chevelle, it also was fitted with the 396 Turbo-Jet V-8.

1968 SS 396

Model availability	two-door Malibu hardtop and convertible; El Camino
Wheelbase	112 inches
Length	197.1 inches
Width	75.7 inches
Height	52.7 inches (hardtop); 53.2 inches (convertible)
Weight	3,844 pounds (hardtop)
Base price	$2,875 (hardtop); $3,102 (convertible)
Track (front/rear, in inches)	59
Wheels	14x6 stamped steel
Tires	F70x14
Suspension	independent upper/lower A-arms, coil springs and stabilizer bar in front; solid axle, upper and lower trailing arms, and coil springs in back
Steering	recirculating ball
Brakes	four-wheel drums
Engine	325-horsepower 396-cubic-inch Turbo-Jet V-8 (L35), std.
Bore & stroke	4.094 x 3.76 inches
Compression	10.25:1
Fuel delivery	single four-barrel carburetor
Transmission	three-speed manual
Axle ratio	3.31:1
Production	62,785 (includes El Camino SS 396)

Dark lower-body accents were standard (except with darker paint choices) for the 1968 SS 396. This convertible also demonstrates the optional D96 pinstriping (running over the nose and down the lower body sides), which reportedly couldn't be combined with the standard accent treatment after December 1, 1967. D96 cars built after that date did not have dark lower body panels regardless of paint choice.

1968 SS 396

The A-body's 115-inch wheelbase was traded for a 112-inch stretch in 1968, at least for the two-door Malibu. Four-door Chevelles got a longer 116-inch chassis. On top of the frame in either case was a restyled body that looked considerably more like a Coke bottle. Though they lost 3 inches between their wheels, two-door Chevelles for 1968 remained about as long overall as their 1967 predecessors, meaning there now was some serious overhang up front, which helped make the lengthened 1968 hood appear even longer. At the same time, flush-mounted rear glass in place of 1967's recessed window further enhanced the shortened nature of the rear deck. A case of ponycar envy?

Contributing to the 1968 SS 396's new sleek look were hideaway windshield wipers, standard equipment for both the new luxury-minded Concours Chevelle and all Malibus. SS 396 exterior treatment carried over in similar fashion with two exceptions: gone was the rear quarter script, and engine identification was now relegated to an almost unnoticeable tag incorporated within the side marker lamp bezels up front, new features for 1968 inspired by ever-tightening federal safety standards. A contrasting black lower body treatment also was new this year for the SS 396.

Mechanicals were once more familiar, with the three 396 V-8s offered again at the same output levels.

Below left
SS 396 fender identification was revised for 1968. Only the displacement numbers were advertised, and rather obscurely at that within the new safety-conscious side marker lights. *Mike Mueller*

Below
A new Coke-bottle Chevelle body appeared for 1968, as did a shorter wheelbase for the two-door Malibu: 112 inches, compared to the previously used 115-inch stretch. Notice the red D96 stripes on this 1968 SS 396. *Mike Mueller*

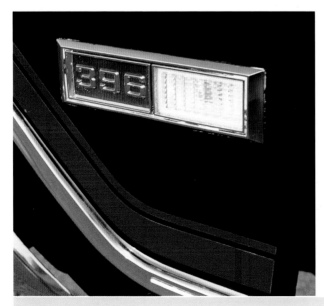

1968 El Camino SS 396

1968 El Camino SS 396

1968 El Camino SS 396

Introduced in 1959, Chevrolet's half-car/half-truck rolled into temporary retirement in 1960, but was reborn on the new A-body platform in 1964. Initially available with nearly every option that helped make its Chevelle running mate such an overnight sensation, the downsized El Camino could play as well as it worked, a fact not lost on potential buyers. Chevrolet sold 36,615 that first year, more than twice the number of 1964 Rancheros unloaded by Ford.

Like the Chevelle, the El Camino could've been fitted with a host of hot small-blocks in 1964 and 1965 right up to the 350-horsepower L79. But unlike the Chevelle, the early A-body El Camino couldn't wear Super Sport garb. Even the 396 big-block was an option in 1966, as were bucket seats, a console, and the SS 396 Chevelle's mag-style wheelcovers. Yet the complete SS image remained unavailable.

All that changed in 1968 when Chevrolet introduced an honest-to-goodness El Camino SS 396, complete with those revered badges, an attractive blacked-out grille, and that bulging hood. "Fancier than a truck, more utilitarian than a passenger car, able to leap past sports cars in a single bound, the El Camino [SS 396] will fill needs that the owner never knew he had." Or so claimed a *Car Life* report, which posted an impressive quarter-mile time of 14.80 seconds for the latest member the Super Sport fraternity.

Model availability	two-door utility vehicle
Wheelbase	116 inches
Length	207.1 inches
Width	75.7 inches
Height	55.2 inches
Weight	3,930
Base price	$2,949
Track (front/rear, in inches)	59
Wheels	14x6 stamped steel
Tires	G70x14
Suspension	independent upper/lower A-arms, coil springs and stabilizer bar in front; solid axle, upper and lower trailing arms, and coil springs in back
Steering	recirculating ball
Brakes	four-wheel drums
Engine	325-horsepower 396-cubic-inch Turbo-Jet V-8 (L35), std.
Bore & stroke	4.094 x 3.76 inches
Compression	10.25:1
Fuel delivery	single four-barrel carburetor
Transmission	three-speed manual
Axle ratio	3.31:1
Production	5,190

A full-fledged El Camino SS 396 finally appeared in 1968. Production of this high-powered hauler was 5,190.

1969 SS 396

1969 SS 396

Model availability	two-door Malibu hardtop and convertible; two-door 300 Deluxe sport coupe and sedan; El Camino
Wheelbase	112 inches
Length	196.9 inches
Width	76 inches
Height	52.8 inches (hardtop)
Curb weight	3,335 pounds (hardtop)
Price	RPO Z25 cost $347.60
Track (front/rear, in inches)	59
Wheels	14x7 five-spoke
Tires	F70x14 Wide Oval
Suspension	independent upper/lower A-arms, coil springs and stabilizer bar in front; solid axle, upper and lower trailing arms, and coil springs in back
Steering	recirculating ball
Brakes	front discs, rear drums
Engine	325-horsepower 396-cubic-inch Turbo-Jet V-8 (L35), std.
Bore & stroke	4.094 x 3.76 inches (bore was increased late in the year to 4.126 inches, boosting actual displacement to 402 cubic-inches)
Compression	10.25:1
Fuel delivery	single four-barrel carburetor
Transmission	three-speed manual
Axle ratio	3.31:1
Production	86,307 (includes El Camino SS 396)

1969 SS 396

After selling 57,595 Super Sport Chevelles (plus 5,190 of the El Camino SS) in 1968, Chevrolet came back with another 86,307 (Chevelles and El Caminos) in 1969, making the SS 396 America's best-selling muscle car, an honor Pontiac's GTO had owned since its 1964 inception. Chevelle Super Sports then went on to outsell GTOs by 37 percent from 1969 to 1971. How the worm can turn.

Above
The preferred Turbo Hydra-Matic automatic transmission carried on alone into 1969 as the Powerglide option was finally deleted. The TH-400 option also was made available behind the L78 V-8 (as demonstrated here) for the first time that year. *Mike Mueller*

In other news for 1969, Chevrolet changed the way it offered the SS 396 to power-hungry customers. In 1968, the SS 396 model lineup included a Malibu sport coupe, convertible, and El Camino. Beginning the following year, an SS 396 buyer had to check off RPO Z25, which was offered for those same three body styles, plus two new ones in the low-priced 300 series. Both the 300 Deluxe sport coupe and 300 Deluxe sedan could have been transformed into an SS 396 in 1969, the only year a Super Sport Chevelle could have been anything other than a top-of-the-line Malibu or Custom El Camino.

Priced at $347.60, RPO Z25 was basically the same SS 396 package offered from 1966 to 1968, with a couple of nice additions. Standard power still came from the 325-horsepower 396 backed by a three-speed manual, and a beefed-up chassis remained as well. But also standard in 1969 were power front disc brakes and a set of new five-spoke SS wheels. The brakes consisted of 11-inch rotors and single-piston calipers, while the wheels featured small SS center caps and bright trim rings. Set off by chrome wheel opening moldings, these sporty 14x7 rims were the only wheels available for the 1969 SS 396 and represented a marked departure from the dog-dish caps that had been standard from 1966 to 1968.

As for the transformation of the mundane 300 Deluxe models into an SS 396, this job required a few more parts switches here and there. First, roof rail drip gutters, larger taillight bezels, and the upper body accent stripe were added, as were upper and lower rear cove moldings. The 300 Deluxe's rocker moldings were deleted and the "300 Deluxe" fender script was, of course, traded for the new SS 396 badge.

Inside, the dash and steering wheel both got the SS identification, but the 300 sedan door panels didn't–this was because the 300's doors had vent windows and the Malibu hardtops didn't, meaning a different panel was required by the former. And because only Malibu models featured hideaway windshield wipers, the wiper arms on the 300 Deluxe SS 396 didn't retract beneath the cowl edge of the twin-bulge Super Sport hood. From there, however, everything else was basic Z25, right down to the sport wheels at the corners and bright

exhaust extensions in back.

No breakdowns are available, but suffice it to say that the 300 Deluxe SS 396 was a rare bird in 1969. And its 300 sedan running mate was indeed a queer duck—it was the only SS 396 model ever offered with a B-pillar "post." All others were hardtops or convertibles.

New on the options list in 1969 were weight-saving aluminum cylinder heads (for the L78 396 only) and louder-than-loud low-restriction chambered exhausts. Basically a set of flow-through pipes with eight sets of 11 baffles running their 45-inch length (two smaller baffled pipes were included farther back), chambered exhausts (RPO NC8) were street legal, although the local constabulary may have been more than willing to question that fact. Reportedly, chambered exhausts were included

with the L34 396 before December 1968 then were moved to the options list.

Introduced as well at extra cost in 1969 was the F41 sport suspension, which did the existing F40 heavy-duty option one better. Offered for the Chevelle since 1964, the F40 package simply stiffened the springs and shocks. RPO F41 traded the 0.937-inch front sway bar for an unyielding 1.125-inch unit and also added an 0.875-inch rear stabilizer bar, along with special-duty bushings, reinforced lower control arms in back, and beefier springs and shocks.

Changes came in the transmission lineup as well. The optional Powerglide automatic was finally deleted, leaving the preferred Turbo Hydra-Matic to carry the load. And Turbo Hydra-Matics also were offered behind the brutal L78 for the first time, as were all manuals, including the "special" MC1 three-speed and M20 wide-ratio four-speed, gearboxes that previously had been spared the wrath of 375 hoppin'-mad horses. The M21 close-ratio four-speed remained L34 and L78 exclusives, and the M22 Rock Crusher, introduced in 1966, was again offered only along with RPO L78.

Above
Adding the Z25 option to a 300 Deluxe coupe or sedan in 1969 required deleting various trim pieces, including rocker moldings and "300 Deluxe" fender badges. Roof rail drip gutters and larger taillight bezels were added, as were upper and lower rear cove moldings, these to delineate the Super Sport's blacked-out cove panel. *Mike Mueller*

Left
Along with vent windows in the doors and those B-pillar "posts," the 300 Deluxe sedan SS 396 also featured one other oddity: exposed windshield wipers. Vent wings disappeared on Malibu models in 1968, the same year that hidden wipers were also introduced for the top-shelf Chevelle. The low-priced 300-series sedan, however, continued using vent wings and mounting the wipers in plain sight. *Mike Mueller*

Inside, the dash and steering wheel both got the SS identification, but the 300 sedan door panels didn't—this was because the 300's doors had vent windows and the Malibu hardtops didn't, meaning a different panel was required by the former.

Above
That four-speed stick is connected to the optional M21 close-ratio gearbox. Notice the vinyl-coated rubber floor covering; trading carpeting for rubber floor mats was just one of various means used to keep costs down in the 300-series Chevelle. *Mike Mueller*

Right
Chevrolet introduced the L89 aluminum-head option for the Chevelle Super Sport's L78 396 only in 1969. These weight-saving heads did not change the L78's 375-horsepower rating. L89/L78 production in 1969 was 400. *Mike Mueller*

1969 COPO 9562

1969 COPO 9562

Model availability	two-door Malibu coupe and hardtop
Wheelbase	112 inches
Length	196.9 inches
Width	76 inches
Height	52.8 inches
Price	$4,100
Track (front/rear, in inches)	59
Wheels	15x6 stamped steel, 14x7 SS five-spokes or 15x7 Rally rims
Tires	F70x14 or F70x15 Goodyear Wide Tread GT
Suspension	independent upper/lower A-arms, heavy-duty coil springs and stabilizer bar in front; solid axle, upper and lower trailing arms, and heavy-duty coil springs in back
Steering	recirculating ball
Brakes	front discs, rear drums
Engine	425-horsepower 427-cubic-inch L72 V-8
Bore & stroke	4.251 x 3.76 inches
Compression	11:1
Fuel delivery	single 800-cfm Holley four-barrel carburetor
Transmission	four-speed manual or Turbo Hydra-Matic automatic
Axle ratio	4.10:1 in heavy-duty 12-bolt axle with Posi-Traction
Production	325 (estimated)

1969 COPO

The rule was plain enough: no engines larger than 400-cubic-inches could be ordered for the Chevelle prior to 1970. What a shame, because the Corvette's 427-cube big-block could've slipped right in with only a few turns of a wrench. Performance products chief Vince Piggins knew how simple this swap was, and he also recognized a way to circumvent corporate policy to perform the switch right on a Chevrolet assembly line.

Piggins' trick involved COPO paperwork. Meant for special fleet orders by volume customers like trucking firms and police departments, COPOs proved especially useful to Piggins because they didn't require upper-management approval. All that was needed was a go-ahead from the engineering office and almost any equipment combination could be put together with little sweat. Of course, if the process worked for trucks and cop cars, given a little inside assistance, it could also be applied to performance automobiles.

Piggins first began considering the COPO loophole to produce 427-powered Camaros and Chevelles as early as July 1968. At the time, Pennsylvania Chevrolet dealer and former Chevy racer Don Yenko was marketing his own 427 Camaros and was looking both to expand into the Chevelle realm and make these packages easier to handle—easier by letting the factory take care of the engine swaps his mechanics had been performing since 1967. The result was the COPO 9561 Camaro, the factory-built 427 F-body used as a base for the Yenko Super

As was the case on the outside, no clues existed beneath the hood as to a COPO Chevelle's true identity—notice the absence of any decals on the air cleaner lid of the 425-horse L-72 427 big-block. Yenko Chevrolet re-rated the L-72 at 450 horses for the COPO Chevelles it converted into Yenko SC models. *Mike Mueller*

Above
Although it has the blacked-out Super Sport grille, this mysterious '69 Chevelle is not an SS 396; it is a COPO car equipped with the Corvette's L-72 427 big-block. The SS 396's hood with twin "power bulges" is also present. Estimates put production of 1969 COPO Chevelles at about 320 or so. Both hardtop and post-sedan models were built. *Mike Mueller*

Right
Some COPO Chevelles used the SS steering wheel. This particular model is also fitted with the Turbo Hydra-Matic automatic, making it even more rare. Four-speeds expectantly dominated the production run. *Mike Mueller*

Car conversion in 1969.

Yenko also began offering his S/C Chevelle that year, using COPOs to acquire specially equipped 427 A-bodies. Once he primed the COPO pump, 427 Chevelles became available to any Chevrolet customer in the know, although few recognized the opportunity. The COPO code in this case was 9562.

All COPO 9562 Chevelles relied on the 425-horsepower L-72 Corvette 427 featuring 11:1 compression, a 0.520-inch solid-lifter cam,

Corvette-powered COPO Chevelles became Yenko Super Cars in 1969 at Don Yenko's dealership in Canonsburg, Pennsylvania. Yenko Chevrolet also offered 427-equipped Camaros and Novas that year, all done up in similar striping. *Mike Mueller*

big-valve heads (2.19-inch intakes, 1.72 exhausts), and a huge 800-cfm Holley four-barrel carb on an aluminum intake. Also included on the COPO 9562 High Performance Unit parts list was a heavy-duty radiator and the L-72's oil pan, left-hand exhaust manifold, and clutch fork assembly and housing. Completing the package was a special heavy-duty 12-bolt Positraction rear end with 4.10:1 gears and various beefed-up components. The Turbo Hydra-Matic 400 was available, while manual transmission choices included the M21 and M22 Rock Crusher four-speeds.

The COPO Chevelle's exterior left witnesses scratching their heads. Included were the SS 396's twin-bulge hood, blacked-out grille and rear cove panel, D96 upper-body accent stripes, and chrome exhaust extensions, but the cars weren't Super Sports. No SS exterior nomenclature appeared anywhere, nor was

the 427's presence tipped off by an emblem or decal, not even under the hood. Although a few 427 Chevelles apparently came with SS steering wheels, basically all remaining features were pure Malibu. Contrary to the quasi-SS look given these COPO cars, at least one 427 Chevelle came with Malibu lower-body trim.

Also contrary to 1969 SS 396 specifications, most COPO Chevelles rolled on 15x7 Rally wheels. Fourteen-inch Rallys were a Malibu option in 1969, but Super Sports came only with the exclusive 14x7 five-spoke SS rim, which some COPO cars did use. Optional 15-inch "COPO tires," RPO ZP1, also were offered, and would've included either standard 6-inch-wide rims with hubcaps or the wider Rally wheels. Reportedly never used on any other Chevrolet products, ZP1 tires were four-ply Goodyear Polyglas F70-15s with "Goodyear Wide Tread GT" in raised white letters.

According to Chevy big-block expert Fran Preve, Tonawanda engine plant records show 277 L-72 427s were produced for MQ-code manual-transmission COPO 9562 applications, while another 96 MP-code L-72s were intended for use with Turbo Hydra-Matics. But this combined total, 373, represents engines manufactured, not cars built. Speculating a bit, Preve estimated that perhaps as many as 323 COPO Chevelles were released, with 99 of those known to have gone from the Baltimore assembly plant to Yenko Chevrolet in Canonsburg, Pennsylvania.

1970 SS 396

The name remained the same even though the Chevelle Super Sport's big-block was enlarged slightly to 402 cubic-inches late in 1969. SS 396 coupes and convertibles continued rolling on into 1970. *Mike Mueller*

1970 SS 396	
Model availability	two-door Malibu hardtop and convertible; El Camino
Wheelbase	112 inches
Length	197.2 inches
Width	76 inches
Height	52.8 inches (hardtop)
Weight	3,990 pounds (hardtop)
Price	RPO Z25 cost $445.55
Track (front/rear, in inches)	59
Wheels	14x7 five-spoke
Tires	F70x14
Suspension	independent upper/lower A-arms, coil springs and stabilizer bar in front; solid axle, upper and lower trailing arms, coil springs and stabilizer bar in back
Steering	recirculating ball
Brakes	front discs, rear drums
Engine	350-horsepower 402* cubic-inch Turbo-Jet V-8 (L34) *still referred to as 396 Turbo-Jet V-8
Bore & stroke	4.126 x 3.76 inches
Compression	10.25:1
Fuel delivery	single four-barrel carburetor
Transmission	four-speed manual or Turbo Hydra-Matic automatic
Axle ratio	3.31:1
Production	53,599 (includes El Camino SS 396)

1970 SS 396

Listed again as RPO Z25, the SS 396 package for 1970 regained some of its earlier exclusivity as it once more was offered only for Custom El Caminos and Malibu hardtops and convertibles. No more post sedans. Along with revised exterior touches (for a nicely freshened Chevelle body), the Z25 deal included front disc brakes, F70 rubber on 14x7 SS wheels, bright wheelhouse trim, dual exhausts with chrome extensions, and appropriate interior identification. New standard features included an aggressive domed hood, exclusive Super Sport instrumentation borrowed from the new Monte Carlo, and the coveted F41 sport suspension.

Z25 buyers in 1970 also could have chosen between an M20 four-speed or TH-400 automatic—no three-speed, heavy-duty or otherwise, was available. Standard SS 396 power now

came from the 350-horsepower L34 big-block as the L35 didn't return. The optional 375-horsepower L78 carried over one more time for its final appearance. Optional L89 aluminum heads returned as well but were cancelled early in the year—only 18 pairs were installed in 1970 SS 396s before the axe fell.

Other intriguing options included RPOs D88 and ZL2. D88 was a sport stripe kit, which first appeared late in 1969. Featuring twin contrasting stripes (either black or white) running over the hood and rear deck, the D88 kit proved to be far more desirable than previous Super Sport stripe treatments.

The D88 stripes were added when the ZL2 option, the legendary Cowl Induction hood, was ordered. Featuring a vacuum-operated flap at the rear of yet another bulge stacked on top of the already bulging SS hood, the ZL2

lid allowed cooler, denser outside air from the high-pressure area that normally develops at a windshield's base to force its way into the Rochester four-barrel below whenever the hammer went down. Underneath, a large rubber ring sealed a special open-element air cleaner to the Cowl Induction hood's dirty side. During normal operation, the carb drew air through a typical snorkel. But when the rpms jumped and that flap opened, the ZL2 ductwork supplied as much air as the big-block could suck, helping an SS 396 blow the competition away.

Above
The Z25 SS 396 package was priced at $455.15 for the El Camino Custom in 1970. *Mike Mueller*

Below left
Standard for an El Camino SS 396 in 1970 was a 350-horsepower big-block. Optional muscle was supplied by the 375-horse L78 396. *Mike Mueller*

Below right
El Camino Super Sports came with "SS" steering wheels like their 1970 Chevelle cousins. But they didn't get the "SS 396/454" door panel emblems because they had vent windows—the required hand crank took the spot where the emblem belonged. Malibu coupes and convertibles for 1970 did not have vent windows, and thus had room for the extra interior identification. *Mike Mueller*

1970 SS 454

1970 SS 454

Model availability	two-door Malibu hardtop and convertible; El Camino
Wheelbase	112 inches
Length	197.2 inches
Width	76 inches
Height	52.8 inches (hardtop)
Curb weight	3,885 pounds (hardtop)
Price	RPO Z15 cost $503.45
Track (front/rear, in inches)	59
Wheels	14x7 five-spoke
Tires	F70x14
Suspension	independent upper/lower A-arms, coil springs and stabilizer bar in front; solid axle, upper and lower trailing arms, coil springs and stabilizer bar in back
Steering	recirculating ball
Brakes	front discs, rear drums
Engine	360-horsepower 454-cubic-inch Turbo-Jet V-8 (LS5), std.
Bore & stroke	4.25 x 4.00 inches
Compression	10.25:1
Fuel delivery	single four-barrel carburetor
Transmission	four-speed manual or Turbo Hydra-Matic automatic
Axle ratio	3.31:1
Production	8,773 (includes El Camino SS 454)

The SS 454 package was listed under RPO Z15 in 1970. Available for Malibu coupes and convertibles and the El Camino Custom, the Z15 option was priced at $503. Along with typical badges, the 1970 SS 454 package also added wheel opening moldings, a black-accented grille, and exclusive sport wheels. A black resilient rear panel also was included in the El Camino's case. *Mike Mueller*

1970 SS 454

By 1970, the SS 396 legacy had become so revered that Chevrolet's hype-masters didn't dare toy with it after the Turbo-Jet big-block was bored out to 402 cubic-inches late in 1969. "Ess-Ess-four-oh-two?" No way. It was "Ess-Ess-three-ninety-six" or nothing at all. Unless, of course, it was the new SS 454, the supreme evolution of the Chevelle Super Sport breed.

The Chevelle/El Camino SS 454 was born after GM finally dropped its 400-cube maximum displacement limit for its intermediate models. Two widely different SS 454s were offered, by way of RPO Z15, for 1970, beginning with the relatively tame LS5 version with its 360 horsepower. The other featured the awesome LS6, a big-block bully that *Car Life* called "the best supercar engine ever released by General Motors." Many other critics considered the LS6 to be the best supercar engine, period.

Put together with precision at Chevrolet's big-block V-8 production plant in Tonawanda, New York, the LS6 454 was specially built from oil pan to air cleaner with truly super performance in mind. Unlike the LS5, which was based on a two-bolt main bearing block, the LS6's bottom end was held together with four-bolt main bearing caps. The crank was a tuftrided, forged 5140 alloy steel piece cross-drilled to ensure ample oil supply to the connecting rod bearings. Rods were forged steel, magnafluxed, and equipped with 7/16-inch bolts, compared to the LS5's 3/8-inch units.

Left
Tame in comparison to its 450-horse LS6 big brother, the LS5 nonetheless was no wimp. Rated at 360 horsepower, the milder 454 Mk IV big-block, with its hydraulic lifters, was much easier to live with in everyday use. *Mike Mueller*

Below
LS6 Chevelles actually outnumbered their tamer LS5 brothers in 1970. Production for the 360-horsepower LS5 SS 454 was 4,298. Chevrolet built 4,475 LS6 models that year, including this green coupe. *Mike Mueller*

At the rods' business ends were TRW forged aluminum pistons, which mashed the mixture at a ratio of 11.25:1. LS 5 compression was 10.25:1. An aggressive cam (0.520-inch lift, 316-degree duration) activated solid lifters.

On top were free-breathing closed-chamber cylinder heads with large rectangular ports and big valves: 2.19-inch intakes and 1.88-inch exhausts. A huge 780-cfm Holley four-barrel fed this beast, which was conservatively rated at 450 horsepower, the highest advertised output figure ever assigned to a muscle car engine. Some claim actual output was more than 500 horses. Either way, results on the street were earth-shaking.

"Driving a 450-horsepower Chevelle is like being the guy who's in charge of triggering atom bomb tests," claimed a *Super Stock* report. "You have the power, you know you have the power, and you know if you use the power, bad things may happen. Things like arrest, prosecution, loss of license, broken pieces, shredded tires, etc." Finishing the quarter-mile in a tad more than 13 seconds was no problem for the LS6. "That's LS as in Land Speed Record," concluded *Motor Trend*'s A. B. Shuman.

Even though the 450-horsepower 454 alone cost $1,000 extra, the slightly cranky LS6-powered Chevelle actually outsold its more affordable LS5 brother, 4,475 to 4,298.

Above
The LS6's 450-horsepower factory rating was the highest ever assigned during the muscle car era of the 1960s and 1970s. Estimates put actual output as high as 500 horses. Notice the rubber "doughnut" on the air cleaner—this created a seal to the cowl induction hood's ram-air ductwork. *Mike Mueller*

Above right
Production estimates for 1970 LS6 convertibles range from 20 to 70. Also notice the absence of commonly seen hood stripes and Cowl Induction on this topless LS6. *Mike Mueller*

Right
The dual-snorkel air cleaner on this LS6 454 is the most rare of the three units used in 1970. This type or an open-element air cleaner (with chrome lid) were used whenever the Cowl Induction option wasn't chosen. *Mike Mueller*

Above
Chevrolet's legendary LS6 V-8 was purpose built from top to bottom to dominate the muscle car scene in 1970. The parts list included a bullet-proof forged-steel crank, TRW forged-aluminum pistons, and a sturdy four-bolt block.

Far left
Chevrolet's popular ZL2 option, the Cowl Induction hood, allowed the LS6 to breathe in cooler, denser air from the base of the windshield. *Mike Mueller*

Left
With no displacement limit in place after 1969, Chevrolet engineers were allowed to drop their 454-cubic-inch big-block between Chevelle fenders. Both the familiar SS 396 and new SS 454 were offered for 1970. *Mike Mueller*

1970 Monte Carlo SS 454

1970 Monte Carlo SS 454

1970 Monte Carlo SS 454

General Manager Pete Estes, who had replaced Bunkie Knudsen at Chevrolet in July 1965, put his head together with chief designer David Holls to create the Monte Carlo, which was introduced in September 1969 by Estes' successor, John De Lorean. More or less a stretched Chevelle, the relatively luxurious Monte Carlo was inspired by the Grand Prix, itself a lengthened version of Pontiac's A-body (redefined as a G-car) first seen in 1969. Production of Chevrolet's first Monte Carlo was 145,975, most of them powered by 350-cubic-inch V-8s in 1970.

Adding RPO Z20 meant trading that small-block for the LS5 454 big-block, resulting in what *Car Life* called a "gentleman's bomb," the SS 454 Monte Carlo. Along with the LS5, the $420 Z20 package included a heavy-duty suspension (stiffer springs and shocks, front and rear sway bars, and air-regulated Automatic Level Control) and G70 tires on 15x7 wheels. Outward identification consisted only of twin chrome exhaust tips and black-accented rocker trim incorporating polite "SS454" lettering.

Front disc brakes were standard for all Monte Carlos, and the Turbo Hydra-Matic automatic was a mandatory addition (costing another $222) for the SS 454. Some four-speed manuals may have been installed by special order. Popular options included a vinyl roof, air conditioning, power windows, floorshift with console, special instrumentation, simulated woodgrain dash, and Strato bucket seats.

Monte Carlo SS 454 production in 1970 was 3,823.

Chevrolet rolled out 3,823 1970 Monte Carlo SS 454s. *Car Life* called this luxury-minded machine a "gentleman's bomb." A vinyl roof was optional. *Mike Mueller*

Model availability	two-door coupe
Wheelbase	116 inches
Length	205.8 inches
Width	75.6 inches
Height	52.9 inches
Curb weight	4,140 pounds
Base price	RPO Z20 cost $420.25
Track (front/rear, in inches)	59
Wheels	15x7
Tires	G70x15
Suspension	independent upper/lower A-arms, coil springs and stabilizer bar in front; solid axle, upper and lower trailing arms, coil springs and stabilizer bar in back
Steering	recirculating ball
Brakes	front discs, rear drums
Engine	360-horsepower 454-cubic-inch Turbo-Jet V-8 (LS5)
Bore & stroke	4.25 x 4.00 inches
Compression	10.25:1
Fuel delivery	single four-barrel carburetor
Transmission	Turbo Hydra-Matic automatic, std.
Production	3,823

Adding RPO Z20 meant trading that small-block for the LS5 454 big-block, resulting in what *Car Life* called a "gentleman's bomb," the SS 454 Monte Carlo.

The biggest news for 1971 involved the return of small-block power.

New single headlamps set the 1971 Chevelle apart from its forerunners. Only one Super Sport equipment group, RPO Z15, was offered that year, and an available small-block V-8 returned. This convertible is equipped with the 350-cubic-inch V-8. *Mike Mueller*

1971 SS

1971 SS	
Model availability	two-door Malibu hardtop and convertible; El Camino
Wheelbase	112 inches
Length	197.5 inches
Width	75.4 inches
Height	52.7 inches (hardtop)
Curb weight	3,670 pounds (small-block hardtop)
Base price	RPO Z15 cost $357.05
Track (front/rear, in inches)	60/59.9
Wheels	15x7 five-spoke (Camaro sport-type)
Tires	F60x15
Suspension	independent upper/lower A-arms, coil springs and stabilizer bar in front; solid axle, upper and lower trailing arms, coil springs and stabilizer bar in back
Steering	recirculating ball
Brake	front discs, rear drums
Engine	245-horsepower 350-cubic-inch V-8, std.
Bore & stroke	4.00 x 3.48 inches
Compression	8.5:1
Fuel delivery	single two-barrel carburetor
Transmission	three-speed manual
Production	19,293 (includes El Camino)

1971

Only one SS equipment group, RPO Z15, was listed for the 1971 Chevelle, which featured new single headlamps up front and a revised rear bumper, which now incorporated two round tail-lights at each end. Priced at $357, this package included power front disc brakes, F41 sports suspension with rear stabilizer bar, black-accented grille, domed hood, special instrument panel, bright wheel opening trim, and typical identification. New standard features included 15x7 five-spoke Camaro sport wheels wearing F60 rubber, a remote-control left-hand mirror, and competition-style hood pins. The latter items were previously seen in 1970 when the Cowl Induction hood was installed.

The Heavy Chevy Chevelle (left) was introduced midyear in 1971. It offered some of the Super Sport's flair at a lower cost. All V-8s except for the LS5 454 were available beneath the Heavy Chevy's domed hood.

Both the ZL2 and D88 options carried over from the previous year.

The biggest news for 1971 involved the return of small-block power, the first in Chevelle Super Sport ranks in six years. Engine choices now numbered four: two 350-cid small-blocks and two Mk IV big-blocks. Rated at 245 horsepower, the L65 350 featured 8.5:1 compression as well as two items Chevelle SS buyers also hadn't seen since 1965: a two-barrel carburetor and single exhaust. The L48 350 also used 8.5:1 compression and a single tailpipe, but traded that two-barrel for a four-barrel. L48 output was 270 horsepower. The big-blocks were the 300-horsepower Turbo-Jet 400, which

actually displaced 402 cubic-inches, and the surviving LS5 454, now rated at 365 horsepower. Although magazines did road test a 1971 LS6-powered Chevelle, it failed to make it into regular production.

Transmission choices varied by powerplant. The L65 was backed by either the TH-350 automatic or M20 wide-ratio four-speed. The M11 three-speed manual was the base box behind the L48, while the MC1 heavy-duty three-speed was standard for the LS3 big-block. The M40 TH-400 automatic and M20 four-speed were LS3 options. LS5 buyers got to choose between the TH-400 and M22 Rocker Crusher four-speed.

Gone was the revered "SS 396" badge. Chevelle Super Sport fenders in 1971 simply wore "SS" emblems in small- or big-block applications, unless the LS5 was installed. "SS 454" identification remained for Chevrolet's biggest big-block.

Right
Only the SS 454 received its own individual exterior identification in 1971. This SS convertible, powered by the 402-cid big-block, wears the same "SS" badges seen on small-block cars that year. *Mike Mueller*

Below
Options appearing on this well-stocked 1971 SS convertible include the Turbo Hydra-Matic automatic transmission, Strato bucket seats with center console, tilt steering wheel, power steering, power door locks, air conditioning, and AM/FM radio. *Mike Mueller*

Below right
The 402-cubic-inch LS3 V-8 was rated at 300 horsepower in 1971. Notice the absence of an air cleaner decal. Chevrolet people were no longer so proud of their big-block legacy. *Mike Mueller*

Above
The SS 454 remained the king of the Chevelle Super Sport lineup in 1971 and again was offered in hardtop or convertible forms. *Mike Mueller*

Left
The mighty LS6 didn't survive into 1971 (not in Chevelles, at least; it became a Corvette option that year), but the LS5 did. Advertised LS5 output for 1971 was 365 horsepower, up 5 ponies from 1970. *Mike Mueller*

1971 Monte Carlo SS 454

1971 Monte Carlo SS 454

1971 Monte Carlo SS 454

The Monte Carlo SS 454 returned for 1971, this time with 365 standard horses, five more than offered the previous year. New this year was a black band across the back featuring a small "SS" badge on the right. Special suspension components carried over from 1970, as did the G70 rubber. But 15x7 Rally wheels were not specified as standard equipment–the wide rims listed for the first Monte Carlo SS 454 may or may not have been Rally units.

Z20 production for 1971 was 1,919. While an optional 454 big-block remained a Monte Carlo option after this year, the SS 454 package did not return.

Model availability	two-door coupe
Wheelbase	116 inches
Length	205.8 inches
Width	75.6 inches
Height	52.9 inches
Weight	4,195 pounds
Base price	RPO Z20 cost $484.50
Track (front/rear, in inches)	59
Wheels	15x7 Rally
Tires	G70x15
Suspension	independent upper/lower A-arms, coil springs and stabilizer bar in front; solid axle, upper and lower trailing arms, coil springs and stabilizer bar in back
Steering	recirculating ball
Brakes	front discs, rear drums
Engine	365-horsepower 454-cubic-inch Turbo-Jet V-8 (LS5)
Bore & stroke	4.25 x 4.00 inches
Compression	8.5:1
Fuel delivery	single four-barrel carburetor
Transmission	Turbo Hydra-Matic automatic, std.
Production	1,919

Above
New Super Sport identification in a black band appeared on the 1971 Monte Carlo SS 454's tail. *Mike Mueller*

Right
The Monte Carlo SS 454 made an encore appearance in 1971. Production that year was 1,919. *Mike Mueller*

1972 SS

1972 SS	

Model availability	two-door Malibu hardtop and convertible; El Camino
Wheelbase	112 inches
Length	197.5 inches
Width	75.4 inches
Height	52.7 inches (hardtop)
Curb weight	3,650 pounds (small-block hardtop)
Base price	RPO Z15 cost $357.05
Track (front/rear, in inches)	60/59.9
Wheels	15x7 five-spoke (Camaro sport-type)
Tires	F60x15
Suspension	independent upper/lower A-arms, coil springs and stabilizer bar in front; solid axle, upper and lower trailing arms, coil springs and stabilizer bar in back
Steering	recirculating ball
Brakes	front discs, rear drums
Engine	130-horsepower 307-cubic-inch V-8
Bore & stroke	3.875 x 3.25 inches
Compression	8.5:1
Fuel delivery	single two-barrel carburetor
Transmission	three-speed manual
Production	24,946 (includes El Camino)

1972

Save for restyled front marker lights and a new grille that now encompassed the headlights, the 1972 Chevelle was a near-perfect copy of its 1971 predecessor. And other than a color-keyed remote-control left-hand sport mirror in place of the 1971's plated unit, the Z15 package rolled over almost identically too. The most notable change came where it hurt, as all Chevelle V-8s, including the truly meek Turbo-Fire 307 small-block, became available for the 1972 SS.

As in 1971, all 1972 SS engines featured 8.5:1 compression. Net outputs were 130 horsepower for the 307-cubic-inch small-block, 165 for the L65, 175 for the L48, 240 for the LS3 big-block, and 270 for the LS5 454. An available Powerglide returned for the 307, which, like the L65, was backed in standard form by a three-speed manual. Remaining transmission choices echoed those from 1971.

Chevelle SS buyers in California could only order the two 350-cid small-block V-8s in 1972.

Top
Chevrolet's excellent F41 suspension (with rear stabilizer bar) and front disc brakes remained a part of the Z15 package in 1972. This 1972 SS hardtop is fitted with the 402-cid LS3 big-block V-8, now rated at 240 horsepower. *Mike Mueller*

Above
The sporty four-spoke steering wheel shown here was a Chevelle SS option in 1972. Eagle-eyes might also notice the optional 7,000-rpm tachometer. *Mike Mueller*

Chevelle SS buyers in California could only order the two 350-cid small-block V-8s in 1972.

Top
Revised trim that completely encompassed the Super Sport's blacked-out grille and headlights appeared in 1972. Again, "SS" badges were used for both the 350- and 402-equipped models. This 1972 SS convertible features the 350 small-block. *Mike Mueller*

Right
Standard power for the 1972 Chevelle SS was a wimpy 130-horsepower 307-cubic-inch small-block. The L65 350 V-8 was net-rated at 165 horsepower, its L48 running mate at 175. *Mike Mueller*

Left
This convertible is one of only 1,625 Chevelle SS 454s built for 1972 with the optional M22 "Rock Crusher" four-speed manual transmission. *Mike Mueller*

Below left
Chevrolet's optional LS5 454 V-8 was rated at 270 horsepower in 1972. Compression was a wimpy 8.5:1. *Mike Mueller*

Below
This fabled badge appeared on Chevelle fenders for the last time in 1972. An optional 454 V-8 remained available afterward, but its installation was never played up so prominently again. *Mike Mueller*

1973 SS

Model availability	two-door Malibu Colonnade coupe and station wagon
Wheelbase	113 inches
Base price	RPO Z15 cost $242.75
Wheels	14x7 Rally
Tires	G70x14
Suspension	independent upper/lower A-arms, coil springs and stabilizer bar in front; solid axle, upper and lower trailing arms, coil springs and stabilizer bar (for the SS station wagon) in back
Steering	recirculating ball
Brakes	front discs, rear drums
Engine	145-horsepower 350-cubic-inch V-8
Bore & stroke	4.00 x 3.48 inches
Compression	8.5:1
Fuel delivery	single two-barrel carburetor
Transmission	three-speed manual
Production	28,647

1973

A totally restyled Chevelle body debuted for 1973 and no longer featured a two-door hardtop variation. In its place was GM's Colonnade coupe, a sweeping, pillared roofline shared that year with Buick, Oldsmobile, and Pontiac. RPO Z15 carried over into this new age for one last fling (in Chevelle ranks; it rolled on for the El Camino into the 1980s) and this time was available for the Malibu Colonnade coupe and two Malibu station wagons: a six-passenger two-seater and its eight-passenger, three-seat companion. Nineteen-seventy-three was the only year an SS wagon was offered.

The Z15 package for 1973 included G70 tires on 14x7 Rally rims, dual sport mirrors, and a special instrument cluster with black bezels. SS identification appeared inside on the door panels and steering wheel, while exterior dress-up included a blacked-out grille, color-keyed striping along the lower body sides and wheel openings, bright drip moldings, bright trim for the triangular rear-quarter windows, and SS badges for the grille, fenders, and tail. Those rear badges were mounted on the bumper in the coupe's case, on the tailgate in the wagons. SS wagons also received a rear stabilizer bar.

The available engine list began with the L65 350 small-block, net-rated at 145 horsepower. Next was the L48 350, at 175 horses. Top dog was the LS4 454 big-block, which pumped out 245 ponies.

Z15 installations numbered 28,647 in 1973, the last year for the Chevelle SS. Its replacement for 1974 was the sporty Laguna S-3.

Top left
The Chevelle SS made one final appearance in 1973, this time based on Chevrolet's totally restyled midsize platform. Production of 1973 SS Colonnade coupes was 28,647.

Above
The Laguna S-3 coupe replaced the Chevelle SS for 1974.

06

Above
1965 Gran Sport

Middle
1969 GS-400

Right
1973 Gran Sport Stage 1

High-Class Hot Rod

06

Buick Gran Sport 1965–1974

Like Chevrolet, Buick also entered the great American muscle car race midyear in 1965, in this case with the rather regal Gran Sport. Once again, the plan was so damned simple: drop a big engine into a not-so-big car, then let it eat. In Buick terms, the car was the Special, initially reborn in radically downsized form in the fall of 1960 (as a 1961 model) along with its senior compact cousins from Pontiac and Oldsmobile. Unveiled early in 1961 as well was the Skylark coupe, an upscale Special named after the flashy convertible Buick had rolled off a Motorama stage into regular production in 1953. Neither the next-generation Skylark nor its Special alter-ego were well suited for high-performance applications in the beginning, but all that changed in 1963 when Buick's classy compact graduated into GM's newly formed intermediate ranks. Gone was that innovative-yet-limiting unit-body construction, replaced by a traditional full-frame foundation that would prove to be a much more accommodating home to many more horses.

The big engine that found its way down from full-size ranks into the midsize Skylark in 1965 was Buick's Wildcat 445 V-8, a rather antiquated "nail-head" powerplant that traced its roots back to the division's first modern overhead-valve V-8, introduced for 1953. That nickname referred to this breed's relatively small valves, which in some hacks' minds appeared not much bigger than—you guessed it—the head of a nail. Such slings aside, Buick's big-block bully still churned out 325 horsepower, as well as 445 lb-ft of torque, hence its official moniker.

Displacement for the Wildcat 445 V-8 was 401 cubic-inches, one more than GM supposedly allowed in its intermediate models prior to 1970. But what was a single cube between

friends? Ivory-tower execs apparently couldn't have cared less, or maybe they never even noticed. Buick promotional people helped make the situation easy enough to miss by identifying the first Gran Sport's standard power source as a "400 cu. in." mill in all printed references in 1965.

Motor Trend's Bob McVay fell for this one, repeating the faux figure in his May 1965 Gran Sport road test. But *Hot Rod*'s Eric Dahlquist wasn't fooled, nor were his comrades at *Car Life*—both these magazines reported the correct 401-cubic-inch count in their GS reviews in early 1965.

Simply saying "Zow!," Buick's magazine ads called the Skylark GS a "Superbird," a

- → All 1965 magazine advertisements referred to the first Gran Sport's engine as a 400-cid unit even though it actually displaced 401 cubic-inches.
- → Buick's Rivera also received the Gran Sport treatment in 1965.
- → The full-size Wildcat Gran Sport appeared for one year only in 1966.
- → A true 400-cubic-inch V-8 appeared between Gran Sport fenders in 1967.
- → The small-block GS-340 joined its big-block GS-400 brother in 1967.
- → The GS California debuted for sale in California only in 1967.
- → The GS-350 replaced the GS-340 in 1968.
- → Buick's fabulous Stage 1 V-8 debuted as a full-fledged factory option in 1969.
- → The GS-400 was replaced by the GS-455 in 1970.
- → All Buick GSXs, built for 1970 and 1971, were hardtops.
- → All midsize Gran Sports built from 1973 to 1975 were based on the new Century Colonnade coupe.
- → A GSX trim package option appeared for Buick's compact Apollo in 1974.
- → The last Gran Sport Stage 1 was built in 1974.

Opposite
Buick introduced its supreme Skylark Gran Sport, the GSX, at the Chicago Auto Show in February 1970. This high-profile hauler was offered only in Apollo White or Saturn Yellow. *Mike Mueller*

reference that would take flight again in much more dramatic fashion five years later splashed across Plymouth Road Runner rear quarters. According to Edward Rollert, Buick general manager, the new GS was "a completely engineered performance car designed to appeal to sports car enthusiasts." And being from Flint, where better cars were built, the gentlemanly GS, in the opinion of *Car Life*'s editors, came "off stronger, more distinctive [than high-powered rivals] and with something its owners can appreciate"—that being an incredibly polite asking price—the Gran Sport package added a mere $200.53 to the bottom line of a Skylark coupe, sedan, or convertible in 1965.

The Gran Sport treatment also debuted on Buick's top-shelf Riviera that year and, for one year only, on the full-size Wildcat in 1966. Both the Riviera GS and its midsize running mate carried on until 1975. A small-block Skylark GS joined the original big-block rendition in 1967, and this tandem continued rolling on together after the Skylark was replaced by Buick's new Century in 1973. Nineteen-seventy-four was the last year for the big-block Century GS. Only the 350-cid small-block and cost-conscious 231-cube V-6 were available in 1975. A Century Gran Sport reappeared briefly in 1986, and a Regal GS was offered from 1988 to 2006.

Top left
Buick first used the Skylark name in 1953 for a flashy convertible that rolled right off a Motorama stage onto the street. The original Skylark was built in limited numbers for 1953 (front) and 1954 (rear). *Mike Mueller*

Top right
Buick's upscale compact, the Special, debuted for 1961. New, too, that year was a reborn Skylark, a top-shelf two-door coupe that served as a flagship for the Special line. A 1962 Skylark is shown here. *Mike Mueller*

Above
Buick pioneered the big-engine-in-a-not-so-big-car thing in 1936, introducing its Roadmaster-powered Century. A Century didn't initially reappear after World War II, but it did make a triumphant comeback in 1954. Available as a two-door hardtop and convertible, four-door sedan, and four-door station wagon, the 1954 Century offered "more power per dollar than you can get anywhere else in the American market," according to Buick ads. A 200-horsepower Roadmaster V-8 was standard that year for automatic-equipped Centurys. *Mike Mueller*

Right
Both Oldsmobile and Buick's "senior compacts" used this innovative 215-cubic-inch aluminum V-8 from 1961 to 1963. In 1962 it was recast (using iron) into a V-6, and this engine evolved to later power Buick's tough Grand National and sensational GNX during the 1980s.

1965 Gran Sport

1965 Gran Sport

1965

For $200.53 in 1965, a Skylark GS buyer got the Wildcat 445 V-8 backed by a floorshift three-speed manual, typical heavy-duty suspension upgrades, and a beefier convertible frame. For the record, the nail-head V-8's valves measured 1.875 inches on the intake side, 1.50 on the exhaust. A 600-cfm Carter AFB four-barrel fed this big-block, and compression was 10.25:1. Optional transmissions included a prerequisite four-speed manual and Buick's so-fine two-speed Super Turbine 300 automatic. Standard gear ratios were 3.08:1 behind the auto box, 3.36:1 behind the four-speed, and standard brakes were 9.5-inch drums front and rear. Also part of the deal were oversized 7.75x14 tires on typical steel wheels, but those rims could've been replaced by optional 14x6 five-spokers done in gleaming chrome.

Bucket seats, a console, and tachometer (mounted on the console) were optional inside, as was a limited-slip differential out back. All of Buick's typical soft touches were available as well, including air conditioning, power steering, power brakes, and so on. Indeed, "gentleman's hot rod" was a fair description for a fully loaded Gran Sport.

Right
A Riviera Gran Sport debuted along with the Skylark GS in 1965, and a Wildcat GS (shown here) appeared for 1966 only.

Model availability	two-door coupe, hardtop, and convertible
Wheelbase	115 inches
Length	203.4 inches
Width	73.9 inches
Height	54 inches (coupe)
Curb weight	3,720 pounds (coupe)
Base price	GS package cost $200.53
Track (front/rear, in inches)	58
Wheels	14x6 stamped steel
Tires	7.75x14
Suspension	independent upper/lower A-arms, coil springs and stabilizer bar in front; solid axle, control arms and coil springs in back
Steering	recirculating ball
Brakes	four-wheel drums
Engine	325-horsepower 401-cubic-inch "Wildcat 445" V-8
Bore & stroke	4.1875 x 3.640 inches
Compression	10.25:1
Fuel delivery	single 600-cfm Carter AFB four-barrel carburetor
Transmission	three-speed manual
Axle ratio	3.36:1 std. w/manual transmission; 3.08:1 std. w/automatic transmission
Production	15,780

Buick ads in 1965 called the new Skylark GS a "Superbird" or "a howitzer with windshield wipers." The 14-inch chromed wheels seen here were available that year at extra cost. *Mike Mueller*

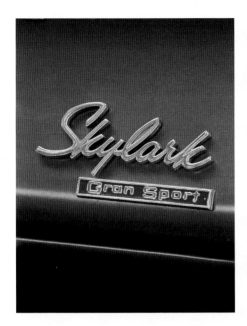

Indeed, "gentleman's hot rod" was a fair description for a fully loaded Gran Sport.

Above
Buick's original Gran Sport legacy rolled on from 1965 to 1975 for both the division's midsize models and the luxurious Riviera. A Century GS reappeared in 1986 and a Regal Gran Sport was built from 1988 to 2006. *Mike Mueller*

Above Center
From 1965 to 1972, Buick's midsize Gran Sport was based on the Skylark. In 1973, the Skylark was superseded by the new Century. *Mike Mueller*

Above right
Bucket seats and a console (with tachometer) were optional inside the 1965 Gran Sport. A floor-shifted three-speed manual transmission was standard behind the Wildcat 445 V-8. *Mike Mueller*

Right
It actually displaced 401 cubic-inches, but Buick paperwork referred to the 1965 Gran Sport's standard V-8 as a 400-cubic-inch engine. That was the limit for General Motor's midsize models at the time. "Wildcat 445" came from this engine's torque output: 445 lb-ft. *Mike Mueller*

1966 Gran Sport

1966 Gran Sport

Model availability	two-door coupe, hardtop and convertible
Wheelbase	115 inches
Length	204 inches
Width	75 inches
Height	53.2 inches (coupe and hardtop); 54 inches (convertible)
Curb weight	3,479 pounds (coupe), 3,428 pounds (hardtop), 3,532 pounds (convertible)
Base price	$2,956 (coupe), $3,019 (hardtop), $3,167 (convertible)
Track (front/rear, in inches)	58/59
Wheels	14x6 stamped steel
Tires	7.75x14
Suspension	independent upper/lower A-arms, coil springs and stabilizer bar in front; solid axle, control arms and coil springs in back
Steering	recirculating ball
Brakes	four-wheel drums
Engine	325-horsepower 401-cubic-inch "Wildcat 445" V-8
Bore & stroke	4.1875 x 3.640 inches
Compression	10.25:1
Fuel delivery	single 600-cfm Carter AFB four-barrel carburetor
Transmission	three-speed manual
Axle ratio	3.36:1 std. w/manual transmission; 2.93:1 std. w/automatic transmission
Production	13,816

1966

Buick sold 15,780 Skylark Gran Sports in 1965, and then followed that up with 13,816 more in 1966. Once again the GS was available in sedan, hardtop, or convertible forms, but this time around, all three were classed in their own segregated model group wearing their own series numbers in the 44600 range. Other Skylarks were 44400-series models.

Additional distinctiveness appeared in 1966 by way of a standard black-out treatment for the Gran Sport's grille and rear cove panel, simulated vents on the hood and fenders, and bodyside paint stripes. Gone was the somewhat "square" Buick hood ornament that appeared, in some opinions, out of place at the nose of the supposedly groovy 1965 GS.

A blacked-out grille was new for the Skylark-based Gran Sport in 1966, and the not-cool hood ornament seen the previous year was deleted. *Mike Mueller*

All mechanicals carried over more or less unchanged for 1966 save, most notably, the addition of new finned-alloy iron brake drums, created to help cool things down quicker after hard stops. Standard gear ratios this time around were 3.36:1 for manual transmissions and 2.93:1 for the Super Turbine automatic.

Gone was the somewhat "square" Buick hood ornament.

Above
Buick's midsize GS became an individual model in 1966 and remained available as a coupe, hardtop (shown here), and convertible. The production breakdown read 1,835 coupes, 9,934 hardtops, and 2,047 convertibles.

Below
Production of four-speed GS hardtops in 1966 was 2,199. *Mike Mueller*

1967 GS-400

1967 GS-400

Model availability	two-door coupe, hardtop and convertible
Wheelbase	115 inches
Length	205 inches
Width	75.4 inches
Height	53.1 (coupe)
Curb weight	3,439 pounds (coupe), 3,500 pounds (hardtop), 3,505 pounds (convertible)
Base price	$2,956 (coupe), $3,019 (hardtop), $3,167 (convertible)
Track (front/rear, in inches)	58/59
Wheels	14x6 stamped steel
Tires	F70x14
Suspension	independent upper/lower A-arms, coil springs and stabilizer bar in front; solid axle, control arms and coil springs in back
Steering	recirculating ball
Brakes	four-wheel drums
Engine	340-horsepower 400-cubic-inch V-8
Bore & stroke	4.04 x 3.90 inches
Compression	10.25:1
Fuel delivery	single Rochester four-barrel carburetor
Transmission	three-speed manual
Axle ratio	3.36:1 std. w/manual transmission; 2.93:1 std. w/automatic transmission
Production	19,626 (includes GS-340 and GS California)

1967

Buick's 44600-series models (sedan, hardtop, and convertible) were officially renamed "GS-400" for 1967, and this time the numbers didn't lie. In place of the venerable Wildcat 445 V-8 was an all-new big-block that actually did displace 400-cubic-inches. Primarily the work of engineer Clifford Studaker, the 1967 GS-400's exclusive V-8 was created using lightweight thin-wall casting techniques. With less iron present where it wasn't needed, Studaker's thin-wall 400 weighed in at more than 100 pounds less than Chevrolet's Mark IV big-block and was only 72 pounds heavier than Chevy's ever-present small-block.

Additional improvements included better-breathing heads with bigger valves, free-flowing header-style exhaust manifolds, and a beefier lower end featuring a crankshaft with 3.25-inch main bearing journals, compared to 3.00-inch for the good ol' nail-head. Valves now measured 2.00 inches across on the intake side, 1.625 on the exhaust. Compression was again 10.25:1, but the mixture in this case was fed by a 678-cfm Quadrajet four-barrel atop a well-plumbed dual-plane intake. Advertised output was 340 horsepower.

Adorning the 1967 GS-400 were simulated hood scoops and a distinctive single-bar grille sporting a familiar red-painted "GS" badge. The blacked-out cove in back incorporated the new "GS-400" tag. F70x14 tires, with either whitewalls or red stripes, were also new for 1967, as were optional front disc brakes. Buick's much-improved three-speed Super Turbine automatic also debuted on the options list this year.

Left
A new 400-cubic-inch big-block V-8 appeared for the midsize Gran Sport in 1967. Advertised output was 340 horsepower. Compression was 10.25:1.

Above

Two Skylark Gran Sports were offered for 1967, the big-block GS-400 and small-block GS-340, shown here. Only two exterior colors, Platinum Mist or Arctic White, were offered for the 1967 GS-340. Production was 3,692, all hardtops. *Mike Mueller*

Inset

The standard GS-340 interior was kept simple to keep costs down. *Mike Mueller*

Appearing for the first time as well was the GS-340, a less costly variation on the Gran Sport theme using a less powerful 260-horsepower 340-cubic-inch small-block V-8. Introduced in February 1967 in hardtop form only, the GS-340 was created, in Buick's words, to put "performance in the range of budget car buyers." It was also "a lot of car for any car buff." The exclusive exterior, offered only in Platinum Mist or Arctic White paint, may have been dressed up rather flashily with high-profile red accents, but the GS-340's interior was taxi-cab bare with a bench seat and little else. Transmission choices included the three-speed manual and Buick's old two-speed Super Turbine automatic. Base price was $2,845, compared to $3,019 for a 1967 GS-400 hardtop.

A third Skylark Gran Sport also appeared in 1967, but for California customers only. Appropriately named the California GS, this cost-conscious sedan came standard with the GS-340's small-block backed by an automatic transmission, a bench seat, vinyl top, and special "California" script added to the GS badges. California GS production for 1967 was 3,692. The total annual count for all Skylark Gran Sports, small- and big-block, was 19,626.

1967 GS-340

1967 GS-340

Model availability	two-door hardtop
Wheelbase	115 inches
Length	205 inches
Width	75.4 inches
Height	53.2
Curb weight	3,283 pounds
Base price	$2,845
Track (front/rear, in inches)	58/59
Wheels	red-painted 14-inch sport wheels
Tires	7.75x14
Suspension	independent upper/lower A-arms, coil springs and stabilizer bar in front; solid axle, control arms and coil springs in back
Steering	recirculating ball
Brakes	four-wheel drums
Engine	260-horsepower 340-cubic-inch V-8
Bore & stroke	3.75 x 3.85 inches
Compression	10.25:1
Fuel delivery	single Carter four-barrel carburetor
Transmission	three-speed manual
Axle ratio	3.23:1
Production	3,692

A third Skylark Gran Sport also appeared in 1967, but for California customers only.

Below left
The GS-340's small-block was a 340-cubic-inch V-8 topped by a four-barrel carburetor. Advertised output was 260 horsepower. *Mike Mueller*

Below
Red accents appeared on the GS-340's hood, lower bodysides, and wheels. This package was offered for 1967 only. *Mike Mueller*

1968 GS-350

1968 GS-350

1968

Buick's restyled Skylark body made the biggest news this year, as least as far as the GS-400 was concerned. Most everything rolled over identically beneath that softly sculpted skin, with a notable exception involving a name change as the Super Turbine 400 automatic transmission was now the Turbo Hydra-Matic 400. The three-speed Turbo Hydra-Matic option was limited to the GS-400, and some Buick sources still referred to this auto box as the Super Turbine 400. Body-style availability changed, too, for 1968 as the big-block Gran Sport was only offered in hardtop and convertible forms. No more GS-400 sedans.

The small-block GS came only as a hard-top, while the GS California—now marketed nationwide—was again only available as a sedan dressed up with a vinyl roof. GS California production for 1968 was 4,831, all with two-speed Super Turbine 300 automatic transmissions.

New for the GS-400's small-block little brothers was an enlarged 350-cubic-inch V-8 that necessitated another name change as "GS-350" predictably supersede 1967's GS-340. Output for the GS-350's bigger, better small-block was 280 horsepower. Once again a three-speed manual was standard for both the GS-350 and GS-400, but in the former's case was available with either a floorshift or mundane column shift—all previous manual-transmission GS Skylarks featured floor-mounted shifters. While a four-speed manual was again optional (now stirred with a Hurst stick) behind both blocks, small or big, the 350 V-8 was limited to the two-speed Super Turbine option.

The peak year for Buick's midsize Gran

Model availability	two-door hardtop
Wheelbase	112 inches
Length	200.6 inches
Width	75.6 inches
Height	52.8 inches
Curb weight	3,375 pounds
Base price	$2,926
Track (front/rear, in inches)	59
Wheels	14x6 stamped steel
Tires	7.75x14
Suspension	independent upper/lower A-arms, coil springs and stabilizer bar in front; solid axle, control arms and coil springs in back
Steering	recirculating ball
Brakes	four-wheel drums
Engine	280-horsepower 350-cubic-inch V-8
Bore & stroke	3.80 x 3.85 inches
Compression	10.25:1
Fuel delivery	single Carter four-barrel carburetor
Transmission	three-speed manual
Axle ratio	3.23:1
Production	8,317

Right
GM's wonderfully restyled A-body shell worked as nicely for the 1968 Skylark as it did for its corporate cousins from Pontiac, Chevrolet, and Oldsmobile that year. In place of the GS-340 came the 1968 GS-350, predictably fitted with Buick's 350-cubic-inch small-block V-8.

1968 GS-400

1968 GS-400

Model availability	two-door hardtop and convertible
Wheelbase	112 inches
Length	200.6 inches
Width	75.6 inches
Height	52.8 inches (hardtop), 52.7 inches (convertible)
Curb weight	3,514 pounds (hardtop), 3,547 pounds (convertible)
Base price	$3,127 (hardtop), $3,271 (convertible)
Track (front/rear, in inches)	59.4/59
Wheels	14x6 stamped steel
Tires	F70x14
Suspension	independent upper/lower A-arms, coil springs and stabilizer bar in front; solid axle, control arms and coil springs in back
Steering	recirculating ball
Brakes	four-wheel drums
Engine	340-horsepower 400-cubic-inch V-8
Bore & stroke	4.04 x 3.90 inches
Compression	10.25:1
Fuel delivery	single Rochester four-barrel carburetor
Transmission	three-speed manual
Axle ratio	3.42:1 std. w/manual transmission; 2.93:1 std. w/automatic transmission
Production	26,345 (includes GS-350 and GS California)

Sport was 1968, with total production reaching 26,345. Of these, 13,197 were big-blocks, 13,148 were small-blocks. Barely noticed among all these Gran Sports was the new Stage 1 Special Package, a dealer-installed option that on paper pumped up the 400 V-8 another five horses, thanks mostly to a more aggressive cam and a boost to 11:1 compression. Anyone who took a Stage 1 GS to the strip knew that the published 345-horsepower rating was a joke, which *Car Life* proved by burning up the quarter-mile in only 14.4 seconds in an automatic transmission example. With headers and slicks, that time was cut to 13.50 clicks. Fifty extra horsepower was more like it.

Below
The GS-350 was sold only as a hardtop in 1968, while the small-block GS California was offered only in pillared coupe form. Production of 1968 GS-400 convertibles (shown here) was 2,454.

Below right
Skylark GS-400s were available only in hardtop and convertible forms in 1968. GS-400 hardtop (shown here) production that year was 10,743.

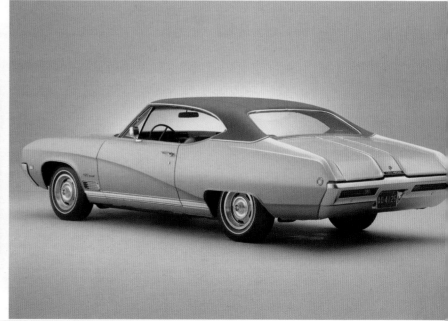

1969 GS-400

1969 GS-400

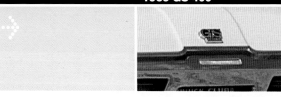

1969

A revised centrally mounted hood scoop announced the 1969 Gran Sport's arrival, and wouldn't you know it—that scoop was finally fully functional for both the GS-400 and GS-350. Breathing in the cooler, denser outside air in both cases were the same V-8s used in 1968, once again backed by a three-speed manual in base form. A floorshift was standard for the GS-400 hardtop and convertible, a column shift for the GS-350 hardtop. Only 58 three-on-the-tree GS 350s were built for 1969, following the 106 released the previous year.

New on the GS-350 options list was the Turbo Hydra-Matic 350 automatic, a junior TH 400, if you will. As before, the GS California was limited to Buick's new TH 350, with 3,574 built before the vinyl-roofed sedan's three-year run came to an end. The Turbo Hydra-Matic 400 remained the optional automatic for the GS-400, and a Hurst-shifted four-speed was offered, as expected, behind either engine.

Model availability	two-door hardtop and convertible
Wheelbase	112 inches
Length	200.7 inches
Width	75.6 inches
Height	53 inches (hardtop), 53.7 inches (convertible)
Curb weight	3,549 pounds (hardtop), 3,594 pounds (convertible)
Base price	$3,181 (hardtop), $3,325 (convertible)
Track (front/rear, in inches)	59.4/59
Wheels	14x6 stamped steel
Tires	F70x14
Suspension	independent upper/lower A-arms, coil springs and stabilizer bar in front; solid axle, control arms and coil springs in back
Steering	recirculating ball
Brakes	four-wheel drums
Engine	340-horsepower 400-cubic-inch V-8
Bore & stroke	4.04 x 3.90 inches
Compression	10.25:1
Fuel delivery	single Rochester four-barrel carburetor
Transmission	three-speed manual
Axle ratio	3.55:1 std. w/manual transmission; 3.07:1 std. w/automatic transmission
Production	26,345 (includes GS-350 and GS California)

Left
A restyled hood scoop mounted in the center of the hood was new for the 1969 Skylark Gran Sport, once more offered in GS-350 hardtop (left), GS-400 (right), and GS California forms. A convertible model again was only available for the GS-400.

Left
Buick's 340-horsepower 400-cubic-inch big-block V-8 remained the heart of the GS-400 in 1969. Both the GS-400 and GS-350 came standard with functional hood scoops that year. *Mike Mueller*

Below left
"GS" identification appeared in the grille, on each quarter-panel, and in the center of the rear deck lid in 1969. *Mike Mueller*

Making the biggest splash for 1969 was the Stage 1 package, which was now an official factory option for both hardtop and convertible GS-400 renditions. Included in this deal was a modified Rochester Quadrajet four-barrel, hotter cam, heavier valve springs, improved oiling, heavy-duty cooling, and low-restriction exhaust system with 2.5-inch pipes and low-restriction mufflers. A three-speed manual with a floorshift was standard behind the Stage 1 400 V-8, as were 3.64:1 gears. Only 13 three-speed Stage 1s were built for 1969: 9 hardtops and 4 convertibles. Four-speed installations numbered 415 hardtops, 77 convertibles. Another 963 (832 hardtops, 131 convertibles) were fitted with the optional TH-400 automatic, which also was modified (high-stall torque converter, higher shift points) for the Stage 1 application.

Chrome engine dress-up and appropriate Stage 1 badges on the hood scoop represented icing on the cake. As for the real meat, the Stage 1 400 was again laughingly rated at 345 horsepower. Adding the optional Stage 2 cam reportedly added another 5 horses, yet another doubtful figure. Putting the pedal to the metal once more revealed a Stage-equipped Buick's true identity. With headers, an aftermarket intake and carb, and a track-ready 4.78:1 rear axle, *Hot Rod* magazine's testers managed to run a 1969 GS Stage 2 well into the 12s down the quarter-mile. "If [the car] had a GTO sheet metal wrapper on it, you couldn't build enough of them," wrote *HRM*'s Steve Kelly.

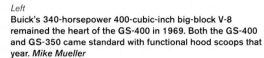

Production of GS-400 convertibles was 1,564 in 1969. Another 212 topless Gran Sports were sold with the Stage 1 V-8. *Mike Mueller*

Right
A deluxe steering wheel was standard inside the GS-400 in 1969. Notice the optional console with U-handle shifter on this Turbo Hydra-Matic model. *Mike Mueller*

Putting the pedal to the metal once more revealed a Stage-equipped Buick's true identity.

Only 13 three-speed Stage 1s were built for 1969.

Left
Production of 1969 GS-350 hardtops was 6,305. New that year on the GS-350 options list was GM's Turbo Hydra-Matic 350 automatic transmission.

Below
A dealer-offered "Special Package" in 1968, Buick's famed Stage 1 big-block V-8 became an official factory option in 1969. Stage 1 production that year was 1,468, including 1,256 GS hardtops and 212 convertibles.

1970 GS-455

1970 GS-455

1970

A thoroughly modernized Skylark body showed up this year to rave reviews, but those in the Gran Sport camp were more interested, at least early on, in General Motors' decision to lift its infamous 400-cid lid on its midsize models. Gone was the GS-400, replaced by the new GS-455, powered by Buick's most massive V-8 yet. Engineers created this 455-cid beast by boring out the division's existing big-block (previously maxed out at 430 cubes for full-size models) to 4.3125 inches. Three versions appeared for 1970: a 370-horsepower 455 for the big Buicks, a 350-horsepower running mate for the GS-455, and its Stage 1 upgrade, again conservatively rated, this time at 360 horsepower. Torque output for the Gran Sport 455 V-8 was a whopping 510 lb-ft at a lazy 2,800 rpm.

After watching a Gran Sport Stage 1 455 scorch the quarter-mile in a scant 13.38 seconds, *Motor Trend*'s Bill Sanders called this ground-shaking Buick an "old man's car inbred with a going street bomb. Performance verges on a precipitous mechanical hysteria," he continued. "The first time you put your foot to the boards a premonition of impending whiplash emanates from the base of the Achilles tendon."

GS-455 hardtops numbered 5,589 in 1970, while the convertible count was 1,184. Stage 1 production was 2,465 hardtops and only 232 convertibles, including one drop-top sold with the standard three-speed manual transmission. Sixteen three-speed Stage 1 hardtops were built.

The small-block Gran Sport hardtop was simply labeled "GS" in 1970. Its heart was now a muscled-up 350 V-8 rated at 315 horsepower. A column-shift three-speed was again standard, with 48 of these built, joined by another 176 floorshift base models. The total 1970 GS tally (three-speed, four-speed, and TH 350 automatic) was 9,948.

Model availability	two-door hardtop and convertible
Wheelbase	112 inches
Length	202.2 inches
Width	77.3 inches
Height	53 inches (hardtop), 53.3 inches (convertible)
Curb weight	3,562 pounds (hardtop), 3,619 pounds (convertible)
Base price	$3,283 (hardtop), $3,469 (convertible)
Track (front/rear, in inches)	59.4/59
Wheels	14x6 stamped steel
Tires	F70x14
Suspension	independent upper/lower A-arms, coil springs and stabilizer bar in front; solid axle, control arms and coil springs in back
Steering	recirculating ball
Brakes	four-wheel drums
Engine	350-horsepower 455-cubic-inch V-8, std.
Bore & stroke	4.3125 x 3.90 inches
Compression	10:1
Fuel delivery	single Rochester four-barrel carburetor
Transmission	three-speed manual
Axle ratio	3.42:1 std. w/manual transmission; 2.93:1 std. w/automatic 3.64:1 std. w/455 Stage 1 V-8
Production	20,096 (includes GSX and GS-350)

Below
A totally new Skylark body appeared for 1970, as did a new standard engine for the big-block Gran Sport: Buick's 455-cubic-inch V-8. Production of 1970 Stage 1 Gran Sport hardtops (shown here) was 2,465.

1970 GSX

1970 GSX

Model availability	two-door hardtop
Wheelbase	112 inches
Length	202.2 inches
Width	77.3 inches
Height	53 inches
Curb weight	3,875 pounds
Base price	$4,479
Track (front/rear, in inches)	59.4/59
Wheels	15x7 five-spoke
Tires	G60x15 Goodyear Polyglass GT
Suspension	independent upper/lower A-arms, coil springs and stabilizer bar in front; solid axle, control arms, coil springs and stabilizer bar in back
Steering	recirculating ball
Brakes	power front discs, rear drums
Engine	350-horsepower 455-cubic-inch V-8, std.
Bore & stroke	4.3125 x 3.90 inches
Compression	10:1
Fuel delivery	single Rochester four-barrel carburetor
Transmission	four-speed manual or Turbo Hydra-Matic automatic
Axle ratio	3.42:1, std. w/455 V 8 ; 3.64:1 std. w/Stage 1 V-8
Production	678 (includes both engines)

1970 GSX

Truly huge headlines were made on February 9, 1970, when Buick introduced its gonzo GSX at the Chicago Auto Show. Along with a hot suspension, 15x7 sport wheels shod in fat G60 Goodyear Polyglas GT rubber, and power front disc brakes, the GSX featured one of the original muscle car era's highest-profile images. Spoilers appeared front and rear, joined by black body-side accent stripes, twin black hood strip-trimmed in red pinstriping, color-coordinated headlight bezels (standard GS units were chromed), a hood-mounted tachometer, dual racing mirrors, and splashy GSX identification.

Only two paint choices were offered for the GSX hardtop: Apollo White or Saturn Yellow. Black was the only available shade inside, where bucket seats, a consolette, a Rallye steering wheel, gauges, and a Rallye clock were

all standard.

Beneath the skin was Buick's Rallye Ride Control Package, consisting of heavy-duty front (1.0-inch) and rear (0.875-inch) sway bars, boxed lower control arms, and performance-tuned springs and shocks. Standard power came from the 350-horsepower 455 big-block backed by a four-speed and a limited-slip differential carrying 3.42:1 gears in back. The sum of these parts, identified by Buick options code A9, added roughly $1,100 to a Gran Sport's bottom line in 1970.

Options included the Stage 1 455, priced at $113 for the 1970 GSX. Stage 1 gear cost $199 when ordered for a GS-455 that year. Unlike the GS Stage 1, its 360-horsepower GSX counterpart carried no exterior identification, meaning most challengers on the street never even knew what hit them.

The Turbo Hydra-Matic 400 automatic was available, too, and it also cost less in the GSX. Of the 678 GSX Buick's built for 1970, 479 had the TH 400, 199 featured four-speeds. The Stage 1 GSX count was 400: 282 with automatics, 118 with four-speeds. The breakdown for the 350-horsepower GSX models was 197 automatics, 81 four-speeds.

Below
A hood-mounted tachometer was included in the GSX deal, as were sport mirrors, black hood stripes, and painted headlight bezels. *Mike Mueller*

Above
A trendy rear wing was standard at the GSX's tail. Unlike other 1970 Skylark Gran Sports, the GSX did not receive Stage 1 exterior identification when so equipped that year, as was this Saturn Yellow example. *Mike Mueller*

Right
Both the Gran Sport's base 350-horsepower 455 V-8 and its Stage 1 alter-ego were available for the GSX in 1970. Advertised output for the 455 Stage 1 big-block in 1970 was 360 horsepower. *Mike Mueller*

The GSX featured one of the original muscle car era's highest-profile images.

1971 GS-455

1971 GS-455

GS 455

Model availability	two-door hardtop and convertible
Wheelbase	112 inches
Length	203.2 inches
Width	77.3 inches
Height	53.5 inches (hardtop), 53.9 inches (convertible)
Base price	$3,4493 (hardtop), $3,639 (convertible)
Track (front/rear, in inches)	59.4/59
Wheels	14x6 stamped steel
Suspension	independent upper/lower A-arms, coil springs and stabilizer bar in front; solid axle, control arms and coil springs in back
Steering	recirculating ball
Brakes	four-wheel drums
Engine	315-horsepower 455-cubic-inch V-8, std.
Bore & stroke	4.3125 x 3.90 inches
Compression	8.5:1
Fuel delivery	single Rochester four-barrel carburetor
Transmission	four-speed manual or Turbo Hydra-Matic automatic
Axle ratio	3.08:1
Production	9,170 (includes GSX and GS-350)

Bucket seats and a full console were optional for the 1971 GS.
Mike Mueller

1971

While all Skylark Gran Sports, big-block or small-, were plainly identified on paper simply as "GS" models in 1971, fender badges still included displacement numbers. The standard GS engine, available for both hardtop and convertible, was the 350 small-block, now rated at 260 horsepower due to corporatewide compression cuts. Revised advertised outputs for the optional 455 V-8 and its Stage 1 brother were 315 and 345 horsepower, respectively.

The GSX hardtop returned in similar fashion but now was offered with either engine, 350 or 455. Total production in 1971 was 124. New this year were six available colors: Stratomist Blue, Arctic White, Lime Mist, Platinum Mist, Cortez Gold, and Bittersweet Mist. Other special-order shades were reportedly possible too.

A column-shift three-speed manual was standard behind the 350 small-block, and no floorshift examples were produced. Options again included a floorshift four-speed and Turbo Hydra-Matic 350 automatic. Total small-block GS production in 1971 was 5,986 hardtops and 656 convertibles. Of those hardtops, 25 had three-speeds, 358 had four-speeds, and 5,603 were automatics. The convertible breakdown read 6 three-speeds, 51 four-speeds, and 599 TH-350s.

Transmission choices for the 455-equipped GS numbered two: a four-speed stick and the Turbo Hydra-Matic 400 automatic. Of the 1,481 455 hardtops built for 1971, 103 had the manual and 1,378 the automatic. Another 165 convertibles also were sold: 18 with four-speeds, 147 with automatics. Stage 1 production was 801 hardtops (114 four-speeds, 687 automatics) and 81 convertibles (9 four-speeds, 72 automatics).

Above
Buick dropped 1,481 350-horse 455 V-8s into Gran Sport hardtops in 1971. Notice the plain-Jane "poverty caps" on this 1971 GS. *Mike Mueller*

Inset
While Buick chose to only use the simple name "GS" in promotional paperwork in 1971, the cars themselves at least still featured fender badges that appropriately spelled out engine displacement: "455" or "350." *Mike Mueller*

Right
Functional hood scoops were standard again for the Skylark GS in 1971. Standard for the big-block Gran Sport that year was a 315-horsepower 455 V-8. The optional Stage 1 455 (shown here) found its way into 801 1971 GS hardtops. *Mike Mueller*

Above
Production of Stage 1 GS convertibles in 1971 was only 81. *Mike Mueller*

Below left
Stage 1 455 output for 1971 was a still-healthy 345 horsepower. *Mike Mueller*

Below right
The 1971 Gran Sport's standard bench seat is demonstrated here on this rare Stage 1 convertible. *Mike Mueller*

Above
The GSX returned for 1971 and that year could've been ordered with either big- or small-block power. More paint choices also appeared, including this special-order red. *Mike Mueller*

Right
Stage 1 buyers again could choose between a four-speed manual or Turbo Hydra-Matic automatic transmission in 1971. *Mike Mueller*

Far right
Bucket seats, a console with tachometer, and a Hurst-shifted four-speed are present and accounted for inside this fully loaded 1971 GSX. The Rallye steering wheel was standard for all Gran Sports that year. *Mike Mueller*

1972 GS-455

1972 GS-455

Model availability	two-door hardtop and convertible
Wheelbase	112 inches
Length	203.3 inches
Width	76.8 inches
Height	53.5 inches (hardtop), 53.8 inches (convertible)
Base price	$3,4493 (hardtop), $3,639 (convertible)
Track (front/rear, in inches)	59.4/59
Wheels	14x6 stamped steel
Suspension	independent upper/lower A-arms, coil springs and stabilizer bar in front; solid axle, control arms and coil springs in back
Steering	recirculating ball
Brakes	four-wheel drums
Engine	225-horsepower 455-cubic-inch V-8, std.
Bore & stroke	4.3125 x 3.90 inches
Compression	8.5:1
Fuel delivery	single Rochester four-barrel carburetor
Transmission	four-speed manual or Turbo Hydra-Matic automatic
Axle ratio	3.08:1
Production	8,575 (includes small-block GS)

1972

Net-rated output figures dropped published power further for the last of the Skylark-based Gran Sports in 1972. The standard 350 small-block now was tagged at 195 horsepower, the 455 at 225, and the Stage 1 at 270. Other mechanicals carried over from 1971, as did the GSX package, however briefly. Only 44 were sold.

Total 1972 production was 8,575, down from 9,170 the previous year. Breakdowns included 5,896 hardtops and 645 convertibles fitted with the standard 350 small-block. The total for 455-equipped models was 1,225 (1,099 hardtops, 126 convertibles), and the Stage 1 count was 809, consisting of 728 hardtops and 81 convertibles. Only 21 standard three-speed small-block Gran Sports were built this year: 16 hardtops and 5 convertibles.

Left
As in 1971, the 1972 Skylark Gran Sport appeared in hardtop and convertible forms with either engine, 350 small-block or 455 big-block.

Below
Total Gran Sport production fell to 8,575 in 1972. Notice the optional sunroof on this 1972 GS hardtop.

1973 GS

1973

Last used by Buick in 1958, the revered Century nameplate replaced Skylark as GM's divisions reintroduced their midsize platforms for 1973. Still rolling on a 112-inch wheelbase, the new Century was some 200 pounds heavier than its predecessor thanks to increases in width, height, and length. Extra attention to noise insulation also helped tip the scales further to the right. More than one driver lauded the 1973 Gran Sport for its quietness, something not commonly associated with earlier muscle cars. But this was Buick's brand of muscle,

Below
Total Gran Sport production for 1973 was 6,637, including 728 Stage 1 models, shown here. The base engine was a 350 small-block topped by a two-barrel carburetor, a GS first. *Mike Mueller*

1973 GS

Model availability	two-door Century Colonnade coupe
Wheelbase	112 inches
Length	208.4 inches
Width	78 inches
Height	53.7 inches
Base price	GS package cost $173
Track (front/rear, in inches)	61.5/60.7
Suspension	independent upper/lower A-arms, coil springs and stabilizer bar in front; solid axle, control arms, coil springs and stabilizer bar in back
Steering	recirculating ball
Brakes	front discs, rear drums
Engine	150-horsepower 350-cubic-inch V-8, std.
Bore & stroke	3.80 x 3.85 inches
Compression	8.5:1
Fuel delivery	single two-barrel carburetor
Transmission	three-speed manual
Axle ratio	3.08:1
Production	6,637

"a pleasant blend of performance and elegant luxury," according to one magazine review.

To leave the lot with a Gran Sport in 1973, a Buick buyer had to add the GS package to a Century Colonnade coupe—no more individual model series. Along with Gran Sport identification in a blacked-out grille, on the deck lid, and down the rear quarters, the GS option also included heavy-duty suspension with stiffer sway bars front and rear. All Century models featured standard front disc brakes.

Something other than a four-barrel made its way beneath a Gran Sport's hood for the first time in 1973 as the base engine this year was a two-barrel-fed 350 small-block rated at 150 horsepower. Next up on the options list was a 190-horsepower 350 with a four-barrel carb and dual exhausts. Dual exhausts were included in the deal when the 225-horsepower 455 big-block was ordered. While this V-8 was also available in most Buicks in 1973, the still-hot Stage 1 version, now rated at 270 horsepower,

was limited to the Gran Sport. Optional transmissions for all Gran Sports included a Hurst-shifted four-speed manual and the two Turbo Hydra-Matic automatics.

Production of 350-equipped (two- and four-barrel) Gran Sports in 1973 was 4,930. Another 979 225-horsepower 455 model were built, and the count for the relatively potent Stage 1 was 728.

Above
The Century nameplate reappeared in 1973 for Buick's restyled midsize models, and the Gran Sport variation reverted back to its original status as an options group. Only a GS Colonnade coupe was offered. *Mike Mueller*

Below left
Buick's last 455 Stage 1 V-8 was net-rated at 270 horsepower in 1973, making it one of Detroit's last surviving muscle mills. Only Pontiac's 455 Super Duty V-8 was more formidable that year. *Mike Mueller*

Below right
Either a Hurst-shifted four-speed (shown here) or GM's excellent Turbo Hydra-Matic automatic transmission went behind the 455 Stage 1 big-block in 1973. *Mike Mueller*

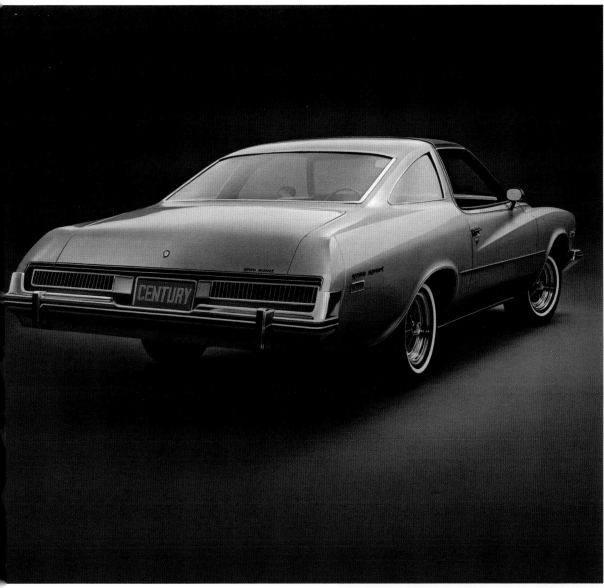

1974 GS

1974 GS	
Model availability	two-door Century Colonnade coupe
Wheelbase	112 inches
Length	208.4 inches
Width	79 inches
Height	53.5 inches
Base price	GS package cost $175
Track (front/rear, in inches)	61.5/60.7
Suspension	independent upper/lower A-arms, coil springs and stabilizer bar in front; solid axle, control arms, coil springs and stabilizer bar in back
Steering	recirculating ball
Brakes	front discs, rear drums
Engine	150-horsepower 350-cubic-inch V-8, std.
Bore & stroke	3.80 x 3.85 inches
Compression	8.5:1
Fuel delivery	single two-barrel carburetor
Transmission	three-speed manual
Axle ratio	3.08:1
Production	3,355

Above
Buick's last big-block Gran Sport was built in 1974. The Century GS rolled on into 1975, but only with small-block (and V-6) power. A 1974 GS is shown here.

1974

The book closed on the big-block Gran Sport this year as the 455 V-8 was limited to big Buicks beginning in 1975. Thus came an end to the Stage 1 story too. Engine availability rolled over unchanged from 1973 with one exception: an optional 455 two-barrel was offered for the last big-block GS. The production breakdown was 2,298 small-blocks, 141 455 two-barrels, 438 455 four-barrels, and 478 Stage 1s. Another 1,288 Century Gran Sports (some with V-6 power) followed in 1975, but it just wasn't the same without the Stage 1 around to maximize muscle.

The book closed on the big-block Gran Sport this year as the 455 V-8 was limited to big Buicks beginning in 1975.

07

Above
1967 Camaro SS 350

Middle
1968 Camaro SS 396

Right
1973 Camaro Type LT

Hold Your Horses

07

Chevrolet Camaro SS 1967–1972

A world without Camaros? Say it ain't so. Chevrolet's once-popular compact cruiser surely qualified as an American icon, or at least it did from a pop culture point of view. But that didn't stop GM execs from closing the book on its venerable rear-drive F-body legacy in 2002, retiring both the Camaro and its corporate cousin, Pontiac's Firebird, in the process.

→ Camaros were built in two Chevrolet plants from 1967 to 1971, one in Norwood, Ohio, the other in Van Nuys, California. Only Norwood rolled out Camaros from 1972 to 1975. F-body production restarted at Van Nuys in February 1976, and both plants again shared the load until the Norwood plant closed in 1987. Van Nuys carried on alone up through 1992.

→ The Camaro legacy constituted four generations: 1967–1969, 1970–1981, 1981–1992, and 1993–2002. All fourth-generation Camaros were built in Ste. Therese, Quebec, beginning in January 1993.

→ Journalists got acquainted with Chevrolet's sixth model line on September 12, 1966, as Camaro officially joined Corvair, Chevy II, Chevelle, Corvette, and the full-size group.

→ Chevrolet's biggest small-block V-8 to date, at 350-cubic-inches, debuted for 1967 but only beneath Camaro hoods and only as part of the Super Sport package. All other Chevys (save, of course, the Corvair) started offering the optional 350 V-8 in 1968.

→ The first big-block Camaro SS 396 appeared in November 1966.

→ The Camaro Super Sport retired after 1972 and was replaced by the Type LT.

Those of you out there still sniffling back the tears need only look to the car-killing sport-utility to find the villain in this tragic tale. Domestic two-door sport coupes have been a slow-dying breed for quite a while now thanks to Americans' increasingly infectious desire to drive trucks. Ford was among the first to give up the ghost when it issued last rites to its midsize Thunderbird in 1997. About that same time, it became obvious to anyone with eyes in Detroit that there was only room around town for one pony car. Mustangs had been outselling Camaros annually since 1993, and by 1997 the margin had grown to 2-1 in favor of the breed's progenitor.

Five years later, Mustang owners found themselves galloping on alone—but not for long. Dry those eyes, Chevy fans. As we speak, a reborn Camaro is waiting in the wings to once more run wild with its longtime rival. And just like that, it'll be 1967 all over again.

Up to that point 40 years ago, Ford's original Mustang also had owned the road. Nothing in the affordable compact arena could compare, not even Plymouth's Valiant-based Barracuda, the comparable little fun machine that actually burst out of the gates first in April 1964. The innovative vehicle that helped inspire the Mustang, Chevrolet's sporty Corvair Monza, was never a threat, nor was the diminutive Chevy II, its stylish Super Sport alter-ego notwithstanding. Any hopes of disrupting this one-horse race hinged on GM's development of its own new breed. It was time to saddle up or sit out.

Plans for a suitable competitor began per-

Opposite
An unknown number of pace car replicas were created for promotional purposes to mark the Camaro Super Sport's first appearance as the Indy 500 pacer in 1967. All were white with blue stripes and had either 350 or 396 V-8s.

Original plans to name Chevrolet's F-body the "Panther" fell through, leaving a more traditional approach: yet another moniker beginning with the letter "C." *Mike Mueller*

colating in the summer of 1964, fired by soaring sales of a runaway pony that many GM execs—including Styling Vice President Bill Mitchell and Irv Rybicki, Chevy chief designer, had poked fun at early on, just before they started eating its dust. Fortunately, others took the Mustang seriously from the get-go. Recognizing a new sensation when he saw it, Henry Haga in Chevrolet Number Two Studio already had various sketches done when General Manager Bunkie Knudsen got the go-ahead in August to add yet another new model to an already crowded lineup.

Curiously, Knudsen a few years before had shot down Rybicki's idea for a relatively upscale personal coupe based on the Chevy II, claiming that he liked the proposal loads but the company simply didn't need another new model, not with Chevrolet's fifth, the Chevelle, then being readied for its 1964 debut. As Rybicki later recalled, his proposal mimicked much of the Mustang's makeup at a time when no one at GM even knew Ford's world-shaker was in the works. But it was not to be.

Some GM execs wanted to put the Super Nova showcar, widely publicized in 1964, into production as a response to Ford's Mustang.

Same for the sensational Super Nova, another sporty proposal based on the Chevy II platform. Transformed from clay into running concept car by Haga's team late in 1963, the Super Nova was turning heads at the New York Auto Show a few weeks before the Mustang made its historic Big Apple debut at the 1964 World's Fair. This time, Knudsen was all in favor of a rush to market, as were Mitchell and his predecessor, retired GM Styling mogul Harley Earl. GM President John Gordon, however, was not particularly fond of sporty cars, and thus it became his turn to do the shooting. Better to burn out than to fade away.

Fortunately, within four months, all attitudes at General Motors had merged onto the same page, this after more than 100,000 Mustangs had hit the streets on the way to the greatest first-year sales effort ever seen in Detroit. Knudsen was instructed in August 1964 to have Chevrolet's direct response, called the F-car, up

and running by the fall of 1966, a tight deadline for sure. Haga's studio wasted little time sculpting a prototype, code-named XP-836.

Most of the final look showed up in December in the form of a full-size clay that followed in the Mustang's hoofprints in nearly all aspects. The hood was long, the rear deck short, and overall impressions were truly sporty. What set the F-car apart big time was its softly contoured shape, which instantly made Ford's original pony car look stiff and boxy in comparison. As for basic dimensions, the Mustang's new challenger was longer, lower, and wider, and predictably featured a little more passenger room inside.

Also beneath that beautiful skin, once it was morphed into metal, was unibody construction, the same as the Mustang but with additional notable differences. Whereas the existing Ford was fully unitized with stamped steel sections welded onto the body up front to carry the

Thirty years of Camaro history was marked in 1997 by an appearance at Indianapolis as the pace car (seen in foreground) for NASCAR's Brickyard 400. Four other Camaros have paced the Indy 500 over the years: (from left to right) 1967, 1969, 1982, and 1993.

engine and suspension components, Chevrolet's newcomer featured a strong, ladder-type front subframe that bolted up to the body. To help hit the short deadline, F-car project engineers simply borrowed this platform from the next-generation Chevy II being prepared for its 1968 introduction. Drivetrains, too, transferred over with no fuss or muss, as did the Chevy II's Mono Plate springs in back. But in the F-car's case, those single-leaf springs were shorter and not parallel—their rear-mounting locations were moved outward to make ample room for an 18-gallon gas tank.

As for its name, company insiders at first called Chevy's new pony car "Panther," a moniker also picked up by the press early on. But this overly aggressive tag didn't stick—after all, it didn't begin with a "C." Reportedly, Merchandising Manager Bob Lund and GM Car and Truck Group Vice President Ed Rollert put their heads together and came up with "Camaro," a traditionally correct word that, in Lund's opinion, had "kind of a ring" to it. In French, it meant "friend," "comrade," or "pal." But in Spanish, it referred to a "shrimp-like creature." Guess which image Chevrolet was counting on.

When Chevrolet General Manager Pete Estes (who had taken over from corporate-ladder-climbing Bunkie Knudsen in July 1965) officially announced the Camaro during a press conference in Detroit on June 29, 1966, he allowed a group of six Michigan State University cheerleaders, holding large block letters, to spell things out. Or so he hoped. Their first try resulted in "CAMAOR" after the last two coeds apparently took wrong turns on the way into the conference room. Once corrected, the sweater-clad lineup still left many witnesses scratching their heads, at least until they were all given English-French dictionaries and encouraged to ignore the Spanish translation.

Calling the 1967 Camaro a "four-passen-

ger package of excitement," Estes went on to explain how the French translation fit because "the real mission of our new automobile [is] to be a close companion to its owner, tailored to reflect his or her individual tastes." Again, like the Mustang, the new Camaro was meant to represent different cars to different drivers, with a budget-conscious six-cylinder starting things off in the basic package. But a flair for fun was the prime attraction, a fact Estes wasn't about to overlook. "The Camaro is aimed at the fast-growing personal sports-type market that was pioneered by Chevrolet's Corvette in 1953 and further defined by the Corvair Monza in the 1960s," he added.

Indeed, the Camaro needed little time after its official press introduction, held September 12, 1966, to impress witnesses with its wide-ranging sporting potential, which in some minds created quite a dilemma for Chevy customers. "The problem is not whether to buy the Camaro," claimed a March 1967 *Car Life* re-

port, "but what kind of Camaro, for [this model] probably wears more faces than any other single car now made."

The 327-cubic-inch V-8 was available from the beginning, as was the bigger, better 350 small-block, created by stroking the 327. The 350 V-8 was not only exclusive to the Camaro in 1967, it also was restricted to the Super Sport rendition, which everyone knew just had to make an appearance in keeping with yet another established tradition. Enhancing the Camaro SS attraction further was the Rally Sport package, a cosmetic option that among other things added trendy hideaway headlights. Additional choices included the SS 396 model, a big-block bully that appeared in November 1966 and acted more like a Clydesdale than a pony. A few weeks later, the legendary Z/28 also became part of the mix, stirring buyers' blood even more.

By New Year's Day 1967, it was Mustang owners doing all the dusty dining.

Above
The last Camaro was also Chevrolet's 35th, inspiring a special anniversary package for SS coupes and convertibles in 2002. Bright Rally Red paint was the only shade available for these commemorative models.

Right
Detroit watchers by 2007 were quite familiar with Chevrolet's latest Camaro, a concept car that teased pony car fans at auto shows for a couple of years before plans to transform it into a production reality were finally announced. Here a Camaro concept rests at the 2006 Atlanta Auto Show. *Mike Mueller*

1967 Camaro SS

1967

The first Camaro was offered with or without a roof and was segregated into two lines, one with the base 230-cubic-inch Turbo-Thrift six-cylinder, the other with a standard 327-cube Turbo-Fire V-8. Output ratings were 140 and 210 horsepower, respectively. A 155-horsepower 250-cubic-inch six (RPO L22) and 275-horsepower 327 (L30) were optional. The L30 V-8 used a four-barrel carburetor, its 210-horsepower little brother a two-barrel.

As mentioned, the 1967 Camaro Super Sport came standard with the new 295-horsepower 350 V-8, topped by a four-barrel carburetor and dressed up with various chrome pieces. One couldn't be had without the other, thus the whole package was listed under RPO L48, identified as the "Camaro SS w/295hp Turbo-Fire 350-cubic-inch engine." The model was called the "SS 350," though that nomenclature only appeared in the grille and on the fuel

Model availability	two-door sport coupe, two-door convertible
Wheelbase	108 inches
Length	184.7 inches
Width	72.5 inches
Height	51.4 inches
Curb weight	3,269 pounds (SS 350 coupe)
Price	RPO L48 cost $210.65, RPO L35 cost $263.30, RPO L78 cost $500.30 (base V-8 coupe: $2,572; base V-8 convertible: $2,809)
Track (front/rear, in inches)	59/58.9
Wheels	14x6 stamped steel
Tires	D70 red-stripe Firestone
Suspension	independent unequal A-arms, coil springs and stabilizer bar in front; single-leaf springs, solid axle with right-side traction bar in back
Steering	recirculating ball
Brakes	hydraulic drums, front and rear
Engine	290-horsepower 350-cubic-inch L48 V-8, 325-horsepower 396 cubic-inch L35 V-8, 375-horsepower 396 cubic-inch L78 V-8
Bore & stroke	4.00 x 3.48 inches, 350 V-8; 4.094 x 3.76 inches, 396 V-8
Compression	10.25:1 (L48 and L35 V-8s), 11:1 (L78 V-8)
Fuel delivery	single four-barrel carburetor
Transmission	three-speed manual standard behind L48; special three-speed standard behind L35 and L78
Axle ratio	3.31:1 standard w/L48; 3.07:1 standard w/L35 and L78
Production	29,270 (L48), 4,003 (L35), 1,138 (L78)

Left
Contrary to the Mustang's fully welded unitized body/frame platform, the Camaro's foundation featured an independent front subframe that bolted up to its body structure. Single-leaf springs were standard in back in 1967.

filler cap. Simple SS identification showed up elsewhere on the fenders and steering wheel. Additional dress-up touches included a color-keyed (black or white) accent stripe around the nose, and the rest of the SS deal consisted of a special hood with simulated vents, red-stripe wide-oval tires on wider 14x6JK wheels, and the F41 heavy-duty suspension.

A yeoman three-speed stick (on the column) was standard behind the L48 small-block. Drivetrain options included the beefed-up, floor-shift M13 three-speed, the wide-ratio M20 four-speed, the close-ratio M21 four-speed, and the Powerglide automatic. Buyers with a few more bucks to spend also could have added

Chevy's new front disc brakes, which again included those attractive Rally wheels. And let's not forget the aforementioned Rally Sport group, a popular package offered for all Camaro models in 1967.

Priced at $105.35, the snazzy RS option (RPO Z22) dressed up both ends of a coupe or convertible, with a distinctive rear taillamp treatment joining those electrically controlled disappearing headlights. RS taillights were solid red with flat-black trim, compared to standard units that used bright trim and incorporated white backup lenses. On Rally Sport models, backup lights were moved down into the rear valance panel. Same for the turn signals up front, which

also dropped down into the valance from their regular position in the grille.

Camaro Rally Sports were adorned further with lower bodyside moldings atop black-finished sills (deleted on certain dark-colored cars), bright wheel opening trim and roof drip moldings, and color-keyed upper bodyside stripes. Appropriate badges were included, too,

The 1967 Camaro shared its foundation, as well as various drivetrain components, with the next-generation Nova then being developed for 1968.

though these were superseded whenever RPO Z22 was applied to a Super Sport Camaro—"SS" took precedence over "RS."

The Z22 option was available for either Super Sport, small- or big-block. Like the SS 350, the meaner, nastier SS 396 Camaro was identified on the options list by its engine code, beginning with RPO L35, the tag for the 325-horsepower hydraulic-lifter 396 V-8. A second Mk IV big-block, the bodacious 375-horsepower L78, also was offered, making Chevy's new pony car the indisputable leader of the pack. Ford's equally new big-block Mustang GT, with its comparably tame 390-cubic-inch FE-series V-8, simply was no match for the L78 Camaro in 1967.

The snazzy RS option (RPO Z22) dressed up both ends of a coupe or convertible, with a distinctive rear taillamp treatment joining those electrically controlled disappearing headlights.

Adding the Rally Sport package to a 1967 Camaro Super Sport meant hiding the headlights away behind a fully blacked-out grille. Notice the preproduction bodyside stripe.

Camaro Rally Sports were adorned further with lower bodyside moldings atop black-finished sills.

Left
The Waikiki show car Camaro featured a surfboard rack, rattan seat inserts, and teakwood side panels.

Below
Based on a 1968 Camaro, the Caribe show car featured a headerless windshield and a small pickup box behind that roll bar.

Top
The 350 V-8 was only offered for the Camaro Super Sport in 1967. Base price for the SS 350 package was $210.65. *Mike Mueller*

Above
A bumblebee nose stripe was standard for the Camaro Super Sport in 1967. "SS 350" identification appeared in the grille and on the fuel filler cap in back. *Mike Mueller*

Right
Production for the Camaro SS 350 in 1967 was 29,270, including both coupes and convertibles. *Mike Mueller*

Top left
Created by boring the 327 V-8, the 350 small-block debuted between Camaro fenders in 1967. It appeared in other Chevrolet models the following year. *Mike Mueller*

Above
Mag-style wheel covers (RPO N96) cost $73.75 in 1967. Production was 6,630. *Mike Mueller*

Left
The 350-cubic-inch Turbo-Fire V-8 produced 295 horsepower in 1967. Chrome dress-up was part of the Super Sport package. *Mike Mueller*

1967 Camaro Super Sport came standard with the new 295-horsepower 350 V-8.

Above
Two 396 Turbo-Jet V-8s were offered for the 1967 Camaro SS: the 325-horsepower L35 and 375-horsepower L78. The former featured solid lifters and 11:1 compression. *Mike Mueller*

Top right
The big-block SS 396 joined the Camaro lineup in November 1966 and instantly blew Ford's 390 Mustang away. *Mike Mueller*

Right
The L35 396 big-block added $263.30 to a Camaro SS bottom line in 1967. L35 production that year was 4,003. *Mike Mueller*

The bodacious 375-horsepower L78 also was offered, making Chevy's new pony car the indisputable leader of the pack.

Top Left
A walnut-grained sport steering wheel was a $31.60 option in 1967. *Mike Mueller*

Top right
The U17 instrumentation option, available in 1967 for console-equipped V-8 Camaros only, added this gauge cluster, along with a tachometer. Price for the U17 option was $79. *Mike Mueller*

Left
Attractive Rally wheels with bright trim rings and center caps were included along with optional front disc brakes in 1967. *Mike Mueller*

1968 Camaro SS

1968

Technical updates this year included staggering the rear shock absorbers on all models to help cure an inherent wheel hop problem that, in 1967, had required the installation of a single traction control bar on the right rear corner of V-8 models. Combining the staggered shocks with new multiple-leaf rear springs beneath 1968 Camaro Super Sports did away with the need for the traction bar installation.

Exterior changes were typically minor. Vent windows were deleted, and government-mandated side marker lights were added. The Rally Sport package returned and once more could have been combined with Super Sport equipment to make for one way-cool Camaro. SS

touches carried over in similar fashion, with the most notable difference involving the deletion of the "350" identification from the grille and gas cap on small-block models. New, too, were the SS 396's simulated hood vents, which contained four equally fake carburetor stacks. The 1968 SS 350's vents were the same as those seen the previous year on all Camaro Super Sport hoods.

The Super Sport's bumblebee striping (listed separately as RPO D91) up front made an encore appearance, but this time around it could have been superseded by a new set of stripes that ran over the nose and turned backward down the body-sides, ending near the doors' trailing edges. Optional fiberglass front and rear spoilers (D80) also appeared midyear.

Model availability	two-door sport coupe, two-door convertible
Wheelbase	108 inches
Length	184.7 inches
Width	72.5 inches
Height	51.4 inches
Curb weight	3,855 pounds (SS 396 coupe)
Price	RPO L48 cost $210.65, RPO L35 cost $263.30, RPO L34 cost $368.65, RPO L78 cost $500.30, RPO L89 cost $868.95 (base V-8 coupe: $2,670; base V-8 convertible: $2,908)
Track (front/rear, in inches)	59/58.9
Wheels	14x6 stamped steel
Tires	F70 x 14
Suspension	independent unequal A-arms, coil springs and stabilizer bar in front; multi-leaf springs, solid axle with staggered shocks in back
Steering	recirculating ball
Brakes	hydraulic drums, front and rear
Engine	290-horsepower 350-cubic-inch L48 V-8, 325-horsepower 396 cubic-inch L35 V-8, 350-horsepower L34 V-8, 375-horsepower 396 cubic-inch L78 V-8, 375-horsepower aluminum-head 396 cubic-inch L89 V-8
Bore & stroke	4.00 x 3.48 inches, 350 V-8; 4.094 x 3.76 inches, 396 V-8
Compression	10.25:1 (L48, L34 and L35 V-8s), 11:1 (L78 and L89 V-8)
Fuel delivery	single four-barrel carburetor
Transmission	three-speed manual standard behind 350 V-8; special three-speed standard behind 396 V-8
Axle ratio	3.31:1 standard w/L48, 3.07:1 standard w/L35, 3.31:1 standard w/L34, 3.55:1 standard w/L78 and L89
Production	12,496 (L48), 10,773 (L35), 2,579 (L34), 4,575 (L78), 272 (L89)

Left
A poor man's Corvette? Not a bad description for a Camaro SS convertible, small-block or big, in 1968.

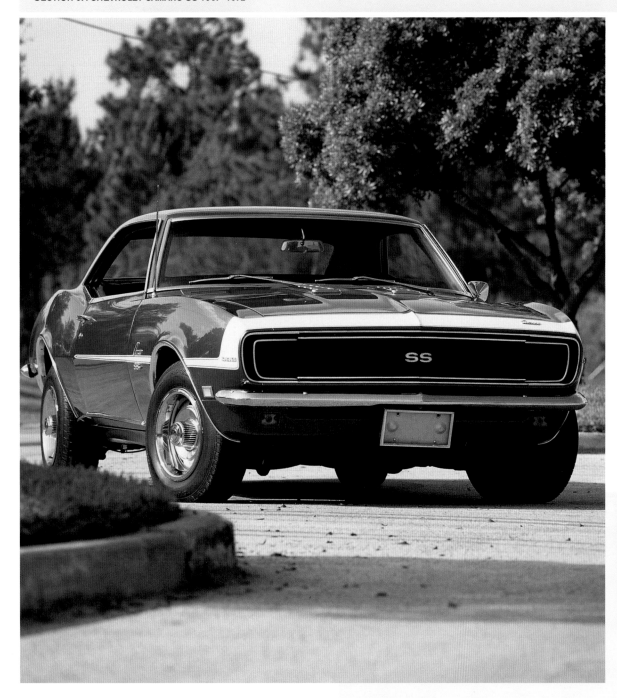

Super Sport drivetrains rolled over with one new addition, as the 350-horsepower L35 396 joined its L34 and L78 big-block brothers. Limited to the L34 only in 1967, the Turbo Hydra-Matic automatic transmission was made available as well behind the L35 in 1968, as was a four-speed manual. Weight-saving aluminum heads (RPO L89) debuted, but their heavy price tag ($868.95) inhibited their popularity. Only 272 sets were sold.

Above left
This 1968 SS 396 is one of 4,575 equipped with the 375-horsepower L78 big-block. RPO L78 added $500.30 to the Super Sport sticker that year. *Mike Mueller*

Above right
Big-block Super Sport hoods in 1968 received unique simulated vents featuring four fake carburetor stacks in each. *Mike Mueller*

Above
A restyled nose and the new ZL2 Cowl Induction hood heightened the Camaro SS attraction in 1969.

1969 Camaro SS

1969 Camaro SS

Model availability	two-door sport coupe, two-door convertible
Wheelbase	108 inches
Length	186 inches
Width	74 inches
Height	51.6 inches, coupe; 51.5 inches, convertible
Curb weight	3,490 pounds (SS 396 coupe)
Price	RPO Z27 (Super Sport Package w/base 350 V-8) cost $295.95, L35 V-8 added $63.20, L34 V-8 added $184.35, L78 V-8 added $316, L89 V-8 added $710.95 (base V-8 coupe: $2,727; base V-8 convertible: $2,940)
Track (front/rear, in inches)	59.6/59.5
Wheels	14x7
Tires	F70 Wide Oval with raised white letters
Suspension	independent unequal A-arms, coil springs and stabilizer bar in front; multi-leaf springs, solid axle with staggered shocks in back
Steering	recirculating ball
Brakes	power front discs, rear drums
Engine	300-horsepower 350-cubic-inch L48 V-8, 325-horsepower 396 cubic-inch L35 V-8, 350-horsepower 396 cubic-inch L34 V-8, 375-horsepower 396 cubic-inch L78 V-8, 375-horsepower aluminum-head 396 cubic-inch L89 V-8
Bore & stroke	4.00 x 3.48 inches, 350 V-8; 4.094 x 3.76 inches, 396 V-8
Compression	10.25:1 (L48 and L35 V-8s), 11:1 (L78 V-8)
Fuel delivery	single four-barrel carburetor
Transmission	three-speed manual standard behind L48; special three-speed standard behind L35 and L78
Axle ratio	3.31:1 standard w/L48, 3.07:1 standard w/L35, 3.31:1 standard w/L34, 3.55:1 standard w/L78 and L89
Production	22,339 (L48), 6,752 (L35), 2,018 (L34), 4,889 (L78), 311 (L89)

1969

Chevrolet's pony car was treated to a major facelift for its third edition, and most critics still agree the change was for the better in a big way. Looking more aggressive all around, the 1969 Camaro Super Sport appeared even hotter when topped off in front with the new ZL2 Cowl Induction hood, a fully functional unit designed by Larry Shinoda. Priced at $79, this lid was limited to SS, Z/28, and COPO applications. Total ZL2 production for 1969 was 10,026. New, too, was an optional body-colored Endura front bumper (RPO VE3), a $42.15 option that attracted 12,650 buyers that year.

The Rally Sport package carried over in similar fashion for 1969, but the Super Sport deal was restructured. Listed as RPO Z27, it included a 300-horse 350 small-block backed by a three-speed manual transmission, special suspension, F70 wide-oval rubber on 14x7 wheels, power front disc brakes, a unique hood, sport striping, and familiar SS identification, all priced rather nicely at $295.95. Creating a Camaro SS 396 was simply a matter of replacing the Z27 group's 350 V-8 with one of the same four optional big-blocks listed in 1968. The aluminum-head L89/L78 combo was again

Above
Chevrolet marked the Camaro's second appearance as an Indianapolis 500 pace car in 1969 with a run of replicas, officially listed under RPO Z11. Z11 production was 3,675. *Mike Mueller*

Far left
As in 1967, Indy pace car Camaros were fitted with both 350 small-blocks and 396 big-block V-8s in 1969. The actual pace car used a 375-horsepower L78 396, shown here. *Mike Mueller*

Left
Power front disc brakes were standard for the Camaro Super Sport in 1969. *Mike Mueller*

Looking more aggressive all around, the 1969 Camaro Super Sport appeared even hotter when topped off in front with the new ZL2 Cowl Induction hood.

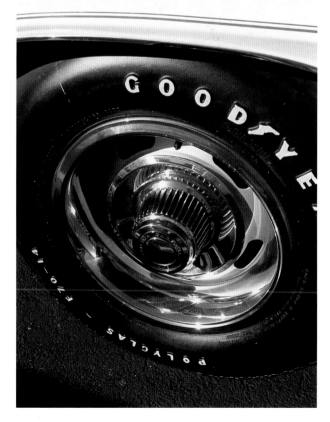

a rarely seen installation, with only 311 made in 1969. Even fewer and farther between was the new JL8 power-assisted four-wheel disc option, priced at $500.30. Only 206 JL8 applications are known for 1969 Camaros.

Last but certainly not least, a Camaro SS was chosen to pace the Indianapolis 500 for the second time in 1969. In 1967, a blue-striped, white-painted SS/RS convertible had led the field around the Brickyard, and Chevrolet followed that up with an unknown number of pace car replicas, all colored similarly with either 350 small-block or 396 big-block V-8s. Two years later, a fully documented run of Indy pace car replicas appeared, officially listed under RPO Z11. All 3,675 of these were SS/RS convertibles done in Dover White paint with Hugger Orange stripes and orange hound's-tooth interiors. Rally wheels and Cowl Induction hoods were included in all cases too.

A similarly adorned pace car replica coupe appeared with many of the same features, including both Super Sport and Rally Sport equipment. A promotional package created for Chevrolet's Southwestern Branch Zone Office, this option was tabbed Z10. No production numbers are available; estimates claim as many as 200 or 300 Z10 coupes were released during the spring of 1969.

1969 COPO

1969 COPO

Model availability	two-door sport coupe
Wheelbase	108 inches
Length	186 inches
Width	74 inches
Height	51.6 inches
Weight	3,300 pounds (COPO 9560)
Price	COPO 9561 cost $489.45, COPO 9560 cost $4,160
Track (front/rear, in inches)	59.6/59.5
Wheels	14x7
Tires	F70 Wide Oval with raised white letters
Suspension	independent unequal A-arms, heavy-duty coil springs and stabilizer bar in front; heavy-duty leaf springs, solid axle with staggered shocks in back
Steering	recirculating ball
Brakes	power front discs, rear drums
Engine	425-horsepower 427-cubic-inch cast-iron L72 V-8 (COPO 9561), 430-horsepower 427 cubic-inch all-aluminum ZL-1 V-8 (COPO 9560)
Bore & stroke	4.25 x 3.76 inches
Compression	11:1 (L72), 12:1 (ZL-1)
Fuel delivery	780-cfm Holley four-barrel carburetor (L72), 850-cfm Holley double-pumper four-barrel carburetor (ZL 1)
Transmission	four-speed manual or heavy-duty Turbo Hydra-Matic automatic
Axle ratio	4.10:1 Positraction in heavy-duty 12-bolt housing
Production	69 (COPO 9560); COPO 9561 total not known—reportedly the Tonawanda engine plant produced 1,015 L72 V-8s for Camaro installations in 1969.

1969 COPO

Like the Chevelle, the Camaro was limited to no more than 400-cubic-inches of engine prior to 1970. But again, that rule didn't stop Vince Piggins, who once more worked his COPO magic in 1969. Two 427-powered Camaro models appeared that year thanks to Piggins and a little help from a pair of quick-thinking Chevy dealers.

Yenko Chevrolet in Pennsylvania had been transforming SS 396 pony cars into Corvette-powered screamers for two years when Don Yenko met with Chevy officials in the summer of 1968 to discuss the possibility of a factory-built 427 Camaro, a package that would save him the trouble of making further engine swaps. Piggins' response was COPO number 9561, which

specified the assembly-line installation of the Corvette's L72 427 big-block into a special run of 1969 Camaros.

Rated at 425 horsepower, the L72 featured 11:1 compression, a lumpy solid-lifter cam, closed-chamber heads, and a big 780-cfm Holley four-barrel on an aluminum dual-plane intake. Also included in the COPO 9561 deal was the ZL2 hood, a heavy-duty Harrison radiator, heavy-duty springs, and a beefed-up Posi-Traction rear with 4.10:1 gears. Optional 4.56:1 cogs were offered, and a buyer could opt for a four-speed or automatic transmission.

The production count for COPO 9561 is not known. Reportedly, Chevrolet's Tonawanda engine plant turned out 1,015 L72 427s (193

automatics, 822 manuals) for F-body installations in 1969, but how many of those actually went into Camaros sold to the public is undocumented. The first 100 L72 Camaros went to Yenko that year, and at least another 100 apparently followed later, all to be decked out in "Yenko S/C" striping. Berger Chevrolet in Michigan also reportedly took delivery of 50 COPO Camaros for its own special promotion.

No mystery whatsoever surrounds the second COPO F-body created in 1969. Essentially every nut and bolt on the famed ZL-1 Camaro has been fingerprinted and filed away for posterity. Exactly 69 of these big-block beasts were built (22 with automatics, 47 with four-speeds) using COPO number 9560, and all were clearly meant for racing duty only.

Unlike the comparatively tame L72, the ZL-1 427 plain and simply wasn't suited for civilized operation. Its beefed-up block (with cast-iron cylinder sleeves) and race-ready open-chamber heads were cast in weight-saving aluminum, as was its cavernous open-plenum intake and bell housing. Atop that intake was a huge 850-cfm Holley double-pumper, just the monster needed to keep the air/fuel flowing through the ZL-1's big valves and large round ports. A truly radical mechanical cam bumped those valves, and compression was a severe 12:1. Though Chevrolet laughingly rated the aluminum 427 at 430 horsepower, actual output easily soared past 500 horses at a dizzying 7,000 rpm.

Magazine road testers in 1969 wasted little time making a mockery of that token 430-horse tag. *Cars* testers managed a 13.16-second, 110.21-mile-per-hour quarter-mile pass in a four-speed ZL-1 Camaro right out of the box. Veteran racer Dick Harrell added headers (with full exhausts) and slicks to an automatic ZL-1 and produced an 11.85/119.06 run for *Super Stock* magazine. Uncapping the headers resulted in an 11.64/122.15 time slip, and later tests pushed the outside of the envelope even further into the

Fred Gibb ordered 50 COPO 9560 Camaros for his lot in LaHarpe, Illinois, with the first two arriving on New Year's Day 1969.

Right
Only 69 COPO 9560 Camaros were built in 1969: 22 with automatic transmissions, 47 with four-speeds. *Mike Mueller*

mid-teens. In 1971, a Pro Stock ZL-1 Camaro using twin Holley Dominator carbs set an AHRA record of 9.63 seconds at 143 miles per hour.

It was Dick Harrell, working in concert with Illinois Chevrolet dealer Fred Gibb, who inspired the ZL-1 Camaro's creation. Like Yenko, Gibb and Harrell approached Piggins in 1968 with a request to use COPO paperwork to build 427 Camaros, both L72s and ZL-1s. NHRA drag racing rules then specified that at least 50 examples of a particular production car be built to legalize that vehicle for stock class competition. Again, no problem.

Gibb ordered 50 COPO 9560 Camaros for his lot in LaHarpe, Illinois, with the first two arriving on New Year's Day 1969. Another 19 cars were built and went to various dealers across the country who, like Gibb, quickly found out how tough it was to market this high-strung, high-priced Camaro.

Base price for a typical V-8 Camaro in 1969 was $2,727. COPO 9560 tacked on an-

other $4,160.15, or just about the amount Gibb figured the entire car would cost. An official price was still in the works when he placed his order; he guessed that $4,900 would be tops. Nearly all the cars had arrived in Illinois before GM sent the bill in March. A bit overwhelmed, he somehow managed to send 20 ZL-1s back to the Norwood, Ohio, plant, where they were reluctantly redistributed.

Atop that intake was a huge 850-cfm Holley double-pumper, just the monster needed to keep the air/fuel flowing through the ZL-1's big valves and large round ports.

The COPO 9560 package included the ZL-1 427, ZL2 hood, Harrison radiator, transistorized ignition, heavy-duty suspension, and the equally tough 12-bolt Posi-Traction rear end with 4.10:1 gears. Boosting the bottom line further were a few mandatory options: power front discs and either a Muncie M21 close-ratio four-speed or a Turbo Hydra-Matic 400 auto box, both with aluminum cases. Chevy's mean-and-nasty M22 Rock Crusher four-speed was available at extra cost, as were those loud, cackling, chambered exhausts.

Above
A 12-bolt rear end containing 4.10:1 Posi-Traction gears was standard for the ZL-1 Camaro in 1969. *Mike Mueller*

Left
The 427-cubic-inch ZL-1 V-8's cylinder block and heads were all made of aluminum. Output was a token-rated 430 horsepower. Compression was 12:1. *Mike Mueller*

Right
In Chevrolet's COPO applications, the Corvette's 427-cubic-inch L72 V-8 was rated at 425 horsepower. Yenko people upped the advertised ante to 450 horses when they converted a 1969 COPO Camaro into a Yenko Super Car.
Mike Mueller

Below
COPO Camaros were used by Yenko Chevrolet to create a special run of Yenko S/C Camaros in 1969. Beneath that striped hood went a 450-horsepower Corvette big-block.
Mike Mueller

Above
The COPO 9561 engine was the Corvette's L72 427 big-block. The cylinder block and closed-chamber heads were cast-iron. The carburetor was a 780-cfm Holley four-barrel. *Mike Mueller*

Below
Save for the standard ZL2 hood, next to nothing gave away the identity of an L72 Camaro in 1969. This COPO 9561 car is fitted with optional spoilers front and rear. *Mike Mueller*

Above
Pure paradox—Chevrolet's Air Injection Reactor system was required in 1969, even on the high-performance L72 427, shown here. The race-ready ZL-1 also got this plumbing, although it undoubtedly didn't use it for long in 1969. *Mike Mueller*

1970-1/2 Camaro SS

1970

Pony car watchers eagerly awaited a veritable rebirth for GM's F-body in the fall of 1969. Hank Haga's styling studio had been busy fashioning a new and improved Camaro dating back to late 1966, and the word just couldn't help but get out. But when Chevrolet's new models were announced in September, a 1970 Camaro failed to appear. At first. Various glitches, combined with designers' desires to unveil no new F-body before its time, worked in concert to delay its introduction. Buyers initially were told to take 1969 leftovers and like it. Some didn't. Some sued.

Below
Various delays pushed the revamped Camaro's introduction back to February 1970, meaning the 1969 models carried over unchanged early in the year, as the license plate on this press release photo attests.

Model availability	two-door sport coupe
Wheelbase	108 inches
Length	188 inches
Width	74.4 inches
Height	50.5 inches
Curb weight	3,670 pounds (w/base 350 V-8)
Price	RPO Z27 (Super Sport Package w/base 350 V-8) cost $289.65, L34 V-8 added $152.75, L78 V-8 added $385.50 (base V-8 coupe: $2,839)
Track (front/rear, in inches)	61.3/60
Wheels	14x7
Tires	F70 Wide Oval with raised white letters
Suspension	independent unequal A-arms, coil springs and stabilizer bar in front; multi-leaf springs, solid axle with staggered shocks in back
Steering	recirculating ball
Brakes	power front discs, rear drums
Engine	300-horsepower 350-cubic-inch L48 V-8, 350-horsepower 402-cubic-inch L34 V-8, 375-horsepower 402 cubic-inch L78 V-8
Bore & stroke	4.00 x 3.48 inches, 350 V-8; 4.126 x 3.76 inches, 402 V-8
Compression	10.25:1 (L48 and L34 V-8s), 11:1 (L78 V-8)
Fuel delivery	single four-barrel carburetor
Transmission	four-speed manual or Turbo Hydra-Matic automatic
Axle ratio	3.31:1
Production	34,780 (L48), 1,864 (L34), 600 (L78)

GM execs meanwhile continued teasing the pony car–buying public. "We will give an entirely new direction to this market," claimed Chevrolet General Manager John De Lorean in a January 1970 *Motor Trend* interview. Chevy's upcoming new Camaro, in his words, would be "so sensational that I think we will more than make up for lost ground."

Indeed, almost all was forgiven when a totally fresh Camaro finally did emerge in February 1970. Low, long, and wide, this sleek machine was commonly praised for the way its expensive-looking facade and markedly upgraded feel masked its affordable, compact nature. Warmly welcomed updates beneath its sexy skin included standard front disc brakes.

Above
This preproduction mockup shows the small, individual bumpers that would be included as part of the 1970 Rally Sport package.

Left
A full-width bumper was standard for the Camaro SS in 1970.

Almost all was forgiven when a totally fresh Camaro finally did emerge in February 1970.

"Innovations in design and engineering make the new Camaro different from any car now offered," crowed John De Lorean.

"Innovations in design and engineering make the new Camaro different from any car now offered," crowed De Lorean during a press conference held on February 13, a Friday, no less. "Its expensive-looking body and highly improved handling, ride, and sound insulation create a completely new car." According to *Detroit News* columnist Bob Irvin, the so-called 1970-1/2 Camaro was "a beautiful looking automobile, one that makes the Mustang and Barracuda seem like last year's models."

Though a convertible version wasn't offered, the Super Sport and Rally Sport renditions remained. Still tabbed Z27, the SS package featured power brakes, special trim, F70 tires on 14x7 wheels, a black-painted grille, hideaway windshield wipers, and appropriate SS identification inside and out. The 350 small-block remained the base V-8 and produced 300 horsepower. Optional engines included the L34 and L78 big-blocks, once more rated at 350 and 375 horsepower, respectively. Both were labeled 396 Turbo-Jet V-8s even though a slight bore job had increased actual displacement to 402 cubic-inches. Transmission choices included a wide- or close-ratio four-speed or the Turbo Hydra-Matic automatic.

Less prominent without its hideaway headlights, the Z22 Rally Sport group nonetheless was quickly identified by the two small bumpers found up front in place of the standard Camaro's full-width unit. Various bright accents and black-out treatments, along with familiar RS identification, completed the deal.

1971 Camaro SS

1971 Camaro SS

Model availability	two-door sport coupe
Wheelbase	108 inches
Length	188 inches
Width	74.4 inches
Height	50.5 inches
Weight	3,810 pounds (SS 396)
Price	RPO Z27 (Super Sport Package w/base 350 V-8) cost $313.90, LS3 V-8 added $99.05 (base V-8 coupe: $2,848)
Track (front/rear, in inches)	61.3/60
Wheels	14x7
Tires	F70 Wide Oval with raised white letters
Suspension	independent unequal A-arms, coil springs and stabilizer bar in front; multi-leaf springs, solid axle with staggered shocks in back
Steering	recirculating ball
Brakes	power front discs, rear drums
Engine	270-horsepower 350-cubic-inch L48 V-8, 300-horsepower 402 cubic-inch LS3 V-8
Bore & stroke	4.00 x 3.48 inches, 350 V-8; 4.126 x 3.76 inches, 402 V-8
Compression	8.5:1
Fuel delivery	single four-barrel carburetor
Transmission	four-speed manual or Turbo Hydra-Matic automatic
Axle ratio	3.42:1
Production	8,377 (includes 1,533 w/LS3 V-8)

1971

Only minor changes marked the 1971 Camaro's arrival, and the Super Sport and Rally Sport versions rolled over essentially unchanged. Most notable were power cutbacks for both the base 350 and optional LS3 402 big-block, as compression cuts (down to 8.5:1) were made across the board. Advertised output for the L48 small-block was 270 horsepower, compared to 300 for the LS3 Turbo-Jet.

Only minor changes marked the 1971 Camaro's arrival.

Top
Compression cuts made across the board in Detroit helped detune the big-block Camaro SS 396 for 1971. Advertised output for the LS3 Turbo-Jet V-8 was 300 horsepower that year.

Above
Both the SS and RS packages rolled on basically unchanged for 1971. The Rally Sport shown here was powered by the L48 350 small-block V-8, now rated at 270 horsepower.

1972 Camaro SS

1972 Camaro SS	
Model availability	two-door sport coupe
Wheelbase	108 inches
Length	188 inches
Width	74.4 inches
Height	50.5 inches
Price	RPO Z27 (Super Sport Package w/base 350 V-8) cost $306.35, LS3 V-8 added $96 (base V-8 coupe: $2,819.70)
Track (front/rear, in inches)	61.3/60
Wheels	14x7
Tires	F70 Wide Oval with raised white letters
Suspension	independent unequal A-arms, coil springs and stabilizer bar in front; multi-leaf springs, solid axle with staggered shocks in back
Steering	recirculating ball
Brakes	power front discs, rear drums
Engine	200-horsepower 350-cubic-inch L48 V-8, 240-horsepower 402 cubic-inch LS3 V-8
Bore & stroke	4.00 x 3.48 inches, 350 V-8; 4.126 x 3.76 inches, 402 V-8
Compression	8.5:1
Fuel delivery	single four-barrel carburetor
Transmission	four-speed manual or Turbo Hydra-Matic automatic
Axle ratio	3.42:1
Production	6,562 (includes 970 w/LS3 V-8)

Top
In 1927, Chevrolet introduced its Sport Cabriolet, a closed car that looked like a convertible thanks to a dummy canvas roof covering. No convertible Camaros were available after 1970, leaving jet-setters little choice but to go for the Rally Sport, Super Sport, or Z/28. Most affordable, of course, was the Rally Sport. A 1972 RS coupe is rendered here along with one of those charming Sport Cabriolet Chevys.

Above
Chevrolet cancelled its Camaro Super Sport in 1972, replacing it in 1973 with the sporty Type LT.

The Camaro Super Sport rolled out for one more year before succumbing to sagging popularity.

1972

The Camaro Super Sport rolled out for one more year before succumbing to sagging popularity. Z27 production went from 34,932 in 1969 to 12,476 in 1970, then to 8,377 in 1971. Power again fell off in 1972, as the base L48 350 was net rated at 200 horses, the LS3 Turbo-Jet at 240. Total production for the last Camaro SS was 6,562, of which a mere 970 featured the optional 240-horsepower big-block. In the Super Sport's place for 1973 was the new Type LT Camaro, offered as an individual model with a V-8 only.

08

Above
1967 Z28

Middle
1969 Z28

Right
1974 Z28

Street Racer

08

Chevrolet Camaro Z28 1967-1974

The game was called homologation, a derivative of the Greek *homologos*, roughly meaning "in agreement." Homologation was the process by which a competition version of a regular-production automobile was legalized for on-track duty during stock class racing's heyday back in the 1960s. In most cases, a minimum production standard was the main homologating standard: A company had to build so many street-going examples of a certain car to qualify that machine for a certain racing class. Technical specifications also entered into the equation.

In the case of the Sports Car Club of America's Trans American Sedan Championship, which originated in March 1966, the most important qualification early on involved engine displacement. Soon known simply as Trans-Am racing, this stock class league at first was broken up into two groups, one for compacts with engines displacing less than 2 liters, the other for sedans carrying more than 2 liters, worth of powerplant. Capping the O-2 (over 2 liters) class was a displacement limit of 5 liters, or about 305 cubic-inches. Additional specifications also eventually included a minimum run of 1,000 cars built for sale to the general public.

Ford's Mustang, with its 289-cubic-inch V-8, qualified easily and led the way during Trans-Am road racing's first two seasons, beating up mostly on a bunch of Plymouth

Barracudas and Dodge Darts in 1966. Hitting the road again the following year almost didn't happen, though, as next to no one—save for Ford fans—apparently was interested in watching a one-horse show. Fortunately, additional factory involvement was announced not long after the seven-race 1966 season ended, ensuring at least an encore for Trans-Am competition.

Twelve events followed in 1967, the year both Mercury and Chevrolet joined the fray full force. From there the race was truly on, as American Motors, Dodge, and Plymouth all took to SCCA racing before the bubble burst three years later. With horsepower soon a dirty word around Detroit, all but AMC cancelled their direct support of Trans-Am teams between October 1970 and April 1971. The league itself, in its briefly legendary original form, was history

Opposite
Only 602 Camaro Z28s were built for 1967, all coupes with four-speed manual transmissions.
Mike Mueller

Engineers created the Z28's 302 V-8 by stuffing a 283 crank into a 327 block. That block in 1967 and 1968 featured mundane two-bolt main bearing caps. Four-bolt mains appeared in 1969.

by the end of 1972.

But hold your horses: weren't General Motors' divisions all restricted from direct racing involvement per that infamous executive decree sent down early in 1963? Certainly. But just as Chevrolet engineers had kept the back door open to preferred racers after the 1957 AMA ban on factory racing involvement, so too did certain movers and shakers following GM's own in-house edict six years later. Among those who circumvented the rules more than once during the 1960s was ever-present COPO-man Vince Piggins.

An assistant staff engineer in charge of product promotion in 1966, Piggins was no stranger to a racetrack. The famed NASCAR champion Hudson Hornets of the early 1950s had been his babies, and after Chevrolet took

to stock car racing seriously in 1955, he was brought on board the next year to oversee the company's clandestine competition program. In between that time and 1969, when Piggins shepherded those 427-powered Chevelles and Camaros through the COPO loophole, he was also responsible for the hot little pony car that helped vault the Trans-Am series into the limelight.

On August 17, 1966, Piggins issued a memo to Chevrolet brass outlining his plan to build an SCCA-legal Camaro, a car possessing "performance and handling characteristics superior to either Mustang or Barracuda." Once approved, Piggins' proposed package

was given RPO code Z28, a simply stark label that stuck despite Piggins' pleas for the name "Cheetah."

To meet SCCA homologation standards, the Z28 had to have a back seat (which made it a sedan), a wheelbase no longer than 116 inches, and, as mentioned, an engine no larger than 305 cubic-inches. Too bad the smallest thing then in the Camaro arsenal was the 327 V-8. Original experiments with a high-performance version of the good ol' 283 small-block proved insufficient, leaving engineers no choice but to mix and match existing parts to achieve the desired performance potential while staying within the SCCA limit.

Below
Standard Z28 tires in 1967 were 7.35x15 units adorned with either red or white stripes. *Mike Mueller*

Right
Corvette-style 15-inch Rally wheels were standard for the Z28 in 1967. These rims differed slightly in offset compared to their Corvette counterparts. *Mike Mueller*

The solution was so simple: bolt a 283 crankshaft into a 327 block. Presto, a 302-cube V-8 able to make more than enough horses—290 on paper. In the real world, that advertised number fooled almost no one. "The 290-hp figure quoted for the Z-28 engine seems ridiculously conservative," went a *Car and Driver* claim. "It feels at least as strong as the 327, 350-hp engine offered in the Corvette." According to *Sports Car Graphic*'s Jerry Titus, it was "logical to expect a fully prepared version [of the 302] to produce well in excess of 370 honest ponies." Reportedly, the speed merchants at Traco Engineering coaxed more than 500 horsepower from the 302s they built for Roger Penske's Trans-Am race team.

Although Piggins initially projected a run of at least 10,000 Camaro Z28s for 1967, the actual count was only a mere 602. But it was a start. Though rarely seen at first, Detroit's original Trans-Am pony car was hard to overlook on the street scene. "With the Z-28, Chevy is on the way toward making the gutsy stormer the Camaro should have been in the first place," proclaimed a *Car and Driver* review. Trackside witnesses also were impressed, as Camaro Z28s dominated Trans-Am racing in 1968 and 1969, results that in turn helped sales soar. More than 7,000 Z28s were built in 1968, followed by another 20,000 in 1969.

The Z28 temporarily retired after 1974, then returned triumphantly two years later to continue a legendary legacy that was still running strong when GM cancelled its F-body platform in 2002.

1967

Introduced to the automotive press on November 26, 1966, at Riverside, California, the first Camaro Z28 truly was a well-rounded performer. Along with its exclusive 302-cubic-inch small-block, the package included Chevrolet's superb F41 suspension, a quick-ratio Saginaw

manual steering box, and 3.73:1 rear gears. A Muncie four-speed (with 2.20:1 low) was a mandatory option (no automatics were allowed, either), as were front disc brakes with power assist. Thrown in along with those discs were four 15x6 Corvette-type Rally wheels. Other than these bright rims, the only other outward sign of a '67 Z28's presence were twin racing stripes on the hood and rear deck. The legendary "Z28" emblem didn't debut until midway through 1968.

Popular options included a fiberglass rear spoiler and the Z22 Rally Sport group. The sky was the limit from there, as all available Camaro frills—save for Super Sport equipment and air conditioning—could've been ordered along with RPO Z28, but only for a V-8 coupe. No convertibles were allowed.

Among options exclusive to the Z28 application were tube headers and a fresh-air induction setup. This special air cleaner came boxed in the trunk and featured ductwork that ran from the carburetor to a plenum in the cowl. Ordering RPO Z28 with the dealer-installed headers required shelling out an extra $779.40 in 1967. On its own, the Z28 option cost $358.10. The price was $437.10 with the Cowl Induction equipment and a whopping $858.40 with both the fresh-air ducting and the headers.

As for the heart of this beast, the 290-horse 302 small-block was hot to trot from top to bottom. Though the cylinder block was a typical passenger-car unit with two-bolt main bearings (stronger four-bolt mains came along in 1969), the rugged crank was made of forged steel instead of nodular cast iron. Below that crank went a windage tray to prevent oil sloshing in the pan during hard turns or serious acceleration. On top were L79 big-valve (2.02-inch intakes, 1.60 exhausts) heads and an 800-cfm Holley four-barrel carburetor on an aluminum intake. Compression was 11:1. Along with various chrome dress-up pieces, the 302 V-8 also was

1967 Z28

1967 Z28

Model availability	two-door sport coupe
Wheelbase	108 inches
Length	184.7 inches
Width	72.5 inches
Height	51.4 inches
Curb weight	3,250 pounds
Base price	$3,226
Track (front/rear, in inches)	59/58.9
Wheels	15x6 Rally rims
Tires	7.35x15 red-stripe
Suspension	independent unequal A-arms, coil springs and stabilizer bar in front; single-leaf springs, solid axle with right side trailing link in back
Steering	recirculating ball
Brakes	power front discs, rear drums
Engine	290-horsepower 302-cubic-inch V-8
Bore & stroke	4.00 x 3.00 inches
Compression	11:1
Fuel delivery	800-cfm Holley four-barrel carburetor on aluminum high-rise intake manifold
Transmission	close-ratio M21 four-speed w/ Muncie shifter
Axle ratio	3.73:1
Production	602

treated to deep-groove pulleys, transistorized ignition, a heavy-duty radiator, and a five-blade viscous-drive fan.

Transmission choices numbered two: the M20 wide-ratio four-speed or its M21 close-ratio running mate, both priced at $184.35.

Yet another rare dealer-installed option also broke corporate rules. Supposedly, multiple-carb setups were taboo after 1966 in all GM models save for the Corvette, but leave it to Piggins to promote a cross-ram aluminum intake mounting two Holley four-barrels for the Z28's 302 V-8. The price for this race-ready service part was about $500. It was offered up through 1969.

Left
Optional cowl-induction ductwork was delivered inside a new Z28's trunk in 1967. Adding this air cleaner upped the Z28 package's price from $358.10 to $437.10. *Mike Mueller*

Center
Adding the Custom Interior option (RPO Z87) into the Z28 mix in 1967 required spending an extra $94.80. Included in the Z87 deal were molded front armrests, a deluxe steering wheel, and color-keyed accents on the seats. *Mike Mueller*

Below left
The 1967 Z28's 302 V-8 was advertised at 290 horsepower, a token rating in most opinions. Compression was 11:1. *Mike Mueller*

Below right
A big Holley four-barrel on an aluminum intake fed the Z28's 302-cubic-inch small-block V-8. Heads were big-port L79 units. *Mike Mueller*

Closest thing to a Corvette yet.

Special order Z/28 and you get a Camaro that comes on like Corvette...for a lot less.

Dual exhausts with 2¹⁄₄" diameter pipes and deep tone mufflers.

3.73 rear axle. (Ratios up to 4.88 available when you specify Positraction.)

Big, bold stereo rally stripes. (No mechanical function, but having great psychological value.)

Air spoiler available on request.

Special suspension system, including multi-leaf rear springs with bias-mounted shocks.

15" x 6" wheels and E70 x 15 special nylon cord "Wide Tread GT" high-performance tires.

Limited production 302-cu.-in. V8. 4.0 bore, 3.0 stroke. 11.0:1 compression ratio. 290 rated bhp at 5800 rpm. 290 rated torque at 4200 rpm. Carburetion: 1x4 Holley rated 800 cfm mounted on special tuned aluminum manifold. Special cam. Solid lifters. Curb weight: 3220 lb.

Heavy-duty radiator. Temperature-controlled fan with dual pulleys for fan and water pump.

4-speed and power disc brakes for you to order.

21.4:1 quick-ratio steering. 17.9:1 fast ratio also available.

GM MARK OF EXCELLENCE

The Z/28 CAMARO CHEVROLET

Above left
Save for the Rally wheels, special stripes on the hood and deck lid were the only outward clues as to a Z28's presence in 1967. *Mike Mueller*

Above right
Soon-to-be-legendary "Z28" fender badges appeared on fenders midyear for Chevrolet's second-edition Trans-Am pony car.

Left
After appearing somewhat clandestinely in 1967, the Camaro Z28 was promoted rather prominently in magazine ads the following year.

1968 Z28

1968 Z28	
Model availability	two-door sport coupe
Wheelbase	108 inches
Length	184.7 inches
Width	72.5 inches
Height	51.4 inches
Curb weight	3,250 pounds
Base price	$3,256
Track (front/rear, in inches)	59/58.9
Wheels	15x6 Rally rims
Tires	E70 Goodyear Wide Tread GT w/raised white letters
Suspension	independent unequal A-arms, coil springs and stabilizer bar in front; multi-leaf springs, solid axle staggered shocks in back
Steering	recirculating ball
Brakes	power front discs, rear drums
Engine	290-horsepower 302 cubic-inch V-8
Bore & stroke	4.00 x 3.00 inches
Compression	11:1
Fuel delivery	800-cfm Holley four-barrel carburetor on aluminum high-rise intake manifold
Transmission	close-ratio M21 four-speed w/ Muncie shifter
Axle ratio	3.73:1
Production	7,199

1968

Z28 production soared from 602 to 7,199 in 1968. Basically the same package rolled over, with minor updates including switching from single-leaf springs to four-leaf units with staggered shock absorbers in back. New, larger center caps graced that year's Rally wheels, shod in Goodyear Wide Tread GT E70 tires. New, too, was a third transmission choice, the gnarly M22 Rock Crusher four-speed, priced at an equally mean and nasty $310.70.

Price changes also made news in 1968, as the RPO Z28 tag increased to $400.25. Adding the plenum air cleaner into the mix bumped that number up to $479.25, but the super rare headers cost the same as in 1967. Another dealer-installed option—four-wheel disc brakes—showed up in 1968, this after Trans-Am race teams demonstrated the brakes' merits on SCCA road courses. Very few of these brake packages were sold over dealership parts counters, and the option then became officially listed on the Camaro RPO list as JL8 in 1969.

Above
Z28 production reached a zenith in 1969: the final tally was 20,302. *Mike Mueller*

Below left
New 15x7 Rally wheels were standard for the restyled Z28 in 1969. The rear spoiler was optional. *Mike Mueller*

Below right
The Z28's 302 V-8 featured various upgrades in 1969, not the least of which was a more durable cylinder block with four-bolt main bearing caps. Advertised output remained at a conservative 290 horsepower. *Mike Mueller*

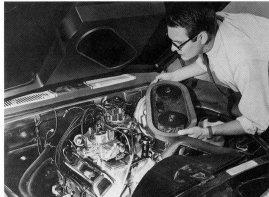

Above
A cross-ram intake sporting two Holley four-barrels was offered over the counter as a service package option for the Z28 from 1967 to 1969.

Above
Camaro Z28s were SCCA Trans-Am champions in 1968 and 1969, thanks in part to the work of the Penske-Sunoco team.

Top left
The truly distinctive hound's-tooth interior was available in four shades in 1969: ivory, yellow, black, and orange, the latter used for that year's Indy 500 pace car replicas. *Mike Mueller*

1969 Z28

1969 Z28	
Model availability	two-door sport coupe
Wheelbase	108 inches
Length	186 inches
Width	74 inches
Height	51.6 inches
Curb weight	3,455 pounds
Base price	$3,266
Track (front/rear, in inches)	59.6/59.5
Wheels	15x7 Rally rims
Tires	E70 x 15
Suspension	independent upper A-arms, lower controls arms, coil springs and stabilizer bar in front; multi-leaf springs, solid axle in back
Steering	recirculating ball
Brakes	power front discs, rear drums (four-wheel discs optional)
Engine	290-horsepower 302-cubic-inch V-8
Bore & stroke	4.00 x 3.00 inches
Compression	11:1
Fuel delivery	800-cfm Holley four-barrel carburetor on high-rise aluminum intake manifold
Transmission	close-ratio M21 four-speed w/ Hurst shifter
Axle ratio	3.73:1
Production	20,302

1969

Chevrolet's nicely restyled 1969 Camaro body suited the Z28 to a T, even more so when topped off by the functional ZL2 hood with its rear-facing scoop, introduced on November 25, 1968. Nearly all standard features carried over unchanged, and the Rally Sport package was again available, featuring prominently styled headlight doors. The rarely seen JL8 four-wheel-disc package was a $500.30 option.

Notable upgrades included a more durable 302 cylinder block refitted with four-bolt main bearing caps, a thicker front stabilizer bar, and wider 15x7 wheels, although some early models apparently used 1968's 15x6 rims. Two different tires were installed in 1969: The E70 Goodyear Wide Tread GT was joined by Firestone's Sport Car 200. New, too, was a more precise, definitely preferred Hurst shifter in place of the clunky Muncie stick used in 1967 and 1968.

Various changes were made to the Z28 equipment group during the year, as more than one individual component came and went. Low-restriction, chambered exhausts were briefly included in RPO Z28, as were a tachometer, rear deck spoiler, and chrome exhaust tips. Prices ranged from $485.15 to $522.40. One little-known variation involved deleting the stripes on the hood and deck lid.

1970-1/2 Z28

1970-1/2 Z28

Model availability	two-door sport coupe
Wheelbase	108 inches
Length	188 inches
Width	74.4 inches
Height	50.5 inches
Curb weight	3,580 pounds
Base price	$3,794
Track (front/rear, in inches)	61.3/60
Wheels	15x7
Tires	F60 Goodyear Polyglas
Suspension	independent upper A-arms, lower controls arms, coil springs and stabilizer bar in front; multi-leaf springs, solid axle w/stabilizer bar in back
Steering	recirculating ball
Brakes	power-assisted front discs, rear drums
Engine	360-horsepower 350-cubic-inch V-8
Bore & stroke	4.00 x 3.48 inches
Compression	11:1
Fuel delivery	780-cfm Holley four-barrel carburetor
Transmission	four-speed manual or Turbo Hydra-Matic automatic
Axle ratio	3.73:1 posi-Traction
Production	8,733

Various glitches helped delay the second-generation Camaro's debut until February 1970, thus the "1970-1/2" reference. Z28 production that year was 8,733. *Mike Mueller*

1970-1/2

Another excitingly new Z28 fit into the redesigned 1970-1/2 Camaro like Raquel Welch in her furs from *One Million Years B.C.* (the 1966 British film rather firmly established the fully loaded actress as a leading lady–a reference to her profile, not theatrical merits). "It's quiet, quick, beautiful, and all the parts look and act as though they belong together," claimed *Sports Car Graphic*'s Paul Van Valkenburgh–in reference to the car, of course.

Next to the cranky, hot-tempered, 1969 Z28 with its loud, skittish, rough-idling 302 small-block, the next-generation Z was a kinder, gentler machine, a still-strong performer that *Car Life* claimed was "as close to a mild-mannered racing car as the industry has come." Real men who preferred a real racer complete with a real racer's really bad nature preferred the first-gen-

eration Z28, as rough a ride as Detroit had ever let loose in polite society. But drivers who liked to compete on the street with someone like Ms. Welch along for the trip were more than thrilled by the 1970-1/2 model's more cooperative, better-balanced brand of pony car performance.

The new Camaro's improved chassis and better-insulated body meant that, in most cases, that trip was smoother and quieter. And it remained exciting. As *Car Life*'s staff concluded, "Despite the added weight and tougher emissions controls, [the '70-1/2 Z28 is] faster than ever, and in a way that makes the car driveable by anybody."

Inspiration for that claim came beneath the second-generation Z28's even longer hood. Behind that pointed prow was a new power source, a truly muscular mill with a sports car pedigree. A new option for the 1970 Corvette,

the 350-cubic-inch LT-1 V-8 replaced the Z28's 302 that year. Beneath fiberglass hoods, the LT-1 was rated at 370 horsepower. As the new heart of the Z28, it wore a 360-horsepower advertised-output sticker. Either way, most bystanders then agreed that the LT-1 was probably the greatest small-block V-8 to yet scream down the pike. With a much wider, more usable powerband than its 302 predecessor, the 360-horsepower 350 was even more responsive–to both full-throttle bursts and slow-speed operation.

Such relatively civilized compatibility allowed engineers to offer the Turbo Hydra-Matic automatic (albeit a beefed-up version with a high-stall torque converter) as a Z28 option for the first time. Previous models had all been Muncie four-speeds. The M40 Turbo Hydra-Matic option cost $290.40 when paired with

Above
Chevrolet's LT-1 350 produced 370 horsepower under fiberglass hoods in 1970. It was downrated slightly to 360 horses for the 1970-1/2 Z28. *Mike Mueller*

Top right
Z28 buyers in 1970 could choose between a Muncie four-speed or Turbo Hydra-Matic automatic transmission. The Hurst stick seen here controls the M21 close-ratio four-speed. Additional options included power steering, a tilt wheel, and an AM pushbutton radio. Bucket seats were standard for all Camaro models in 1970. *Mike Mueller*

RPO Z28. The Muncie four-speed, in either M20 wide-ratio or M21 close-ratio form, cost $205.95.

The LT-1's extra 48 cubes were allowed entry into the Z28's engine bay thanks to an SCCA rules change. Previously, destroking a production engine to meet the 305-cubic-inch Trans-Am limit was not allowed. But this left Dodge and Plymouth out of the picture, because no mixing and matching of Chrysler hardware could bridge the gap between the 273- and 318-cubic-inch Mopar small-blocks. SCCA officials then changed their minds about destroking in 1970, a move that allowed the 340-equipped T/A Challenger and AAR 'Cuda to qualify for Trans-Am competition. With that done, it became only logical at Chevrolet to leave the 302 hybrid behind in favor of the larger 350 small-block.

Like the '69 302, the LT-1 featured big-port heads, solid lifters, rugged four-bolt main bearing caps, a tough forged-steel crank, a high-volume oil pump, and a baffled oil pan with windage tray. TRW impact-extruded pistons again squeezed the air/fuel mixture at an 11:1

ratio. On top, a 780-cfm Holley four-barrel found a home on a revised aluminum intake that allowed more clearance for lower hood lines. A heavy-duty radiator was included, and a beefier 11-inch clutch replaced the 10.34-inch unit previously used for four-speed models.

Brakes were 11-inch front discs, 9.5-inch rear drums, with power-assist made mandatory. Heavier F41 springs and staggered shocks again appeared but were joined by a new rear sway bar.

Priced at $572.95 in 1970, RPO Z28 included a rear spoiler, chrome exhaust tips, and new 15x7 sport wheels wearing F60 Wide Oval rubber. Special stripes, "Z28" identification, a blacked-out grille, and various deluxe trim pieces completed the deal.

Above
One of the highlights of the new F-body design for 1970 was its lengthened, pointed prow. The Z28's blacked-out grille drew even more attention up front. *Mike Mueller*

Center
New 14x7 wheels, chrome exhaust tips, and a rear deck spoiler all came standard on the Z28 in 1970. *Mike Mueller*

1971 Z28

1971 Z28

Model availability	two-door sport coupe
Wheelbase	108 inches
Length	188 inches
Width	74.4 inches
Height	50.5 inches
Curb weight	3,560 pounds
Base price	$4,005
Track (front/rear, in inches)	61.3/60
Wheels	15x7
Tires	F60x15
Suspension	independent upper A-arms, lower controls arms, coil springs and stabilizer bar in front; multi-leaf springs, solid axle w/stabilizer bar in back
Steering	recirculating ball
Brakes	power-assisted front discs, rear drums
Engine	330-horsepower 350-cubic-inch V-8
Bore & stroke	4.00 x 3.48 inches
Compression	9:1
Fuel delivery	Holley four-barrel carburetor
Transmission	four-speed manual or Turbo Hydra-Matic automatic
Axle ratio	3.73:1 posi-Traction
Production	4,862

1971

A compression cut from 11:1 to 9:1 dropped the Z28's output down to 330 horsepower in 1971, a bad year for the king of the Camaros as production fell as well, from 8,733 the previous year to 4,862. Impressions remained exciting as all-important RPO Z28 components again rolled over, but the 350 Turbo-Fire's lost horses, working in concert with changing attitudes concerning high performance, meant a dimming future for Chevrolet's Trans-Am pony car. All 1971 Z28s featured front and rear spoilers. RPO Z28 cost $786.75.

Z28 production fell to 4,862 for 1971, a trend that led to the car's temporary retirement three years later.

1972 Z28

1972

Z28 production fell again, to 2,575, in 1972, as inhibiting emissions controls limited the 350 V-8 further. Advertised output dropped to 255 horsepower. Spoilers were dropped from the Z28 package, priced at $769.15.

Below
Output dropped to 255 horsepower for the 1972 Z28's 350 small-block, helping explain why sales dropped again, this time to 2,575.

Model availability	two-door sport coupe
Wheelbase	108 inches
Length	188 inches
Width	74.4 inches
Height	50.5 inches
Price	Z28 Special Performance Package cost $796.15
Track (front/rear, in inches)	61.3/60
Wheels	15x7
Tires	F60x15
Suspension	independent upper A-arms, lower controls arms, coil springs and stabilizer bar in front; multi-leaf springs, solid axle w/stabilizer bar in back
Steering	recirculating ball
Brakes	power-assisted front discs, rear drums
Engine	255-horsepower 350-cubic-inch V-8
Bore & stroke	4.00 x 3.48 inches
Compression	9:1
Fuel delivery	Rochester four-barrel carburetor
Transmission	four-speed manual or Turbo Hydra-Matic automatic
Axle ratio	3.73:1 posi-Traction
Production	2,575

1973 Z28

1973 Z28

Model availability	two-door sport coupe
Wheelbase	108 inches
Length	188 inches
Width	74.4 inches
Height	50.5 inches
Curb weight	3,689 pounds
Price	Z28 Special Performance Package cost $502.05 w/Type LT coupe
Track (front/rear, in inches)	61.3/60
Wheels	15x7
Tires	F60x15
Suspension	independent upper A-arms, lower controls arms, coil springs and stabilizer bar in front; multi-leaf springs, solid axle w/stabilizer bar in back
Steering	recirculating ball
Brakes	power-assisted front discs, rear drums
Engine	245-horsepower 350-cubic-inch V-8
Bore & stroke	4.00 x 3.48 inches
Compression	9:1
Fuel delivery	Holley four-barrel carburetor on cast-iron intake manifold
Transmission	four-speed manual or Turbo Hydra-Matic automatic
Rear axle	Posi-Traction
Production	11,574

Civilized hydraulic lifters replaced the solid units used by all previous Z28s in 1973, meaning optional air conditioning could finally enter the equation.

Optional air conditioning became available for the Z28 in 1973, but this only signaled just how soft the once-brutal street racer had become.

1973

Civilized hydraulic lifters replaced the solid units used by all previous Z28s in 1973, meaning optional air conditioning could finally enter the equation. Output for the quieter 350 Turbo-Fire was 245 horsepower. Priced at $598.05, RPO Z28 was available that year for the base V-8 Camaro coupe and the new Type LT, which replaced the retiring Super Sport. When combined with the Type LT, the Z28 package's price dropped to $502.05 due to various shared features. Production actually jumped dramatically that year to 11,574. But this rise had as much to do with the disappearances of nearly all rivals as it did with the car's own merits.

1974 Z28

A mild Camaro makeover and new, rather garish graphics made news in 1974.

Above
Z28 popularity jumped in 1974, but the decision had already been made to kill the car off at year's end. Prominent graphics were new that year.

Below
Chevrolet's Camaro Z28 made a triumphant return midyear in 1977. A 185-horsepower 350 small-block V-8 was standard.

1974 Z28	
Model availability	two-door sport coupe
Wheelbase	108 inches
Length	188 inches
Width	74.4 inches
Height	50.5 inches
Price	Z28 Special Performance Package cost $796.15
Track (front/rear, in inches)	61.3/60
Wheels	15x7
Tires	F60x15
Suspension	independent upper A-arms, lower controls arms, coil springs and stabilizer bar in front; multi-leaf springs, solid axle w/stabilizer bar in back
Steering	recirculating ball
Brakes	power-assisted front discs, rear drums
Engine	245-horsepower 350-cubic-inch V-8
Bore & stroke	4.00 x 3.48 inches
Compression	9:1
Fuel delivery	four-barrel carburetor
Transmission	four-speed manual or Turbo Hydra-Matic automatic
Rear axle	Posi-Traction
Production	13,802

1974

A mild Camaro makeover and new, rather garish graphics made news in 1974, the last year for the original Z28. Though sales didn't fall off markedly for once—the 1974 count was 13,802—the decision to end the legacy was already made. Fortunately, the Z28 reappeared midyear in 1977 as an individual model. RPO Z28 components carried over unchanged from 1973 to 1974, as did the 350 Turbo-Fire V-8's advertised output, thanks to the addition of the more-efficient High Energy Ignition (HEI).

09

Above
1967 Firebird and 1954 Firebird I

Middle
1968 Firebird 400 H.O.

Right
1970 Firebird Formula

Hot to Trot

09

Pontiac Firebird 1967–1974

More than one Detroit-watcher in the know in 1966 knew it had to be on its way. As a United Press International report in July claimed, "the Mustang corral is getting crowded. Another new entry into the sports-type auto field is due to make a late debut either in late fall or early winter." Word was already out about Mercury's upscale pony car, the Cougar, scheduled for a 1967 release. Chevrolet's highly anticipated response to the wildly popular Mustang, initially named Panther, was in the works, too, though the badge would read "Camaro" when this all-new F-body was announced to the press in June 1966. It was now Chevy's corporate cousin's turn. "Reports coming out of Detroit keep insisting that Pontiac will have a car similar to the Camaro on the 1967 market," wrote Henry Ward in the *Pittsburgh Press* in August. Not if John De Lorean had anything to say about it.

No, the Pontiac chief wasn't against taking on the Mustang on its sports-type turf. He simply wanted something more than a mildly disguised Camaro—much more, in truth. Like his predecessor, Pete Estes, De Lorean had long been in favor of knocking off another Chevrolet product, the legendary Corvette. Sporty two-seat experiments had been popping up around Pontiac dating back to the Corvette-based Bonneville Special showcar in 1954, and this later was followed by a customized two-place Tempest called the Monte Carlo, which made the auto show rounds rather excitingly in 1962. Estes loved the supercharged Monte Carlo, but his corporate superiors didn't—end of story.

More to De Lorean's liking was a fresh, ground-up creation born in 1963. Originally tagged XP-833, this sweet, sexy two-seater

reached clay mockup stage in August 1964 just as Chevrolet was given two thumbs way up for its F-body project. While Estes more or less ignored the F-car, De Lorean took XP-833 and ran with it. Engineer Bill Collins was tasked with developing this proposal, by then named Banshee. As many as six working prototypes were built, but still no one up in General Motors' ivory tower paid any attention.

De Lorean stepped in as Pontiac general manager after Estes moved over to Chevrolet in July 1965. Now with some serious sway in executive ranks (per common GM practice, he also was made corporate vice president), the new divisional boss wasted little time stepping up his campaign to make the Banshee a production reality by 1967. First came an extensive presentation, lavishly made by Collins for GM

Opposite
John De Lorean might have wanted something entirely different, but GM Design chief Chuck Jordan (right) and Pontiac studio head Jack Humbert were more than proud of the first Firebird.

Left
Former chief engineer John De Lorean stepped in as Pontiac general manager after Pete Estes moved up the corporate ladder in July 1965.

F-body pony car, was then introduced to the public on February 23, 1967. "The Firebird is named after a legendary Indian symbol which promised action, power, beauty and youth," explained a Pontiac press release. "It was first used in 1954 on General Motors' dramatic gas turbine powered car, Firebird I."

While not exactly De Lorean's dream, Pontiac's new pony car still impressed some critics with a sporty flair all its own. "It may be the first step toward a true four-passenger GT car in the best European sense," claimed a *Road & Track* report. Nearly all reviews at the same time pointed out that GM's F-body was very much a dressed-up Camaro, but that wasn't necessarily a bad thing considering how successful Chevy's F-car quickly became. Even the PMD general manager had to concede that one-upping Chevrolet could only lead to good things. "With the introduction of the Firebird we hope to attract new car buyers who want to step up to something extra in styling as well as performance in this segment of the market," said De Lorean while introducing Pontiac's variation on the long-hood/short-deck theme.

Like the Camaro, the Firebird was a budget-conscious compact in base form. Optional extra performance came by way of the Firebird 400, superseded in 1970 by the Formula 400. The highest-flying Pontiac pony car was, of course, the Trans Am, introduced for 1969. For more on this bodacious breed, see the following chapter.

As was the case in GTO ranks, the Firebird's hottest 400 V-8s were the Ram Air renditions, which again weren't fully promoted by that name in official Pontiac paperwork until 1970. 'Bird watchers in 1967 certainly knew what the Ram Air 400 was even though that moniker was nowhere to be found in the company's sales literature or on order forms. As mentioned previously within these pages, the Ram Air I, II, III, and IV jargon, historically correct or not, is used freely here to keep things simple.

president James Roche's benefit, detailing De Lorean's proposition. About the same time, a four-place version of his sporty dream machine also was developed to perhaps slide more easily past corporate killjoys. Roche gave neither plan any consideration, yet designers were still working on De Lorean's pet project as late as February 1966.

Initial progress on a just-in-case Pontiac version of the F-car already was under way by then. And in March 1966, GM executive vice president Ed Cole finally told De Lorean to give his play toys a rest and "make a car out of the Camaro." Handicapped by the short time involved, PMD designers nonetheless did a

nice job of creating their own pony apart from the Camaro, thanks both to the addition of a purely Pontiac beak (measuring 5 inches longer than the Camaro's) and a few chassis tweaks thought up too late to be included in Chevrolet's package. Pontiac's F-car was better balanced thanks to an engine located farther back than the Camaro's. Also, radius rod traction bars were added at the rear to inhibit axle hop under hard acceleration.

As for a name, Banshee wouldn't do, and some observers thought Pontiac might pick up Chevrolet's Panther moniker. But in the end PMD label-hangers looked to Native American mythology for inspiration. Firebird, GM's second

1967 Firebird 400

1967 Firebird 400

Model availability	two-door hardtop or convertible
Wheelbase	108.1 inches
Length	188.8 inches
Width	72.6 inches
Height	51.5 inches, hardtop
Weight	3,549 pounds (hardtop), 3,885 pounds (convertible)
Base price	$2,777 (hardtop), $3,177 (convertible)
Track (front/rear, in inches)	59/60
Wheels	14x5J stamped steel
Tires	E70x14
Suspension	independent unequal A-arms, coil springs and stabilizer bar in front; single-leaf springs, solid axle with anti-windup traction bars in back
Steering	recirculating ball
Brakes	hydraulic drums, front and rear
Engine	325-horsepower 400-cubic-inch V-8 (325-horsepower 400-cubic-inch Ram Air V-8, optional)
Bore & stroke	4.12 x 3.75 inches
Compression	10.75:1
Fuel delivery	single four-barrel carburetor
Transmission	three-speed manual, std.
Axle ratio	3.08:1, std.

Top
Twin hood scoops were standard for the 1967 Firebird 400, available in both hardtop and convertible forms. A beefed suspension too was included when the big-block was installed. This particular example has nonstock traction bars in back. *Mike Mueller*

Above
The base W66 400 V-8 was a $273.83 option for an automatic-equipped Firebird in 1967. The W66 price was $358.09 in manual transmission applications. *Mike Mueller*

Far left
Pontiac's ever-present hood tach option made its way into Firebird ranks in 1967. It cost $63.19. *Mike Mueller*

Left
A rear spoiler was a dealer-offered item in 1967. *Mike Mueller*

1967
"You'd expect Pontiac to come up with a nifty new sports car like this," announced magazine ads. "But did you expect five?" Pontiac's "Magnificent Five" for 1967 included two Firebirds fitted with the division's innovative overhead-cam six. Another, the "light heavyweight" Firebird HO, came with the 326-cid small-block V-8, while the top two models both were equipped with 400 big-blocks. Standard for the Firebird 400 was a beefed suspension and a hood sporting two nonfunctional scoops.

The base Firebird 400, available in hardtop and convertible forms, featured the 325-horsepower W66 V-8. Adding the optional L67 Ram Air 400, also advertised at 325 horsepower, made those two scoops fully functional, which in turn allowed those ponies to breathe a little easier. Maximum output for the Ram Air 400 arrived at 5,200 rpm, 400 revs above the standard big-block's power peak. This translated into 100 miles per hour coming on after only 14.4 seconds down the quarter-mile, according to a *Car and Driver* test.

The Firebird's Ram Air V-8s all produced fewer horsepower compared to their GTO counterparts until 1970 due to a carburetor restriction that kept the two rear throttle plates on those Rochester four-barrels from opening fully when pedal met metal. This allowed Pontiac's pony car to remain within another GM-mandated limit, this one involving a maximum power-to-weight ratio, specified at 10:1. Reportedly, Ram Air 400 production for 1967 was 63 hardtops, 2 convertibles.

1968 Firebird 400

1968 Firebird 400

Model availability	two-door hardtop or convertible
Wheelbase	108.1 inches
Length	188.8 inches
Width	72.8 inches
Height	50.0 inches, hardtop
Weight	3,550 pounds (hardtop)
Base price	$3,216 (hardtop), $3,431 (convertible)
Track (front/rear, in inches)	60/60
Wheels	14x5J stamped steel
Tires	F70x14 redlines
Suspension	independent unequal A-arms, coil springs and stabilizer bar in front; multi-leaf springs, solid axle with anti-windup traction bars, and staggered shock absorbers in back
Steering	recirculating ball
Brakes	hydraulic drums, front and rear
Engine	330-horsepower 400-cubic-inch V-8 (335-horsepower 400-cubic-inch HO V-8, 335-horsepower 400-cubic-inch Ram Air I V-8, and 340-horsepower 400-cubic-inch Ram Air II V-8, all optional)
Bore & stroke	4.12 x 3.75 inches
Compression	10.75:1
Fuel delivery	single four-barrel carburetor
Transmission	three-speed manual, std.
Axle ratio	3.08:1, std.

1968

Performance-oriented upgrades for the second-edition Firebird included staggered shocks and multi-leaf springs in back to further battle axle hop. Output went up to 330 horsepower for the W66 400, 335 for the Ram Air I. Another option, the L74 400 HO, also rated at 335 horses, appeared in 1968, as did the midyear Ram Air II, advertised at 340 horsepower. Behind the Ram Air II was either a four-speed manual or Turbo Hydra-Matic automatic. F70x14 redline or whitewall tires were standard for the 1968 Firebird 400.

Above
Four different 400 V-8s were offered in 1968: the base 330-horse W66, the 335-horse Ram Air I, the new L74 400 HO (shown here), and the midyear 340-horse Ram Air II. *Mike Mueller*

Right
Split exhaust extensions cost $21.06 when ordered for big-block 'Birds (and 350 HO models) in 1968. The price was $10.53 in other dual-exhaust applications. *Mike Mueller*

Output went up to 330 horsepower for the W66 400, 335 for the Ram Air I.

1969 Firebird 400

1969 Firebird 400

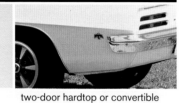

Model availability	two-door hardtop or convertible
Wheelbase	108.1 inches
Length	191.1 inches
Width	73.8 inches
Height	49.6 inches, hardtop
Curb weight	3,575 pounds (hardtop)
Base price	$3,262 (hardtop), $3,460 (convertible)
Track (front/rear, in inches)	60/60
Wheels	14x5J stamped steel
Tires	F70x14 redlines
Suspension	independent unequal A-arms, coil springs and stabilizer bar in front; multi-leaf springs, solid axle with anti-windup traction bars, and staggered shock absorbers in back
Steering	recirculating ball
Brakes	hydraulic drums, front and rear
Engine	330-horsepower 400-cubic-inch V-8 (335-horsepower 400-cubic-inch Ram Air III V-8, and 345-horsepower 400-cubic-inch Ram Air IV V-8, optional)
Bore & stroke	4.12 x 3.75 inches
Compression	10.75:1
Fuel delivery	single four-barrel carburetor
Transmission	three-speed manual, std.

1969

Echoing advancements made for the 1968 GTO, the restyled 1969 Firebird wore a new semimonochromatic nose featuring composite headlight surrounds. Additional advancements behind that facade included the Ram Air III 400 (L74), still wearing a 335-horsepower rating, and the outrageous, rarely seen Ram Air IV (L67), conveniently tagged with a conservative 345-horsepower output figure. The 330-horse-power W66 400 remained the base big-block for the Firebird 400. Costing an extra $832, the impressive Ram Air IV Firebird featured 3.90:1 standard gears in back. A truly short 4.33:1 axle was optional. For more on Ram Air III and IV specifics, see the GTO chapter.

Above
Pontiac introduced its overhead-cam six-cylinder for Firebirds and Tempests in 1966. Adding a four-barrel carburetor and split exhaust manifolds transformed the OHC six into the sporty Sprint, which initially produced 207 horsepower. Maximum Sprint six output reached 230 horses before this short story came to an end in 1969.

Below
The 330-horsepower W66 400 remained the base big-block for the Firebird 400 in 1969. New options included the Ram Air III and Ram Air IV 400s. *Mike Mueller*

Above
Like the 1968 GTO, the 1969 Firebird was fitted with a new composite nose. Popular options on this Firebird 400 convertible include a hood tach and Rally II wheels. *Mike Mueller*

Right
Base price for a Firebird convertible in 1969 was $3,045. The Firebird 400 sport option (with base three-speed manual transmission) cost $416.01 for topless models that year. Choosing a four-speed manual or the Turbo Hydra-Matic automatic lowered that figure to $331.76. *Mike Mueller*

Left
Far and away the hottest Firebird 400 variation for 1969 was the Ram Air IV version with its conservatively rated 345 horses. A Ram Air IV convertible (shown here) certainly was a rare 'Bird that year. *Mike Mueller*

Below left
The optional Rally II wheel cost $84.26 when ordered alone in 1969. The price was $63.19 when combined with the Decor Group. *Mike Mueller*

Below right
The Custom sports steering wheel was a $50.55 option in 1969. It cost $34.76 when ordered along with the $62.14 Decor Group. *Mike Mueller*

Above
General Motors' all-new F-body shape suited the 1970 Firebird just fine. Replacing the Firebird 400 that year was the equally new Formula, which kept up the pace with Pontiac's 330-horse 400 V-8 (now labeled L78) carrying over as standard equipment. *Mike Mueller*

Left
More-aggressive-looking hood scoops were standard at the 1970 Firebird Formula's shapely nose. Ram Air was optional. *Mike Mueller*

Below
A heavy-duty suspension with front and rear stabilizer bars was standard equipment beneath the new Formula. A Hurst-shifted three-speed manual was standard inside. *Mike Mueller*

1970 Formula 400

1970 Formula 400

Model availability	two-door hardtop
Wheelbase	108.1 inches
Length	191.6 inches
Width	73.4 inches
Height	50.4 inches
Weight	3,815 pounds
Base price	$3,370
Track (front/rear, in inches)	61.6/60.3
Wheels	14x7 stamped steel
Tires	F70x14
Suspension	independent unequal A-arms, coil springs and stabilizer bar in front; multi-leaf springs, solid axle and stabilizer bar in back
Steering	recirculating ball
Brakes	front discs, rear drums
Engine	330-horsepower 400-cubic-inch V-8 (335-horsepower 400-cubic-inch Ram Air III V-8, and 345-horsepower 400-cubic-inch Ram Air IV V-8, optional)
Bore & stroke	4.12 x 3.75 inches
Compression	10.75:1
Fuel delivery	single four-barrel carburetor
Transmission	Hurst-shifted three-speed manual, std.
Production	7,708

1970

After hustling to put together a revamped Pontiac pony car for 1969, Jack Humbert's stylists turned their attentions to a total makeover the following year. A convertible didn't return, but who cared? Like its Camaro counterpart, the midyear 1970 Firebird was a really big hit, inside and out.

"It's exciting in a way that Detroit could never master before," claimed a *Car and Driver* review. "The bucket seats are low and the backrests are no longer upright like church pews. You lean back, as if in the arms of a Maserati. As an option you can reach for a small, black-padded [steering wheel] that is surely fresh

from a Formula One car. The tachometer has been turned so that the red line is straight up, and a small clock fits into the right side of the dial, strongly suggesting the instrumentation on a high-revving Japanese motorcycle. It is functional styling at its best." High praise, indeed.

The 1970 lineup was revised, with the base Firebird offered in six-cylinder or V-8 forms. Next was the Esprit, featuring a standard 255-horsepower 350-cubic-inch small-block V-8 (L30) or an optional two-barrel 400 (L65), rated at 265 horsepower. In place of the Firebird 400 was the new Formula 400, and at the top was the flagship Trans Am.

Standard Formula 400 equipment included a Hurst-shifted three-speed manual transmission, front and rear stabilizer bars, F70x14 tires on 7-inch-wide wheels, heavy-duty Firm Control shock absorbers, dual sport mirrors, deluxe steering wheel, and a unique fiberglass hood with two rather dramatic scoops dominating its leading edge. Standard power came from the newly named L78 400, rated at 330 horsepower. The 335-horse L74 Ram Air III big-block was optional, as was the road-hugging Trans Am suspension. Adding the optional L74 put those twin scoops to work sucking in ambient atmosphere. They were simply cool looking when the L78 was installed.

1971 Formula

1971 Formula

Model availability	two-door hardtop
Wheelbase	108.1 inches
Length	191.6 inches
Width	73.4 inches
Height	50.4 inches
Weight	3,473 pounds (Formula 350)
Base price	$3,440 (Formula 350), $3,540 (Formula 400), $3,625 (Formula 455)
Track (front/rear, in inches)	61.6/60.3
Wheels	14x7 stamped steel
Tires	F70x14
Suspension	independent unequal A-arms, coil springs and stabilizer bar in front; multi-leaf springs, solid axle and stabilizer bar in back
Steering	recirculating ball
Brakes	front discs, rear drums
Engine	255-horsepower 350-cubic-inch L30 V-8, std. (300-horsepower 400-cubic-inch L78 V-8, 325-horsepower 455-cubic-inch L75 V-8, and 335-horsepower 455-cubic-inch HO V-8, all optional)
Bore & stroke	3.875 x 3.75 inches (350), 4.12 x 3.75 inches (400), 4.15 x 4.21 inches (455)
Compression	8.2:1 (L30 350, L78 400 and L75 455); 8.4:1 455 HO
Fuel delivery	single four-barrel carburetor
Transmission	heavy-duty three-speed manual with Hurst shifter, std.
Production	7,802 (all engines)

1971

All Firebirds (except the Trans Am) received fake fender vents in 1971, and the Formula could've been dressed up more by adding the T/A's rear spoiler as an option. Formula features carried over in similar fashion for 1971, but the base engine was now the 255-horse L30 small-block V-8. The L78 400 big-block, rated this time at 300 horsepower, was optional, as were two 455-cubic-inch V-8s, the 325-horse L75,

and its 335-horse LS5 running mate, known as the 455 HO. Formula buyers also could've added the Y96 Handling Package, which featured the Trans Am's springs, stabilizer bars, and F60 raised-white-letter tires on 15x7 honeycomb wheels. The Y96 price was $205.37.

1972

Little changed for the latest Firebird Formula, save for engine output ratings. The base L30 small-block was now net-rated at 175 horsepower. Options included the 250-horsepower L78 400 and 300-horsepower 455 HO. A power-flex fan was included with both big-blocks. Production for the 455 HO Formula was 276.

Top
Pontiac's 350-cubic-inch small-block V-8 became the Formula's base engine in 1971. The 400-cube big-block, now rated at 300 horsepower, was optional.

Above
Advertised output for the Formula's base small-block V-8 fell to 175 net-rated horsepower in 1972. The optional L78 400 and 455 HO big-blocks produced 250 and 300 horses, respectively. The honeycomb wheels seen here were optional, as was the Ram Air hood.

Like the legendary 421 Super Duty of 1962–1963, the short-lived LS2 was bad to the bone.

1973

Production breakdowns for the 1973 Formula read 4,771 with the base L30 350 V-8, 4,622 with the 230-horsepower L78 big-block, and 730 with the 250-horsepower L75 455 V-8. Another 48 were built with one of the greatest engines ever unleashed by Pontiac engineers, the LS2 455 Super Duty.

Like the legendary 421 Super Duty of 1962–1963, the short-lived LS2 was bad to the bone. There was one big difference: while the original was an uncivilized beast, its 455-cube successor was amazingly traffic-friendly, as well as emissions-legal, thanks mostly to a relatively skinny hydraulic cam and certainly mild compression. It also still could've easily blown away most of Detroit's unfettered, smog-spouting rivals had it debuted five years earlier. "Just when we had fast cars relegated to the museum section, Pontiac has surprised everyone and opened a whole new exhibit," claimed a 1973 *Car and Driver* report on the 455 Super Duty.

Everything about the LS2 was super-duper, beginning with its new beefy block, burly nodular-iron crank, and bullet-proof forged-iron rods. Also inside were 8.4:1 TRW forged-aluminum pistons and a heavy-duty oil pump. A Rochester Quadra-Jet four-barrel delivered the fuel/air, while free-flowing cast-iron headers hauled away spent gases. But the real stars of the show were the cylinder heads, which were lovingly massaged by the horsepower hounds at Air Flow Research to move the good air in, bad air out better than anything Pontiac engineers had ever concocted. The end result was a low-compression, high-powered big-block that could rev surely and strongly to 6,000 rpm, even on 91-octane fuel, while still remaining kind to the environment. Or was it?

1972 Formula

1972 Formula	
Model availability	two-door hardtop
Wheelbase	108.1 inches
Length	191.6 inches
Width	73.4 inches
Height	50.4 inches
Weight	3,424 pounds (Formula 350)
Base price	$3,221 (Formula 350)
Track (front/rear, in inches)	61.6/60.3
Wheels	14x7 stamped steel
Tires	F70x14
Suspension	independent unequal A-arms, coil springs and stabilizer bar in front; multi-leaf springs, solid axle and stabilizer bar in back
Steering	recirculating ball
Brakes	front discs, rear drums
Engine	175-horsepower 350-cubic-inch L30 V-8, std. (250-horsepower 400-cubic-inch L78 V-8 and 300-horsepower 455-cubic-inch HO V-8, optional)
Bore & stroke	3.875 x 3.75 inches (350), 4.12 x 3.75 inches (400), 4.15 x 4.21 inches (455)
Compression	8.0:1 (L30 350), 8.2:1 (L78), 8.4:1 455 HO)
Fuel delivery	single four-barrel carburetor
Transmission	three-speed manual with Hurst shifter, std.
Production	5,249 (all engines)

Left
The Formula family was officially named by engine in 1973, with the pecking order predictably reading Formula 350, Formula 400, and Formula 455. The Formula 400 (shown here) featured the L78 400 big-block, rated at 230 horsepower.

1973 Formula

1973 Formula

Model availability	two-door hardtop
Wheelbase	108.1 inches
Length	192.1 inches
Width	73.4 inches
Height	50.4 inches
Weight	3,318 pounds (Formula 350)
Base price	$3,276 (Formula 350); $3,373 (Formula 400); $3,430 (Formula 455); $3,951 (Formula SD-455)
Track (front/rear, in inches)	61.6/60.3
Wheels	14x7 stamped steel
Tires	F70x14
Suspension	independent unequal A-arms, coil springs and stabilizer bar in front; multi-leaf springs, solid axle and stabilizer bar in back
Steering	recirculating ball
Brakes	front discs, rear drums
Engine	175-horsepower 350-cubic-inch L30 V-8, std. (230-horsepower 400-cubic-inch L78 V-8, 250-horsepower 455-cubic-inch L75 V-8, 290-horsepower 455-cubic-inch Super Duty V-8, optional)
Bore & stroke	3.875 x 3.75 inches (350), 4.12 x 3.75 inches (400), 4.15 x 4.21 inches (455)
Compression	7.6:1 (L30 350); 8.0:1 (L78 400, L75 455, and LS2 Super Duty)
Fuel delivery	single four-barrel carburetor
Transmission	three-speed manual with Hurst shifter, std.
Production	10,171 (all engines)

Above
The king of the 455 V-8 family was the Super Duty rendition, which initially was rated at 310 horsepower when introduced to the press in June 1973. That advertised figure fell to 290 horses by the time the 455 SD became a Formula and Trans option early in 1973.

Clever PMD engineers had noticed that the EPA's required engine testing only ran for about 50 seconds. They then put together an ingenious system that automatically shut off the exhaust gas recirculation valve after 53 seconds. This trick allowed the 455 Super Duty to breathe easier while making 310 net-rated horses. Of course, it also meant the LS2 spit out unacceptable contaminants, this after supposedly passing emissions testing with apparent flying colors.

Unfortunately, those clean-air cops were clever too. They immediately smelled a rat and the ruse was quickly uncovered. Pontiac was then forced to remove its EGR inactivating system and retest the Super Duty by March 15, 1973. To pass this second test, engineers had to trade their original SD cam (with 0.480-inch lift) for a truly tame 0.401-inch-lift unit. Advertised output then dropped to 290 horsepower, which was still nothing to sneeze at.

The 455 SD was originally introduced, in 310-horse form, to the press by Herb Adams,

chief of the Special Products Group, on June 28, 1972, at GM's Milford Proving Grounds. Initial reports claimed the Super Duty option would become available that fall for the Grand Am, Grand Prix, Le Mans, and both Firebirds, the Trans Am and Formula. Deliveries, however, were delayed until April 1973 by those testing hassles, and by then only the two F-bodies were fitted with the Super Duty punch. Quarter-mile performance was reported at 13.8 super seconds.

1974 Formula

Model availability	two-door hardtop
Wheelbase	108.1 inches
Length	196 inches
Width	73.0 inches
Height	49.2 inches
Weight	3,548 pounds (Formula 350)
Base price	$3,614 (Formula 350); $3,711 (Formula 400); $3,768 (Formula 455); $4,289 (Formula SD-455)
Track (front/rear, in inches)	61.6/60.3
Wheels	14x7 stamped steel
Tires	F70x14
Suspension	independent unequal A-arms, coil springs and stabilizer bar in front; multi-leaf springs, solid axle and stabilizer bar in back
Steering	recirculating ball
Brakes	front discs, rear drums
Engine	170-horsepower 350-cubic-inch L30 V-8, std. (200-horsepower 400-cubic-inch L78 V-8, 250-horsepower 455-cubic-inch L75 V-8, 290-horsepower 455-cubic-inch Super Duty V-8, optional)
Bore & stroke	3.875 x 3.75 inches (350), 4.12 x 3.75 inches (400), 4.15 x 4.21 inches (455)
Compression	7.6:1 (L30 350); 8.0:1 (L78 400, L75 455, and LS2 Super Duty)
Fuel delivery	single four-barrel carburetor
Transmission	three-speed manual with Hurst shifter, std.
Production	14,462 (discounting 455 Super Duty)

1974

Pontiac sold another 57 Formulas 455 SDs before reality finally caught up with this passionate Poncho. The 455 SD was cancelled at year's end and thus came a definite close to Detroit's original muscle car era. All purported performance machines to follow were more or less imposters, though it should be said that Pontiac's Trans Am did manage to pull off its pretender role rather ably into the 1980s before re-emerging as a true muscle car. The attractive Formula remained in the Firebird family until 1981.

The Formula clan for 1974 was broken down by engine, with the Formula 350 featuring the 170-horsepower L30 small-block. The Formula 400 relied on the 200-horsepower L78 big-block, and the Formula 455 used the 250-horsepower L78 V-8. Last but certainly not least was the Formula SD 455 with its 290-horsepower LS2 big-block.

Above
A new nose appeared for the Firebird clan in 1974. The Formula 400 (shown here) that year was fitted with a 200-horsepower L78 big-block V-8. The Formula 455's base engine produced 250 horsepower. Optional for one more year was the big, bad 455 Super Duty, still rated at 290 horsepower.

The 455 SD was cancelled at year's end and thus came a definite close to Detroit's original muscle car era.

10

Above
1969 Trans Am

Middle
1971 Trans Am

Right
1974 Super Duty Trans Am

Lengthy Legacy

10 ···▷

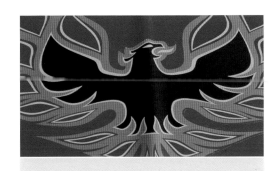

Pontiac Trans Am 1969–1974

Excusing Chevrolet's Corvette (which commonly isn't classed as a muscle car because it is considered to be in a class all its own) from the conversation, Pontiac's Trans Am was the only hot-to-trot machine to remain on the market continuously from Detroit's high-performance heydays in the 1960s into the modern era. Born in 1969, the Firebird-based T/A rolled nonstop until General Motors closed the book on its long-running, still-revered F-body line in 2002.

As its name should have implied, Pontiac's high-profile pony car was originally created, like its Camaro Z28 cousin, to make the Firebird a force in SCCA road racing. But contrary to their Chevrolet counterparts, Pontiac's competition-conscious engineers initially found that road to be a bumpy ride. Vince Piggins and crew triumphantly put Chevy's new pony car into the race with little difficulty in 1967, and the Z28 copped a Trans-Am championship the following year. Firebirds, meanwhile, remained in the stock-class circuit's shadows, primarily because no workable mixing and matching of available cranks and blocks could be easily conjured from the PMD parts book to produce an SCCA-legal power plant, one displacing no more than 5 liters.

Canadian businessman Terry Godsall did take the Firebird road racing in 1968, relying on a loophole based on the belief that all Pontiac models produced for sale in Canada were available with Chevrolet V-8s. This purported fact allowed him to use the Z28's 302-cube hybrid small-block in his SCCA-legal racing 'Birds. In truth, many Pontiacs sold north of the border were Chevy-powered. Canadian Firebirds, on the other hand, were all built in Norwood, Ohio, using typical Pontiac engines. A scam? Basically, yes. But apparently SCCA officials couldn't have cared less—the more the merrier, perhaps?

Pontiac's legit in-house efforts to make the SCCA scene were well under way even as the Canadian ruse was taking root. Fostering visions of a PMD performance machine comparable to Chevy's Corvette from the beginning of his firm's pony car development effort, Pontiac chief John De Lorean wasn't about to let Pete Estes' Camaros run away without a little supposedly friendly competition. Supported by upbeat engineers like Steve Malone, Bill Collins, and Herb Adams, De Lorean rode herd over various proposals intended to match up with Chevy's Z28, as well as Ford's upcoming Boss 302 Mustang.

- → The Trans Am made its public debut at the Chicago Auto Show on March 8, 1969.
- → Though engineers claimed the first Trans Am's rear wing worked well to create downforce at speed, the car's nose did the opposite—front end lift was a real problem in 1969.
- → Only eight Trans Am convertibles were built in 1969. Another topless T/A didn't appear until 1991.
- → All 1969 Trans Ams featured Cameo White paint with blue accents.
- → Second-generation Trans Ams ran from 1970 to 1981.
- → Big-block power remained standard for the Trans Am up through 1979.
- → Annual Trans Am production surpassed 100,000 for the first time in 1979.
- → Optional turbocharging appeared in 1980.
- → Turbo V-6 power debuted in 1989.
- → Special anniversary Trans Am models were offered in 1976 (marking Pontiac's 50th birthday), 1979, 1984, 1989, 1994, and 1999.
- → Pontiac's last Trans Am was built in 2002.

Opposite
Trans Am production that first year was 697, including 8 convertibles. All were painted Cameo White with blue accents. *Mike Mueller*

The NASCAR V-8 reportedly dynoed at 585 horsepower, while its 400-cid cousin produced roughly 500 horses.

Chevrolet took its Camaro SCCA road racing in 1967. Pontiac then tried the same trick with its Firebird in 1969, resulting in the first Trans Am, a muscle car icon that rolled on uninterrupted until 2002. *Mike Mueller*

Among these projects was Adams' "PFST," or Pontiac Firebird Sprint Turismo, a machine inspired by racer/car-builder John Fitch's "Fitchbird" GT conversion kit offered for PMD pony cars in 1967. Reportedly a dozen or so PFST club racers were built early in 1968, some with V-8 power, others with Pontiac's overhead-cam six-cylinder. About the same time, another prominent racer/builder, Jack Brabham, was invited by De Lorean to contribute his world-class experience to another SCCA-targeted development program. Meanwhile, work also progressed on an SCCA-legal de-stroked V-8, the fabled Ram Air V. Displacing only 303 cubic-inches, this bodacious little big-block, once in production, would allow a hot, homologated Firebird entry into the Trans-Am fraternity.

Ram Air V roots ran back to 1967 when De Lorean turned Malcolm MacKellar's engineering team loose on a racing engine project involving Pontiac's 428-cid V-8. Using cylinder heads copied from Ford's NASCAR-proven tunnel-port 427 design, MacKellar's crew built what would later become known as the Ram Air VI and Ram Air VII V-8s, stillborn screamers that laid the groundwork for other track-ready big-block development.

Attention began turning to the SCCA circuit midway through 1968. To meet Trans-Am racing's 5-liter limit, Special Projects Group engineer Steve Malone de-stroked Pontiac's 400-cid big-block to 303 cubes and added similar tunnel-port heads to create the Ram Air V. Special Projects' engineers also developed two other Ram Air V big-blocks, a 366-cid version targeted for NASCAR competition and a 400-cid running mate originally aimed at GTO buyers as a street/strip power choice. All three Ram Air V engines featured extra-heavy-duty blocks, rods, and cranks; free-flowing, individual-runner exhaust manifolds; and a big 780-cfm Holley four-barrel carb on a special aluminum high-rise intake manifold. The NASCAR V-8 reportedly dynoed at 585 horsepower, while its 400-cid

cousin produced roughly 500 horses.

Estimated output for the 303 V-8 was about 430 horsepower. Initial plans called for at least 1,000 of these tunnel-port big-blocks to find their way into 1969 Firebirds to meet SCCA homologation requirements. An optional "Brabham Firebird" package was also considered early on that year, as well. By the time the dust settled, Brabham's respected moniker was dropped in favor of a more suitable tag, this one in keeping with Pontiac's tradition of borrowing famous world-renowned racing images for its new models. An alternate choice was quite clear: If SCCA racing was the goal, it was only right to name the car Trans Am. Only this time De Lorean couldn't just claim this title as his own. His people had to negotiate a royalty fee with SCCA officials: $5 for every Trans Am Pontiac built.

Undoubtedly, no one at Pontiac figured the Trans Am would have such long legs when they introduced the car to the automotive press in December 1968 at Riverside International Raceway in California. The goal initially was to build just enough T/A Firebirds to go SCCA racing for however long that roller coaster ride lasted. But a competition career never really got off the ground after the 303 V-8 failed to make it into regular production. Fortunately it was another story entirely on the street. Discounting the Corvette once again, nothing out of Detroit could match the Trans Am during the horsepower-starved late-1970s and 1980s as far as born-in-the-U.S.A. four-wheeled excitement was concerned.

1969

Pontiac's Trans Am Performance and Appearance package, option code WS4, was priced at about $1,100 in 1969, depending on transmission choice and body style. Both coupes and convertibles were built: 689 of the former, only 8 of the latter. Appearance features included a blacked-out grille, small "Trans Am"

1969 Trans Am

1969 Trans Am

Model availability	two-door hardtop and convertible
Wheelbase	108.1 inches
Length	191.1 inches
Width	73.9 inches
Height	49.6 inches
Weight	3,654 pounds
Base price	$3,887
Track (front/rear, in inches)	60/60
Wheels	14x7 stamped steel
Tires	F70x14
Suspension	independent unequal A-arms, coil springs and stabilizer bar in front; multi-leaf springs, solid axle and stabilizer bar in back
Steering	recirculating ball w/variable-ratio power steering
Brakes	front discs, rear drums, with power assist
Engine	335-horsepower 400-cubic-inch Ram Air III V-8 (345-horsepower 400-cubic-inch Ram Air IV V-8, optional)
Bore & stroke	4.12 x 3.75 inches
Compression	10.75:1
Fuel delivery	single four-barrel carburetor
Transmission	heavy-duty three-speed manual, std.
Axle ratio	3.55:1 in Safe-T-Track differential
Production	697 (includes 8 convertibles)

decals, Cameo White paint with blue racing stripes, and a matching blue taillight panel. Standard, too, were fender-mounted air extractors, a twin-scooped ram-air hood, and a rear spoiler, all equipment that helped turn heads while performing valuable functions at the same time. The extractors reportedly kept underhood temperatures down, the scoops allowed the big 750-cfm Quadrajet four-barrel beneath to breathe in cooler, denser air. According to Herb Adams, the 60-inch-wide rear wing created 100 pounds of downward force at 100 miles per hour.

Beneath that rather beauteous skin was a typically beefed-up chassis: a thickened 1-inch sway bar, heavier front coils and rear leafs, stiffer shocks, and a limited-slip Safe-T-Track differential with 3.55:1 gears. Brakes were power front discs, and variable-ratio power steering was standard too. F70 fiberglass-belted tires on 14x7 steel rims completed the package.

In place of the stillborn 303 V-8 was Pontiac's proven 400-cid big-block. Standard was the 335-horsepower Ram Air III version (L74) backed by a heavy-duty three-speed manual transmission. On the options list was the wide-ratio M20 four-speed, its close-ratio M21 alternative, or GM's ever-present M40 Turbo-Hydra-Matic automatic. Optional, too, was the L67 Ram Air IV 400, conservatively rated at 345 horsepower. Ram Air IV features included an aluminum intake (in place of the L74's cast-iron unit), a heavy-duty four-bolt block, cross-drilled crank, a lumpier cam, and special heads with large round exhaust ports instead of the L74's D-shaped ports.

Above left
Pontiac engineers attempted to downsize the Firebird's 400-cubic-inch big-block V-8 to allow it entry into the SCCA's Trans-Am racing fraternity, resulting in the 303-cube Ram Air V, which made an estimated 430 horsepower. Unfortunately this mean mill never made it into regular production.

Above right
The original Trans Am's standard rear wing reportedly produced 100 pounds of downforce at 100 miles per hour. Too bad the car's nose made way too much unwanted lift at speed. *Mike Mueller*

Right
Rally II wheels were optional for the first Trans Am. *Mike Mueller*

Only 55 Trans Am customers chose the L67 V-8 in 1969: 9 with automatics, 46 with manuals. All eight 1969 Trans Am convertibles featured the L74: 4 automatics, 4 manuals. Transmission breakdown for the 634 L74 hardtops was 114 automatics, 520 manuals.

Right
Unlike its small-block Z/28 cousin from Chevrolet, the 1969 Trans Am came standard with big-block power: Pontiac's 400-cubic-inch Ram Air III V-8 (shown here), rated at 335 horsepower. The awesome 345-horse Ram Air IV was optional.

Below left
A three-spoke steering wheel with simulated wooden rim was standard inside the 1969 Trans Am. Variable-ratio power steering and power front disc brakes also were part of the package. *Mike Mueller*

Below right
A heavy-duty three-speed manual was standard in 1969. Two four-speeds—one close-ratio, one wide-ratio—and the Turbo Hydra-Matic automatic were optional. *Mike Mueller*

1970 Trans Am

1970 Trans Am

Model availability	two-door hardtop
Wheelbase	108 inches
Length	191.6 inches
Width	73.4 inches
Height	50.4 inches
Weight	3,550 pounds
Base price	$4,305
Track (front/rear, in inches)	61.6/60.3
Wheels	15x7 Rally II five-spokes
Tires	F60x15 white-letter
Suspension	independent unequal A-arms, coil springs and stabilizer bar in front; multi-leaf springs, solid axle and stabilizer bar in back
Steering	recirculating ball w/variable-ratio power steering
Brakes	front discs, rear drums, with power assist
Engine	345-horsepower 400-cubic-inch Ram Air III L74 V-8 (370-horsepower 400-cubic-inch Ram Air IV LS1 V-8, optional)
Bore & stroke	4.12 x 3.75 inches
Compression	10.5:1
Fuel delivery	single four-barrel carburetor
Transmission	three-speed manual, std. (four-speed manual w/Hurst shifter and Turbo Hydra-Matic automatic were no-cost options)
Production	3,196

1970

Polar White replaced Cameo White for Pontiac's second-edition Trans Am, which, like its Z28 cousin, showed up late in February 1970 due to various delays encountered while bringing GM's next-generation F-body to market. Now offered only in full-roof form, the 1970 Trans Am also could have been ordered in a second color: Lucerne Blue. Standard striping returned but was redone in one bold center line accented with black edging. The stripe color inside that black border was white on blue cars, blue on white ones. Attractive Rally II wheels

(without trim rings) also became standard features after appearing optionally the previous year. Chrome trim rings for these rims cost $21 in 1970. New, too, on the 1970 standard-equipment list were aerodynamic sport mirrors, a snazzy engine-turned aluminum instrument panel insert, 14-inch Formula steering wheel, and the Rally Gauge Cluster.

Such details definitely appeared trivial considering overall impressions, which arguably stood among Detroit's most creative melding of form and function to date. Everything that helped the 1969 Trans Am stand out in a crowd returned, this time with much more purposefulness. Front fender air extractors were noticeably larger, and a new integral rear deck spoiler was joined by a standard front air dam, the latter to help better deal with the troublesome front-end lift encountered the year before. Special spats added to the wheelhouses' leading edges also

aided aerodynamics. Crowning things was a shaker-style hood scoop that opened to the rear—a Trans Am trademark that remained in place until 1980.

Yet another familiar feature—later affectionately (or not) called the screaming chicken logo—debuted in 1970 in decal form at the Trans Am's Endura nose. Remaining rather humble early on, this decal would eventually grow to cover the car's hood, making it the only hokey aspect of this purposeful machine.

Everything else about the 1970 Trans Am represented the real deal. According to Pontiac ads, this 14-second street stormer featured "gauges that gauge, spoilers that spoil, scoops that scoop." In *Car and Driver's* words, the machine was "a hard-muscled, lightning-reflexed commando of a car, the likes of which doesn't exist anywhere in the world, even for twice the price."

Car and Driver called the second-edition Trans Am "a hard-muscled, lightning-reflexed commando of a car." It surely was one of Detroit's most exciting-looking machines for 1970.

For $4,305, a 1970 Trans Am customer got
this fully functional facade along with the Ram
Air III 400 V-8, now backed by a Hurst-shifted
wide-ratio four-speed manual gearbox. The
close-ratio four-speed and Turbo Hydra-Matic
automatic were no-cost options. L74 output
jumped 10 horses this year, while the optional
Ram Air IV V-8 (renamed the LS1 in 1970) was
pumped up to 370 horsepower.

Only 88 LS1 models were built for 1970:
59 automatics, 29 manuals. Total Trans Am production (LS1 and L74) that year rose to 3,196.

1971 Trans Am

1971 Trans Am

Model availability	two-door hardtop
Wheelbase	108 inches
Length	191.6 inches
Width	73.4 inches
Height	50.4 inches
Weight	3,602 pounds
Base price	$4,464
Track (front/rear, in inches)	61.6/60.3
Wheels	Rally II five-spokes or honeycomb rims (both 15x7)
Tires	F60x15 white-letter
Suspension	independent unequal A-arms, coil springs and stabilizer bar in front; multi-leaf springs, solid axle and stabilizer bar in back
Steering	recirculating ball w/variable-ratio power steering
Brakes	front discs, rear drums, with power assist
Engine	335-horsepower 455-cubic-inch HO V-8 (LS5)
Bore & stroke	4.15 x 4.21 inches
Compression	8.4:1
Fuel delivery	single four-barrel carburetor
Transmission	four-speed manual w/Hurst shifter (Turbo Hydra-Matic automatic was a no-cost option)
Production	2,116

Most noticeable were new standard 15x7 "honeycomb" wheels.

Above
Few notable changes were made to the Trans Am in 1971. Both the familiar Rally II wheels and Pontiac's new honeycomb rims were available that year. The only engine available was the new 455 HO, rated at 335 horsepower.

1971

Few exterior changes marked the Trans Am's march into 1971. Most noticeable were new standard 15x7 "honeycomb" wheels. Fourteen-inch versions of these popular rims were offered optionally on other Pontiac models, and the 15-inch type remained available for Firebirds up through 1976. The familiar Rally II wheels remained on the options list for the 1971 Trans Am, while F60 white-letter tires were standard, as they had been the year before. High-back Vega bucket seats became standard inside in 1971 in place of the low-back buckets seen previously.

Only one engine was available for the third-edition Trans Am, but this big-block was the biggest yet—455 cubic-inches. The 335-horse 455 HO was backed by either the Hurst-shifted close-ratio four-speed or Turbo Hydra-Matic automatic. All other mechanicals rolled over from 1970.

Trans Am production dipped to 2,116 in 1971: 1,231 automatics, 885 manuals. Polar White and Lucerne Blue again constituted the only exterior finishes offered.

1972 Trans Am

1972

A restyled grille, apparently inspired by the honeycomb wheels introduced the year before, represented the easiest way to identify Pontiac's 1972 Trans Am as even fewer changes were made this year. Those honeycomb rims became options this time around with the Rally II wheels returning to the standard-equipment list.

The LS5 455 HO returned, now net rated at 300 horsepower. Remaining mechanicals and features once again carried over, as did paint choices. Production for 1972 was 1,286: 828 automatics and 458 four-speeds.

1972 Trans Am	
Model availability	two-door hardtop
Wheelbase	108 inches
Length	191.6 inches
Width	73.4 inches
Height	50.4 inches
Curb weight	3,564 pounds
Base price	$4,256
Track (front/rear, in inches)	61.6/60.3
Wheels	15x7 Rally II five-spokes, std.
Tires	F60x15 white-letter
Suspension	independent unequal A-arms, coil springs and stabilizer bar in front; multi-leaf springs, solid axle and stabilizer bar in back
Steering	recirculating ball w/variable-ratio power steering
Brakes	front discs, rear drums, with power assist
Engine	300-horsepower 455-cubic-inch HO V-8 (LS5)
Bore & stroke	4.15 x 4.21 inches
Compression	8.4:1
Fuel delivery	single four-barrel carburetor
Transmission	four-speed manual w/Hurst shifter (Turbo Hydra-Matic was a no-cost option)
Production	1,286

Below
A restyled grille, echoing the honeycomb wheel design introduced the previous year, identified a 1972 Trans Am at a glance up front. Paint choices carried over from 1971. *Mike Mueller*

Above
Chrome exhaust tips again were included in the Trans Am package for 1972, as were all those high-profile spoilers, spats, and air extractors. *Mike Mueller*

Left
Now famously familiar on the street scene, the Trans Am's standard shaker hood scoop once again topped only one engine in 1972, the 455 HO big-block V-8. *Mike Mueller*

Right
The 455 HO was rated at 300 horsepower for 1972. Compression was 8.4:1. *Mike Mueller*

Below left
Rally II wheels, with trim rings this time, were standard for the 1972 Trans Am. These flashy honeycomb rims became options that year. *Mike Mueller*

Below right
The standard Trans Am interior carried over essentially unchanged into 1972. Only 458 four-speed models were built that year. The front and rear consoles seen here were optional. *Mike Mueller*

1973 Trans Am

1973 Trans Am

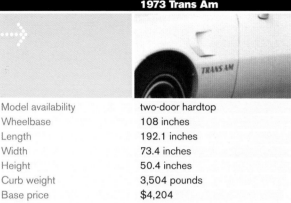

Model availability	two-door hardtop
Wheelbase	108 inches
Length	192.1 inches
Width	73.4 inches
Height	50.4 inches
Curb weight	3,504 pounds
Base price	$4,204
Track (front/rear, in inches)	61.6/60.3
Wheels	15x7 Rally II five-spokes, std.
Tires	F60x15 white-letter
Suspension	independent unequal A-arms, coil springs and stabilizer bar in front; multi-leaf springs, solid axle and stabilizer bar in back
Steering	recirculating ball w/variable-ratio power steering
Brakes	front discs, rear drums, with power assist
Engine	300-horsepower 455-cubic-inch HO V-8 (L75)
Bore & stroke	4.15 x 4.21 inches
Compression	8.4:1
Fuel delivery	single four-barrel carburetor
Transmission	four-speed manual w/Hurst shifter (Turbo Hydra-Matic was a no-cost option)
Production	4,550 (not including 455 Super Duty)

Above

Cameo White returned as an available Trans Am finish for 1973. Lucerne Blue was retired, but two new shades—Buccaneer Red and Brewster Green—appeared. The Trans Am's soon-to-be-familiar flaming firebird hood decal option also debuted this year.

1973

New colors appeared for 1973: Buccaneer Red and Brewster Green. Lucerne Blue was dropped and Polar White was replaced by Cameo White. The wide center stripe running the length of the car was dropped, but this deletion was offset by a new decal option, code WW7, which added a truly large flaming firebird to the hood in front of the familiar shaker scoop. Introduced early in the model run, this $55 option appeared on about half of the 4,802 1973 Trans Ams. All others came standard with the small decal traditionally located at the car's pointed nose.

In both cases, small or large, the decal's colors varied according to paint choice. While the bird itself remained black, the surrounding flames went from orange (with Buccaneer Red) to blue (with Cameo White) to light green (with Brewster Green).

G70 radial rubber appeared as a new option in 1973, and quicker steering became standard. Beneath that ever-present shaker scoop—which was no longer functional—was Pontiac's L75 455 V-8, rated at 250 horsepower. A close-ratio four-speed manual was again standard, with the Turbo Hydra-Matic returning as a no-cost option. Total L75 production was 4,550: 3,130 automatics and 1,420 manuals.

An additional 252 1973 Trans Ams featured the optional 455 Super Duty V-8, a midyear addition that many recognized as Detroit's last gasp as far as true high performance was concerned. Originally announced in June 1972

at 310 horsepower, the 455 SD was quickly downrated to 290 horsepower in regular production form. In either case, super simply was not a big enough word.

"The Last of the Fast Cars comes standard with the sort of acceleration that hasn't been seen in years," announced *Car and Driver* in a road test of a pre-production 310-horsepower Super Duty Trans Am. "How it ever got past the preview audience in GM's board room is a mystery, but here it is—the car that couldn't happen." With an automatic transmission, full exhausts, and street tires, this baby screamed through the quarter-mile in 13.8 seconds, fast by any recollection.

Yet equally quick was its run into the history books. Of the 455 Trans Am Super Dutys built for 1973, 180 featured automatic transmissions, and 72 featured manuals.

1974 Trans Am

1974 Trans Am

Model availability	two-door hardtop
Wheelbase	108 inches
Length	196 inches
Width	73.0 inches
Height	49.2 inches
Curb weight	3,655 pounds
Base price	$4,351 (w/400 V-8);
	$4,408 (w/455 V-8);
	$4,929 (w/455 Super Duty V-8)
Track (front/rear, in inches)	61.6/60.3
Wheels	15x7 Rally II five-spokes, std.
Tires	F60x15 white-letter
Suspension	independent unequal A-arms, coil springs and stabilizer bar in front; multi-leaf springs, solid axle and stabilizer bar in back
Steering	recirculating ball w/variable-ratio power steering
Brakes	front discs, rear drums, with power assist
Engine	225-horsepower 400-cubic-inch L78 V-8, std. (250-horsepower 455-cubic-inch L75 V-8 and 290-horsepoer 455 Super Duty V-8, optional)
Bore & stroke	4.15 x 4.21 inches
Compression	8.0:1
Fuel delivery	single four-barrel carburetor
Transmission	four-speed manual w/Hurst shifter (Turbo Hydra-Matic was a no-cost option)
Production	9,312 (not including 455 Super Duty)

1974

Another 943 Trans Am SDs followed for 1974, with the breakdown reading 731 automatics, 212 manuals. And that was that. Able to prolong the great American muscle car's final demise for a few years, Pontiac engineers simply couldn't keep the dream alive in a world full of catalytic converters and low-octane fuels. In many minds, the same company that kicked off the muscle car race in 1964 suitably signaled its end 10 years later with the Trans Am Super Duty.

Both the 290-horsepower 455 SD and its 250-horsepower L75 little brother were options for the 1974 Trans Am, which featured a new slanted nose and revised tail that did away with the chrome bumper used previously. Standard power this year was supplied by a 225-horse-power 400-cid V-8, also backed by either a

In *Car and Driver*'s words, the machine was "a hard-muscled, lightning-reflexed commando of a car, the likes of which doesn't exist anywhere in the world, even for twice the price."

four-speed or the Turbo Hydra-Matic automatic. The L75 was limited only to the automatic application, and production was 4,648, while the count for the standard 400 Trans Am was 4,664: 1,750 with manual transmissions, 2,914 with automatics. The final 1974 tally, counting all engines, was 10,255, more than twice as many Trans Ams as Pontiac built the previous year.

Trans Am popularity soared from there even though actual performance behind that hot image was sadly lacking. It would take nearly 15 years before the fires again burned so brightly.

Right
The Trans Am's "screaming chicken" hood decal was a $55 option in 1974. *Mike Mueller*

Below
A new tail for 1974 did away with the chrome bumper seen previously. Both Rally II and honeycomb wheels were again available for the Trans Am that year. *Mike Mueller*

Above
Pontiac engineers managed to sneak one last great burst of power out before the life was finally strangled out of the American muscle car. Introduced midyear in 1973, the 455 Super Duty passed emissions tests and still produced 290 real horsepower. It returned for 1974 (shown here) before falling victim to the realities of a changing automotive world. *Mike Mueller*

Top right
Pontiac's 8 track player was a $130 option in 1974. Rockin' out with Ozzy Osbourne while roaring down the road in a Super Duty Trans Am? Priceless. *Mike Mueller*

Right
Super Duty Trans Am production totaled 943 for 1974, including 731 automatics (shown here) and 212 four-speeds. Other options on this legendary muscle machine include deluxe interior appointments, tilt steering wheel, air conditioning, and power windows. *Mike Mueller*

11

Above
1969 Hurst/Olds

Middle
1974 Hurst/Olds

Right
1975 Hurst/Olds Indy 500 Pace Car

Power Shift

OFFICIAL PACE CAR
58TH ANNUAL INDIANAPOLIS 500 MILE RACE
MAY 26, 1974

W-30

11

Hurst/Olds 1968–1975

Personalizing a muscle car was every bit as commonplace 40-some years ago as it is today. Stock steel rims typically were the first things to go back in the 1960s, often replaced by a set of gleaming Cragar S/S five-spoke mags, probably the most coveted custom wheels then, as well as for decades to follow. Also performed regularly was a more functional mod: dumping standard iron exhaust manifolds for a set of free-breathing tube headers, easily the quickest way to free up a few extra horses hiding within that small-block Chevy or big-block Buick.

Aftermarket suppliers in this case were plentiful, but if you wanted to trade that often-clunky, regular-production shifter for a really hot stick, there was only one real choice. If that wasn't a Hurst in your right mitt, it was nothing.

Hands down, nobody built precise, lightning-quick shifters like George Hurst. Factory hot rods have come and gone over the years, and come back again. But the ever-popular Hurst shifter has always been there at arm's reach whenever a need for speed shifting has a risen. What worked so well in the GTO in 1964 continues to do the trick almost a half century later.

The roots of this legacy run back to 1954, when 27-year-old George Hurst was discharged from the Navy. His first business was George Hurst Automotive in Philadelphia, a small shop that did repairs and hop-ups. Popular hot rod

engine swaps quickly became his forte, and he started designing various motor mounts to make these conversions a snap.

He also hand-crafted a fool-proof floorshift for his 1956 Chevrolet, a durable unit featuring much shorter throws than stock units of the day. Right after Christmas 1958, he set out in his floorshifted Chevy in search of buyers for this top-notch performance enhancement. In Detroit, Gratiot Auto Supply immediately ordered as many slick sticks as Hurst could supply, and a *Hot Rod* magazine report soon had gearheads across America clamoring for one. Back home in Philadelphia Hurst took out a $20,000 loan to begin manufacturing his shifters big time.

Earlier in 1958 he had made official an existing partnership with cohort Bill Campbell, resulting in the Hurst-Campbell Company. Anco Industries was formed the following year,

- → Along with GM's B-O-P trio, Chrysler, Dodge, Plymouth, and American Motors all offered Hurst conversion models during the 1960s and 1970s.
- → In 1965, Hurst introduced an especially tough custom wheel called the "Dazzler," which was then promoted as part of Pontiac's GeeTO Tiger giveaway contest. Despite its merits, the Hurst wheel never really got rolling.
- → George Hurst also patented his "Jaws of Life" rescue apparatus in 1965.
- → A second exhibition drag car, Hurst's "Hairy Olds," debuted in 1966 with two Toronado V-8s powering all four wheels.
- → Hurst hired Linda Vaughn as one of various "Hurst Golden Shifter Girls" in 1966. Every bit as affable as she was eye-popping, Vaughn soon became the parade-ground ambassador not only for Hurst but the entire high-performance realm.
- → Save for one, perhaps two four-speed examples built in 1968, all other Hurst/Olds models featured GM's Turbo Hydra-Matic automatic controlled by Hurst's Dual Gate shifter.

Opposite
The Hurst/Olds conversions were made on a hastily prepared assembly line at Demmer Engineering in 1968. *From the files of Hurst/Olds Club of America*

George Hurst opened a small automotive shop in Philadelphia in 1954, then fashioned his first performance-conscious floor shifter, for his own car, four years later. *From the files of Hurst/Olds Club of America*

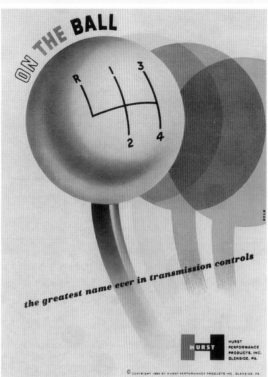

By 1964, Hurst sticks were among the hottest things going in this country's high-performance aftermarket. Hurst died in May 1986.

Along with its legendary shifters, Hurst products also included brake components and custom wheels. The Hurst name also showed up on various mean machines, including the famous "Hemi Under Glass" Plymouth Barracuda exhibition drag cars.

later becoming Hurst Performance Products Inc., Hurst-Campbell's sales division. By 1965, Hurst-Campbell was bringing in more than $20 million annually, triggering the construction of bigger, better digs in Warminster, Pennsylvania. The Hurst Research Center, directed by Jack "Doc" Watson, also opened about the same time outside Detroit in Madison Heights. Hurst-Campbell bought out clutch-maker Schiefer Manufacturing and the Airheart brake company.

Hurst Performance's big break came in 1961 when Bunkie Knudsen and Pete Estes asked George Hurst in for a meeting at Pontiac. Estes had read *Hot Rod*'s appraisal and had a proposition. A deal was then inked and Pontiac began offering Hurst shifters as a parts-counter option. And when the GTO debuted in October 1963, it featured a Hurst stick as standard equipment.

As Jim Wangers later explained in *Automobile Quarterly*, "We quickly learned that one of the first things a new customer would do

after purchasing a high-performance stick shift car was to take it down to the local hot rod shop and install a Hurst. I was finally able to convince both Estes and De Lorean that it meant more to Pontiac to be able to advertise the fact that our cars came equipped with a Hurst right from the factory than it meant to Hurst to say they were original equipment on a Pontiac. This was the first time GM had ever allowed a component supplier's name to be used in advertising."

All GTOs built up through 1974 featured factory-equipped Hurst sticks. Available as well for automatic transmission cars was Hurst's Dual Gate shifter, the so-called "His and Hers" unit, first developed in 1964. The list of Hurst-equipped muscle cars grew fast soon afterward, including Plymouth's Superbird, which in 1970 used easily the most distinctive rendition, the high-arching "Pistol Grip" shifter. Hurst shifters were even created for Volkswagens.

Hurst's multifaceted firm also was the aftermarket home to a large family of modified

factory muscle machines, a group led most prominently by the long-running Hurst/Olds line, first offered in 1968. Hurst got involved that year, too, with Chrysler Corporation, helping both Dodge and Plymouth wedge 426 Hemi V-8s into a limited run of Dart and Barracuda super-stock drag cars. Two years later, Hurst did the 300H, a 440-powered 1970 Chrysler that briefly brought back memories of the famed letter-series beautiful brutes of 1955–1965.

Hurst teamed up with American Motors in 1969 to produce the SC/Rambler, a truly hot 315-horsepower compact adorned inside and out in patriotic red, white, and blue. Additional standard equipment included a Sun tachometer and—you guessed it—a Hurst four-speed stick. The Hurst/AMC alliance also produced the strip-ready AMX S/S in 1969 and the Rebel Machine in 1970.

Appearing in 1970 as well was Pontiac's Grand Prix SSJ, a Hurst conversion that could've been equipped with a 455 V-8 and

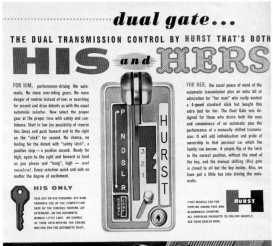

dual gate...

THE DUAL TRANSMISSION CONTROL BY HURST THAT'S BOTH

HIS and HERS

FOR HIM, performance-driving the automatic. No more over-riding gears. No more danger of reverse instead of low, or searching for second and drive detents as with the usual automatic selector. Now select the proper gear at the proper time with safety and confidence. Start in low (no possibility of reverse this time) and push forward and to the right on the "stick" for second. No chance, no feeling for the detent with "safety latch", a positive stop — a positive second. Ready for high, again to the right and forward as hard as you please and "bang", high — not neutral. Every selection quick and safe no matter the degree of excitement.

FOR HER, the usual peace of mind of the automatic transmission plus an extra bit of admiration for "her man" who really wanted a 4-speed standard stick but bought this extra just for her. The Dual Gate was designed for those who desire both the ease and convenience of an automatic plus the performance of a manually shifted transmission. It will add individualism and pride of ownership to that personal car which the family can borrow. A simple flip of the latch to the normal position, without the need of the key, and the manual shifting (His) gate is closed to all but the key holder. Also, we have put a little fun in driving the automatic.

HIS ONLY

THIS KEY OR HIS PERSONAL KEY RING PREVENTS USE OF THE COMPETITION GATE BY THE CURIOUS PARKING LOT ATTENDANT, OR THE AUTOMATIC MINDED LITTLE LADY. NO CHANCE OF THEM OVER-REVVING THE ENGINE WAITING FOR THE AUTOMATIC SHIFT.

FIRST MODELS FOR THE PONTIAC GRAND PRIX AND OLDSMOBILE STARFIRE. ALL CHRYSLER PRODUCTS TO FOLLOW SHORTLY. SEE YOUR DEALER NOW.

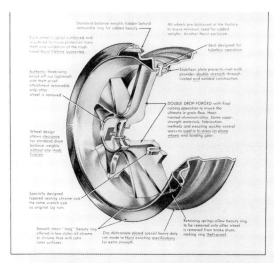

Leave it to Hurst to come up with the safest custom wheel ever made. The only forged wheel in the industry!

The big feature is in the heart of the new Hurst wheel—in the forged, heat-treated aluminum spider. Right from the beginning we decided that a brittle casting or an overweight metal stamping wouldn't be good enough. So we came up with a forging—the strongest, lightest way you can do it. The rim is steel; locked into it is the trim ring, the finishing touch that gives the appearance of a high-priced, fully-cast racing wheel. Hurst's unique, load-distributing stabilizer plate unites the forged aluminum center with the steel rim and makes them one for all eternity. What you have, then, is a high-strength wheel with all dead weight whittled away; a wheel that will absorb shock loads far beyond the failing points of cast, stamped steel or stock wheels. Write us direct for details. Or see the new Hurst wheel at your local speed shop. Hurst Performance Products, Glenside, Pa. 19038.

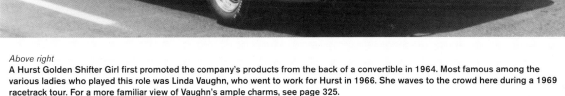

Above right
A Hurst Golden Shifter Girl first promoted the company's products from the back of a convertible in 1964. Most famous among the various ladies who played this role was Linda Vaughn, who went to work for Hurst in 1966. She waves to the crowd here during a 1969 racetrack tour. For a more familiar view of Vaughn's ample charms, see page 325.

Top left
Hurst introduced its Dual Gate shifter for automatic transmissions in 1964. Better known as a "His and Hers" stick, this modification allowed a driver to either manually control an automatic transmission or let it operate normally on its own. Dual Gates quickly became popular options for both Pontiac's GTO and Oldsmobile's 4-4-2.

Left
Custom wheels joined the Hurst Performance Products line in January 1965. These attractive five-spokers featured steel rims mated to forged aluminum centers.

American Racing mags. A second-edition SSJ appeared in 1971, and a few were sold in 1972.

George Hurst was no longer in the picture by then. Hurst-Campbell had gone public in 1968, instantly attracting the Sunbeam Corporation, which acquired controlling inter-

est by buying out Bill Campbell's stock in 1970. Campbell's partner then left soon afterward to pursue other business ventures. Sunbeam itself was bought out in November 1981 by Allegheny International, which sold Hurst to Richard Chrysler of Cars and Concepts in

Detroit. Chrysler had started out in 1966 as a "floor-sweeper" at Hurst, eventually rising to management before leaving to found Cars and Concepts. Hurst was sold again early in 1986, this time to Mr. Gasket's Joe Hrudka. Fifty-nine-year-old George Hurst died on May 15 that year.

Left
Among the various factory hot rods that Hurst helped produce was American Motors' patriotic SC/Rambler, offered for 1969 only. Beneath that boxy hood scoop was a 315-horsepower 390-cube V-8. *Mike Mueller*

Below
Hurst supplied standard-issue floorshifts for many makes, including Chrysler products, which used the unforgettable Pistol Grip design. The Hurst stick here was installed in a 1970 Dodge Coronet R/T. *Mike Mueller*

As Jim Wangers later explained in *Automobile Quarterly*, "We quickly learned that one of the first things a new customer would do after purchasing a high-performance stick shift car was to take it down to the local hot rod shop and install a Hurst."

Hurst logo

1968 Hurst/Olds

1968 Hurst/Olds

Model availability	two-door coupe or hardtop
Wheelbase	112 inches
Length	201.6 inches
Width	76.6 inches
Height	52.8 inches (hardtop)
Shipping weight	3,558 pounds (pillared coupe), 3,568 pounds (hardtop)
Base price	$4,244 (coupe); $4,288 (hardtop)
Track (front/rear, in inches)	59/59
Wheels	14x6 Super Stock II
Tires	G70x14 Goodyear Poly-Glas GT
Suspension	independent unequal A-arms with heavy-duty coil springs and stabilizer bar in front; solid axle with control arms, heavy-duty coil springs and stabilizer bar in back
Steering	recirculating ball w/power assist
Brakes	front discs, rear drums, w/power assist
Engine	390-horsepower 455-cubic-inch V-8
Bore & stroke	4.125 x 4.250 inches
Compression	10.5:1
Fuel delivery	single Rochester four-barrel carburetor w/forced-air induction
Transmission	Turbo Hydra-Matic automatic w/Hurst Dual Gate shifter (as many as two cars featured four-speed manual transmissions)
Axle ratio	3.91:1
Production	515

Above
Hurst and Oldsmobile teamed up to produce 515 Hurst/Olds coupes and hardtops in 1968. All were silver with black accents. The deck lid also was painted black.

1968

The Hurst/Olds heritage dates back to early 1968 when Doc Watson built a special 4-4-2 for his boss using the Toronado's 455-cid big-block V-8. GM's 400-cubic-inch limit was still in place for its midsize models then, so such a combination wasn't possible directly off the assembly line. Nothing, however, prevented aftermarket firms from making such conversions for John Q. Public—witness Don Yenko's Chevy-based shenanigans. With this in mind, Watson approached Olds chief engineer John Beltz with a proposition: Why not let Hurst produce a limited run of 455-powered 4-4-2s for Oldsmobile? The company's marketing experts hated the idea, claiming it would never sell, but Beltz pushed his Hurst/Olds through nonetheless. Initial announcements put the production lid at 500. Orders numbered 900 within two days, 2,600 a day later. Experts indeed.

One Oldsmobile dealer reportedly demand-

ed 26 for his lot in Texas, a ridiculous request considering the 500 cars had to be divvied up among 3,000-odd dealerships nationwide. Some received a pair, most none. In the end, the final tally read 515, and this only because Story Olds in Lansing made its own out-of-the-question demand for those extra cars. At the time Story was the largest Oldsmobile dealer in the world, explaining how it got its way.

Another man especially anxious to get his hands on a Hurst/Olds, Lansing industrialist John Demmer, made it possible to deliver all 515 models in record-breaking time. After seeing the 455 Cutlass his friend Watson had customized for George Hurst, Demmer asked for two identical examples, one for him, another for his son. But the 1968 model year was rapidly winding down by the time Beltz got his plan rolling. No problem. Demmer offered to make Watson's modifications at a plant hastily

opened in a defunct foundry in Lansing. The Demmer Engineering line went into action in April 1968, leaving only 30 days or so to complete all the Hurst/Olds conversions in time to serve as end-of-the-year attractions before the 1969 Oldsmobiles started hitting showrooms.

Legend has it that Oldsmobile delivered those 515 4-4-2s to Demmer Engineering minus engines, leaving the supposedly taboo 455 V-8 installations to the Hurst crew. Watson and Beltz were more than happy to let GM's

micromanaging killjoys believe this, but in truth the cars all came complete off the Olds line in Lansing with the 455s already installed, an easy-enough sleight of hand considering Oldsmobile's biggest big-block was essentially identical at a glance to the 1968 4-4-2's standard 400-cid V-8. Sneaky cusses.

Rated at 390 horsepower, these 455s featured W-30 cylinder heads and all that fresh-air ductwork (with scoops mounted below the front bumper), but they weren't W-30 V-8s. A Toronado 455 short-block was used, as was a milder cam and standard cast-iron intake manifold. W-30 heads weren't supposed to be installed when optional air conditioning was ordered, though at least one of these combinations is known to exist. All but the first (and possibly the second) Hurst/Olds built featured Turbo Hydra-Matic transmissions controlled by Hurst Dual Gate shifters. Another W-30 trademark, those red plastic inner fender wells, also was installed in all cases in 1968, thanks to John Beltz.

Exterior color was consistent in all 515 cases. Hurst's trademark gold with black accents was initially considered, but the Demmer facility couldn't handle the gold paint. A 1968 Toronado shade, Peruvian Silver, was sprayed on instead, complemented with stripes and a deck lid done in black. White pinstriping outlined the black. Two body styles were offered in 1968: Cutlass Holiday hardtop and Cutlass Holiday post coupe. Production was 459 for the former, only 56 for the latter.

1969 Hurst/Olds

1969

A much more distinctive Hurst/Olds appeared for 1969 wearing a fiberglass wing on the deck lid, twin "mailbox" hood scoops, and new paint—gold-accented Cameo White. At least two convertibles were built, one going to Linda Vaughn, while the remaining 912 models were all Holiday hardtops. No post-sedan bodies were used this time around, nor did any four-speed manuals sneak into the mix. The beefed-up three-speed Turbo Hydra-Matic with Hurst Dual Gate shifter was again standard.

All cars, air conditioned or not, featured 455 Toronado V-8s wearing W-30 heads, but a little detuning lowered advertised output to 380 horsepower. A Rochester Quadrajet four-barrel again fed this beast. Big 15x7 Super Stock II wheels replaced the 14x6 SSII rims used in 1968, F60 Goodyear Polyglas GT tires superseded 1968's G70x14 rubber, and Oldsmobile's beefy 4-4-2 suspension carried over.

Model availability	two-door hardtop
Wheelbase	112 inches
Length	201.9 inches
Width	76.2 inches
Height	52.8 inches
Shipping weight	3,716 pounds
Base price	$4,376
Track (front/rear, in inches)	59/59
Wheels	15x7 Super Stock II
Tires	F60x15 Goodyear Poly-Glas GT
Suspension	independent unequal A-arms with heavy-duty coil springs and stabilizer bar in front; solid axle with control arms, heavy-duty coil springs and stabilizer bar in back
Steering	recirculating ball w/power assist
Brakes	front discs, rear drums, w/power assist
Engine	380-horsepower 455-cubic-inch V-8
Bore & stroke	4.125 x 4.250 inches
Compression	10.5:1
Fuel delivery	single Rochester four-barrel carburetor w/forced-air induction
Transmission	Turbo Hydra-Matic automatic w/Hurst Dual Gate shifter
Axle ratio	3.42:1, std.
Production	912 hardtops (plus at least two convertibles)

Left
New for the 1969 Hurst/Olds was a rear wing, reportedly copied from a Cessna airplane. The 14x6 wheels used in 1968 were replaced by 15x7 Super Stock II rims. *Mike Mueller*

Below
A new color scheme appeared in 1969: Cameo White with gold stripes. No post-sedans were built this year. Production was 912 hardtops and two convertibles. *Mike Mueller*

Top
A bit of detuning dropped the Hurst/Olds' 455 big-block down from 390 horsepower to 380 for 1969. *Mike Mueller*

Above
Oldsmobile's W-30 induction plumbing was traded for a pair of boxy hood scoops for the second-edition Hurst/Olds. *Mike Mueller*

Above center
While a couple of four-speeds were installed in 1968, automatics went into all Hurst/Olds conversions made for 1969. Hurst's dual-purpose His and Hers shifter was once more standard. *Mike Mueller*

Top
Save for a dash plaque, the view from behind a Hurst/Olds wheel in 1969 was pure Cutlass. *Mike Mueller*

Above
Hurst's trademark golden touch carried over to the headrests inside a 1969 Hurst/Olds. *Mike Mueller*

The list of Hurst-equipped muscle cars grew fast soon afterward, including Plymouth's Superbird, which in 1970 used easily the most distinctive rendition, the high-arching "Pistol Grip" shifter.

Below
Linda Vaughn does her charming thing at Daytona in February 1969. Only two Hurst/Olds convertibles were built that year, one of them going to Vaughn.

1972 Hurst/Olds

1972 Hurst/Olds

Model availability	two-door hardtop and convertible
Wheelbase	112 inches
Length	203.6 inches
Width	76.8 inches (hardtop)
Height	52.9 inches (hardtop)
Shipping weight	3,520 pounds (hardtop); 3,614 pounds (convertible)
Track (front/rear, in inches)	59/59
Wheels	14-inch Super Stock III
Tires	G60x14 Goodyear Polysteel GT
Suspension	independent unequal A-arms with heavy-duty coil springs and stabilizer bar in front; solid axle with control arms, heavy-duty coil springs and stabilizer bar in back
Steering	recirculating ball
Brakes	front discs, rear drums, w/power assist
Engine	270-horsepower 455-cubic-inch V-8, std. (300-horsepowe W-30 V-8, optional)
Bore & stroke	4.125 x 4.250 inches
Compression	10.5:1
Fuel delivery	single Rochester four-barrel carburetor w/forced-air induction
Transmission	Turbo Hydra-Matic automatic w/Hurst Dual Gate shifter
Axle ratio	3.23:1, std.
Production	499 hardtops, 130 convertibles

1972

GM's decision to drop its 400-cube limit for its intermediate models rendered the Hurst/Olds redundant in 1970. Why mess with an after-market conversion when a 455-powered 4-4-2 was already available right off an Olds assembly line? But the Hurst/Olds did return for 1972, just in time to serve as the official pace car for the 56th running of the Indianapolis 500, making this the first and only time an outsider, not a full-fledged Detroit automaker, sponsored an Indy pacer. The production breakdown was 130 convertibles, 499 hardtops. Cameo White was

again the exclusive finish, but this time was accented with highly reflective gold decals instead of paint.

Standard output was now 270 horsepower for the 1972 Hurst/Olds 455 Rocket V-8. The 300-horse W-30 was optional. The TH-400 automatic, with Dual Gate shifter and console, remained in place as the only drivetrain choice behind either 455 big-block. The W-25 forced-air hood topped things off up front, and power front discs were again standard, as in 1968 and 1969. The heavy-duty Rallye Suspension was also standard in 1972. Super Stock III wheels, done in Hurst Gold and downsized back to 14 inches, went on at the corners wearing new Goodyear G60 tires.

Top
A Hurst/Olds model returned for 1972 and became the first "outsider" to pace the Indianapolis 500. All previous pace cars were full-fledged factory machines. New for H/O hardtops in 1972 was an optional sunroof: reportedly only 220 were installed.

Above
Hurst modified 76 Oldsmobiles for trackside duty during the 56th running of the Indy 500 in May 1972. Forty-two of these were Hurst/Olds convertibles, one of which was driven by Jim Rathmann during the pace lap. Pace car replicas also were sold to the public.

Coupes came with vinyl tops and could've been enhanced with an optional electric sunroof. Reportedly, 220 sunroof-equipped models were built for 1972.

1973 Hurst/Olds

Model availability	two-door Colonnade coupe
Wheelbase	112 inches
Length	211.5 inches
Width	76.5 inches
Height	53.3 inches
Shipping weight	3,900 pounds
Price	$635 for Hurst conversion
Track (front/rear, in inches)	61.4/60.7
Wheels	14-inch Super Stock III
Tires	GR60x14 BF Goodrich Radial T/A
Suspension	independent unequal A-arms with heavy-duty coil springs and stabilizer bar in front; solid axle with control arms, heavy-duty coil springs and stabilizer bar in back
Steering	recirculating ball
Brakes	front discs, rear drums, w/power assist
Engine	250-horsepower 455-cubic-inch L75 V-8 (w/air conditioning); 275-horsepower 455-cubic-inch L77 V-8 (w/o air conditioning)
Bore & stroke	4.125 x 4.250 inches
Compression	8.5:1
Fuel delivery	single Rochester four-barrel carburetor w/forced-air induction
Transmission	Turbo Hydra-Matic automatic w/Hurst Dual Gate shifter
Axle ratio	3.23:1, std. w L75; 3.08:1 w/L77
Production	1,097

Top
Oldsmobile's new Cutlass S Colonnade coupe served as a base for the 1973 Hurst/Olds. New too were color choices: white or black. A custom hood ornament also was included in the H/O package. *Mike Mueller*

Inset
Mylar H/O emblems were imbedded in the 1973 Hurst/Olds opera glass. *Mike Mueller*

Above
A Landau-style half-vinyl roof was standard for the 1973 Hurst/Olds. Dual sport mirrors and bumper rub strips were part of the deal. A sunroof was optional. *Mike Mueller*

1973

Oldsmobile's new Cutlass S Colonnade coupe body served as the base for the 1973 Hurst/Olds, which for the first time was available in two color schemes. Familiar was the Cameo White paint with white vinyl half top, gold stripes, and gold Super Stock III wheels. New was Ebony with a black "wet look" half-vinyl roof and black-painted rims. Also new were [B.F.]

Goodrich Radial T/A tires and standard swivel bucket seats. In between those buckets was a console that once more served as a home to Hurst's Dual Gate shifter. Again, the Turbo Hydra-Matic was the only transmission mated up to the Hurst/Olds 455 V-8.

Air-conditioned cars in 1973 used the 250-horsepower L75 455. Models without air conditioning got a hotter 275-horsepower L77 V-8. A 3.08:1 axle ratio was standard with the former, while the latter featured 3.23:1 gears. Total production for 1973 was 1,097.

Oldsmobile's new Cutlass S Colonnade coupe body served as the base for the 1973 Hurst/Olds, which for the first time was available in two color schemes.

Top left
Snazzy swivel bucket seats and a custom sport steering wheel were standard inside the 1973 Hurst/Olds, as was Hurst's familiar Dual Gate shifter. Owner-added nonstock gauges also appear here. *Mike Mueller*

Center
Where would any too-cool-for-school muscle car owner be in 1973 without his or her optional 8-track stereo? Or the latest top 40 hits? *Mike Mueller*

Above
Standard for air-conditioned Hurst/Olds models (shown here) in 1973 was the 250-horsepower L75 455 big-block V-8. Automatic transmissions once again were installed in all instances. *Mike Mueller*

Left
A thoroughly modern digital electronic tachometer was a $79.95 option in 1973. *Mike Mueller*

1974 Hurst/Olds

1974 Hurst/Olds	
Model availability	two-door Colonnade coupe
Wheelbase	112 inches
Length	211.5 inches
Width	76.5 inches
Height	53.2 inches
Shipping weight	3,993 pounds
Track (front/rear, in inches)	61.4/60.7
Wheels	15x7 Super Stock III
Tires	H60x15 Goodyear Poly-Glas GT
Suspension	independent unequal A-arms with heavy-duty coil springs and stabilizer bar in front; solid axle with control arms, heavy-duty coil springs and stabilizer bar in back
Steering	recirculating ball
Brakes	front discs, rear drums, w/power assist
Engine	230-horsepower 455-cubic-inch W-30 V-8; 180-horsepower 350-cubic-inch W-25 V-8, optional
Bore & stroke	4.125 x 4.250 inches (W-30); 4.06 x 3.39 inches (W-25)
Compression	8.5:1
Fuel delivery	single Rochester four-barrel carburetor w/forced-air induction
Transmission	Turbo Hydra-Matic automatic w/Hurst Dual Gate shifter
Axle ratio	3.42:1
Production	1,800

Top
The Hurst/Olds package carried over essentially unchanged for 1974. The Rallye Suspension, 15-inch Super Stock wheels, heavy-duty cooling, low-restriction dual exhausts, and a louvered hood were again standard. *Mike Mueller*

Above
The band across the roof of a 1974 Hurst/Olds mimicked the roll bar seen on the customized H/O convertible that paced that year's Indianapolis 500. Large triangular rear quarter glass replaced the understated opera windows seen in 1973. *Mike Mueller*

1974

The Hurst/Olds legacy rolled over almost unchanged into 1974, with the most notable update involving engine availability. Cars sold in California were all fitted with a 350-cubic-inch Rocket V-8 rated at 180 horsepower. This engine was optional in all other states and was identified by "W-25" decals on the fenders. A 455 big-block remained the top choice, rated at 230 horsepower, and changed the stick-on identification to W-30. Total production was 1,800: 1,420 with the W-25, 380 with the W-30 455.

A Hurst/Olds was again chosen to pace the Indy 500 in 1974, requiring two specially customized models for actual on-track duty. With a convertible Cutlass no longer available from Oldsmobile, the Hurst folks decided to create their own brand of topless travel. The steel tops were stripped off the two pace cars and a large padded roll bar was put in place.

"With the number of convertible models produced in this country each year on the decline, we think these cars will be real attention grabbers at the Speedway," said Hurst Performance President Will Kay in December

1973. A removable hardtop was created just in case weatherproofing was required at the Brickyard on race day.

The pace car's image was replicated on 1974 Hurst/Olds coupes by a stylized band that ran over the roof, mimicking that roll bar. Large triangular Cutlass S rear quarter windows replaced the small "opera" glass used the previous year.

Top left
A small-block V-8 became available for the Hurst/Olds for the first time in 1974. Mandated in California, optional in other states, this 180-horsepower 350 wore the W-25 tag. The 455 big-block now carried the familiar W-30 code. *Mike Mueller*

Above
The Hurst/Olds W-30 455 V-8 was net-rated at 230 horsepower in 1974. Behind it was GM's Turbo Hydra-Matic 400 automatic transmission. *Mike Mueller*

Below
A convertible Cutlass was no longer offered by Oldsmobile when the Hurst/Olds was chosen to pace the Indianapolis 500 again in 1974. So Hurst simply stripped the roofs off two coupes and added a padded roll bar. Jim Rathmann once again handled pace lap chores on race day in May 1974.

1975 Hurst/Olds

1975 Hurst/Olds

1975

No glass at all graced the rear roof pillars on the 1975 Hurst/Olds, which again came in black or white, but now based on the formal Cutlass Supreme body in place of the semi-fastback Cutlass S shell used in 1973 and 1974. A half-vinyl roof again appeared, mandated in this case by the Hurst/Hatch T-top conversion, a neat idea that proved prone to leaks in practice. New for 1975 was the option to mix and match the vinyl top and body color. Contrasting black-and-white combos were possible this year. Total production was 2,535: 1,242 in black paint, 1,293 in white.

Catalytic converters debuted in 1975, mandating the installation of a single exhaust system. Both the W-25 small-block and W-30 big-block returned, rated this time at 180 and 210 horses, respectively. Production breakdown by engine was 1,324 with the W-25 350, 1,211 with the W-30 455.

Oldsmobile offered its own Hurst/Olds in 1979, a rather attractive package based on that year's Cutlass Calais coupe. Power was supplied by a 170-horsepower 350 V-8, now called the W-30 in the absence of an available big-block. Production was 2,499.

A Cutlass Supreme–based Hurst/Olds appeared in 1983 to mark the breed's 15th anniversary and was a pleasant surprise with its 180-horsepower 307 Rocket V-8. A similar model made an encore appearance in 1984, followed a few years later by a conversion kit in 1988 to honor the 20th anniversary and final edition of the Hurst/Olds.

A conversion kit in 1988 honored the 20th anniversary and final edition of the Hurst/Olds.

Below
Hurst's T-top conversion graced the 1975 Hurst/Olds, which once again came only in black or white. The W-25 small-block and W-30 big-block remained available beneath the hood. *From the files of Hurst/Olds Club of America*

Model availability	two-door Colonnade coupe
Wheelbase	112 inches
Length	211.7 inches
Width	76.5 inches
Height	53.2 inches
Shipping weight	3,793 pounds
Track (front/rear, in inches)	61.4/60.7
Wheels	15x7 Super Stock III
Tires	H60x15 Goodyear Poly-Glas GT
Suspension	independent unequal A-arms with heavy-duty coil springs and stabilizer bar in front; solid axle with control arms, heavy-duty coil springs and stabilizer bar in back
Steering	recirculating ball
Brakes	front discs, rear drums, w/power assist
Engine	210-horsepower 455-cubic-inch W-30 V-8; 180-horsepower 350-cubic-inch W-25 V-8, optional
Bore & stroke	4.125 x 4.250 inches (W-30); 4.06 x 3.39 inches (W-25)
Compression	8.5:1
Fuel delivery	single Rochester four-barrel carburetor w/forced-air induction
Transmission	Turbo Hydra-Matic automatic w/Hurst Dual Gate shifter
Axle ratio	2.73:1
Production	2,535

Index